THE COMPLETE GUIDE TO CHESAPEAKE BAY RETRIEVERS

Karen Harris

LP Media Inc. Publishing
Text copyright © 2021 by LP Media Inc.
All rights reserved.

No part of this book may be reproduced or transmitted in any form or by any means, electronic or mechanical, including photocopying, recording, or by an information storage and retrieval system – except by a reviewer who may quote brief passages in a review to be printed in a magazine or newspaper – without permission in writing from the publisher. For information address LP Media Inc. Publishing, 3178 253rd Ave. NW, Isanti, MN 55040

www.lpmedia.org

Publication Data

Karen Harris

The Complete Guide to Chesapeake Bay Retrievers – First edition.

Summary: "Successfully raising a Chesapeake Bay Retriever Dog from puppy to old age" – Provided by publisher.

ISBN: 978-1-954288-18-8

[1. Chesapeake Bay Retriever – Non-Fiction] I. Title.

This book has been written with the published intent to provide accurate and authoritative information in regard to the subject matter included. While every reasonable precaution has been taken in preparation of this book the author and publisher expressly disclaim responsibility for any errors, omissions, or adverse effects arising from the use or application of the information contained inside. The techniques and suggestions are to be used at the reader's discretion and are not to be considered a substitute for professional veterinary care. If you suspect a medical problem with your dog, consult your veterinarian.

Design by Sorin Rădulescu

First paperback edition, 2021

Cover Photo Courtesy of Emma Totten = @daisy.the.chessie on IG

TABLE OF CONTENTS

Introduction 1

CHAPTER 1:
The All-American Chessie 3
The Origins of the Chessie 3
Chessies and Duck Hunting 4
Cousins to Labrador Retrievers? 6
A Charter Member of the AKC 8
An Underappreciated Breed 10

CHAPTER 2:
Physical and Personality Traits of the Chesapeake Bay Retriever 11
Physical Characteristics 11
Behavioral Characteristics 13
Personality Characteristics 16
Is the Chesapeake Bay Retriever the Right Dog for You? 17

CHAPTER 3:
Finding Your Perfect Chesapeake Bay Retriever 21
How to Find a Chesapeake Bay Retriever Breeder 22
How to NOT Find a Chesapeake Bay Retriever Breeder 23

How to Differentiate Between a Reputable Chessie Breeder
and a Backyard Breeder 25
Questions to Ask a Breeder During a Phone Interview 26
Questions to Ask a Breeder During a Visit 29
Guarantees, Health Certifications, and Breeder's Contracts 31
What Is a Breeder's Contract? 32
How to Pick Out the Perfect Chessie Pup 33
Adopting a Chessie 34
Animal Shelters 34
Chessie Rescue Organizations 37
The Perks of Adopting an Older Chessie 40

CHAPTER 4:

Get Ready for your Chessie's Homecoming 41
What Supplies Do I Need to Have on Hand? 42
How Do I Puppy Proof My House? 45
How Do I Puppy Proof My Garage and Yard? 47
How to Prepare Your Children for Your Chessie's Homecoming . . . 48
Get Your Other Pets Accustomed to Other Animals 49
Find a Veterinarian 51
    Tips for Finding a Good Veterinarian 51
    Questions to Ask When Interviewing Veterinarians 52

CHAPTER 5:

Welcoming Home your Chessie 55
A Smooth Ride Home 56
How to Create a Stress-Free Environment For Your
Chesapeake Bay Retriever 57
How to Help your Chessie through the First Night 58
Set Boundaries from Day One 60
    Establish Physical Boundaries 60
    Start Housetraining 60
    Teach Rules 61
    Start Socializing 61

Preparing for your Chessie's First Vet Visit 62
Finding Puppy Training and Obedience Classes 64
The Benefits of Obedience Classes 64

CHAPTER 6:

Housetraining your Chessie 67
Take Frequent Walks 69
Stay on Schedule 69
What Goes In Must Come Out 69
Be Patient 69
Puppy Pads: A Temporary Solution 70
The Role of Crates in Housetraining 71
Learning the House Rules 73
Ways to Reward Good Behavior 73
    Treats as a Reward 73
    Praise as a Reward 73
    Verbal Cues as a Reward 74
    Timing Is Everything 74
Tips for Correcting Naughty Behavior 74
    Prevent the Bad Behavior 75
    Adopt a Stern Tone 75
    For a Dog, All Attention Is Good Attention 75
    Again, Pay Attention to Timing 76
To Crate or Not to Crate, That Is the Question 76
Creating Safe Zones 77
Tips for Leaving your Chessie Home Alone 77

CHAPTER 7:

Keeping your Chessie Fit and Happy 81
Exercise Requirements of Young Chessies 82
Exercise Requirements of Adult Chessies 83
The Benefits of Walking 84
The Benefits of Running 84
The Benefits of Swimming 85

The Importance of Mental Stimulation	86
Outdoor Exercise	86
Puzzle Feeders and Treat Toys	88
Stay Connected with Technology	88
Doggie TV	90
Chew Toys	90

CHAPTER 8:

Socializing your Chessie — 91

Why Socializing Is So Important	92
Socialize Early and Often	93
Socializing with New People	94
Socializing Your Chessie with Children	95
Meeting Other Dogs	95
Doggie Social Rules	96
Personal Space	96
Mounting	97
Doggie Body Language	97
The Eyes	97
The Hackles	97
The Smile	98
The Tail	98
Chessies and Other Pets	99
Chessies and Livestock	99

CHAPTER 9:

Training your Chessie — 101

Why Is Good Training So Important?	102
Be Consistent	103
Tips for Clear, Consistent Training	105
Positive Versus Negative Reinforcement Training	107
Positive Reinforcement Training	107
Negative Reinforcement Training	109

Pitfalls of Punishment-Based Training ... 110
Pros of Obedience Classes ... 110
Cons of Obedience Classes ... 111

CHAPTER 10:

Teaching your Chessie Basic Commands ... 113
Tips for Making Training Fun for your Chessie ... 113
Basic Training Commands ... 115
    How to Teach your Chessie to Roll Over ... 119
    How to Teach your Chessie to Come ... 121
    How to Teach your Chessie to Give or Drop the Ball ... 122
Tips for Leash Training your Chessie ... 123
Tips for Off-Leash Training your Chessie ... 125

CHAPTER 11:

Nipping Bad Behavior in the Bud ... 127
Bad Behavior Isn't Cute ... 128
Tips for Correcting Problem Behaviors ... 129
Chewing and Destroying Property ... 131
Barking and Growling ... 131
Digging ... 133
Begging ... 134
Jumping Up on People ... 136
Aggression Toward Children ... 136
Aggression Toward Other Animals ... 138
Biting, Nipping, and Mouthing ... 139
Do You Need Training Help from a Professional? ... 141

CHAPTER 12:

Chessies as Hunting Dogs ... 143
Chessies Are Natural Water Dogs ... 144
Chessies Are Natural Hunters ... 145
Tips for Training your Chessie to Hunt ... 147
Be Alert to Outdoor Dangers ... 150

CHAPTER 13:

Chessies and Dog Shows — 155
The Pros and Cons of Dog Shows — 156
Agility Shows with your Chessie — 157
Field Trials with your Chessie — 159

CHAPTER 14:

Your Chessie's Nutrition — 161
Why Is Nutrition So Important? — 162
Tips for Picking the Best Food for your Chessie — 163
Wet or Dry, Which Food Is Best? — 164
The Raw Food Trend — 166
Is a Vegetarian Diet a Good Choice for Your Chessie? — 167
The Pros and Cons of Homemade Dog Food for Your Chessie — 168
Does your Chessie Need Vitamins and Supplements? — 168
What Should You Know About Treats for Your Chessie? — 170
What Should You Know About Table Scraps for your Chessie? — 171
Human Foods That Are Toxic to Chessies — 171

CHAPTER 15:

The Overweight Chessie — 173
How Can I Tell if my Chessie is Overweight? — 173
Health Problems Associated with Excess Weight — 174
Preventing Obesity in your Chessie — 175
Putting your Chessie on a Diet — 175

CHAPTER 16:

Chessies and the Holidays — 177
Christmas Dangers — 178
Easter Dangers — 182
Fourth of July Dangers — 183
Halloween Dangers — 184

CHAPTER 17:

Grooming your Chessie … 185
The Chessie's Unique Coat … 186
- Bathing … 186
- Brushing … 190

Ears, Teeth, and Eyes … 191
- Your Chessie's Ears … 191
- Your Chessie's Teeth … 192
- Your Chessie's Eyes … 194

Trimming your Chessie's Nails … 195
Using a Groomer Versus Grooming Your Chessie Yourself … 197

CHAPTER 18:

Your Chessie's Health … 199
The Benefits of Building a Good Rapport with Your Veterinarian … 200
The Importance of Routine Checkups … 200
Different Kinds of Vaccinations … 202
- Your Chessie's Vaccination Schedule … 204

Tips For Preventing and Treating External Parasites … 204
- Fleas … 204
- Ticks … 205
- Mites … 206
- Lice … 207
- Ringworm … 207

Tips For Preventing and Treating … 207
Internal Parasites … 207
- Heartworms … 207
- Hookworms … 208
- Tapeworms … 209
- Round worms … 209
- Whipworms … 210

The Importance of Spaying and Neutering Your
Chesapeake Bay Retriever … 211
Common Diseases and Medical Conditions in Chessies … 213

The Pros and Cons of Holistic Medicine for Your Chessie ... 218
    Chiropractic Care ... 218
    Massage Therapy ... 218
    Acupuncture ... 219
    Sound Therapy ... 219
    Aromatherapy ... 220
    Acupressure ... 220
Potential Concerns with Holistic Methods ... 220
What You Should Know About CBD Products and your Chessie ... 221
The Pros and Cons of Pet Insurance ... 222

CHAPTER 19:

Traveling with your Chessie ... 225
Making Travel Preparations ... 226
The Importance of ID Tags and Microchips ... 226
Dog Carriers and Travel Crates ... 227
What You Should Know About Flying with Your Chessie ... 227
Tips for Making Car Travel with your Chessie Easier and Safer ... 229
What You Should Know About Staying in a Hotel with your Chessie ... 232
Leaving your Chessie at Home ... 235
    Pros and Cons of Boarding Kennels ... 235
    The Pros and Cons of a Dog Sitter ... 236

CHAPTER 20:

Your Chessie in his Golden Years ... 237
The Changing Care of a Senior Chessie ... 238
Changes to your Senior Chessie's Vision and Hearing ... 238
Changes in your Senior Chessie's Temperament and Behavior ... 239
Nutritional Changes for your Older Chessie ... 241
Exercise Changes for your Older Chessie ... 243
Common Age-Related Ailments in Chessies ... 245
What You Should Know About Dog Euthanasia ... 245
When Your Chessie Crosses the Rainbow Bridge ... 246

Introduction

"No, he's not a Chocolate Lab. He's a Chesapeake Bay Retriever."

Photo Courtesy of Karen Harris

Hank around the campfire

As a Chessie owner, get ready to say that phrase over and over again. A lesser-known cousin to the popular Labrador Retrievers, Chesapeake Bay Retrievers are often confused with Chocolate Labs. Of course, there are some notable differences, which people will point out. You'll undoubtedly hear, "His coat is wavy. Is he a Lab-Poodle mix?" and "Wow, I've never seen a Lab that stocky. He must not miss too many meals."

I owned a female Chessie, named Maizie, for 14 years and got another Chessie, Hank, shortly after we lost Maizie to congestive heart failure eight years ago. That means I have had a Chessie in my life for more than two decades.

I live in the Midwest, far from the shores of the Chesapeake Bay but still in a region popular with duck hunters, yet many people are unfamiliar with the Chessie breed. I find myself often explaining, "No, he is a purebred Chessie. These are water dogs, so their coats are thicker and curlier to keep them warm in the water." To the fat shamers, I say, "Chessies are not as lean and lanky as Labs. The breed is more stoutly built with broad barrel chests."

I have been around my share of Labs and I can see why they are one of the most popular dog breeds in the world. They are happy-go-lucky pups that have never met a stranger. Hank, by comparison, is a bit more reserved and less likely to smother you with licks. That doesn't mean, however, that he lacks in personality. On the contrary. It just means Chessies are the introverts of the Retriever world. They could be higher on the popularity ladder, but they just don't put themselves out there like Labs do.

Although the puppy years were often trying times (remind me to tell you about the time Hank pulled a knife on me...seriously), Hank settled down to become a good boy and loving companion with the eyes of an old soul.

INTRODUCTION

*Photo Courtesy of
Hailley Tucker
Ayse Demircan Photography*

He is observant and far smarter than we give him credit for – I swear he can tell time!

For a dog as intelligent, independent, and athletic as the Chesapeake Bay Retriever, every stage of life offers its own set of challenges and rewards. The information in this book is intended to guide you through life with your own Chessie, from puppyhood to his golden years. You will learn about the Chessie breed and its origins, how to locate a reputable breeder, ways to train your Chessie pup, the Chessie's nutritional requirements, and tips for keeping your new best friend fit and healthy. Along the way, you will hear that story of my knife fight with Hank and a few other tales of his zany Chessie antics.

CHAPTER 1:
The All-American Chessie

The Origins of the Chessie

"Chesapeakes were bred for the stamina and determination to retrieve & withstand the cold temps on the Chesapeake Bay, and to protect what they retrieve. They are a hard driving dog with a natural protection instinct, yet soft in nature to train."

KATHY MILLER
Sandy Oak Chesapeakes

Photo Courtesy of Stephanie Wright

CHAPTER 1 The All-American Chessie

On a blustery September day in 1807, an American ship, the *Canton*, returning to its home port of Baltimore, was approaching the entrance to the Chesapeake Bay from the Atlantic Ocean. There, according to one of the sailors on board, a man named George Law, the *Canton* came upon an English brig floundering in the rough seas. The ship was loaded with codfish from Newfoundland and dangerously close to sinking. Law's journal entry stated that the *Canton* sailors brought the crew of the English vessel aboard their own ship. In addition to the human crew, two puppies were rescued from the sinking ship, described as Newfoundland dogs. When the *Canton* dropped the Englishmen off in Norfolk, Law purchased the two pups from the English captain. He named the male dog Sailor and the female one *Canton*.

Most likely, Sailor and Canton were St. John's water dogs or a similar breed, yet these two dogs are considered to be the parents of the Chesapeake Bay Retriever breed. Law noted in his journal that the pair were not littermates and that Sailor was a "dingy red" color, while Canton was black. Sailor and Canton were separated as pups and raised in different parts of the Chesapeake Bay. They did not mate together. Instead, each dog was bred with other dogs, such as hounds and spaniels, to bring out key duck-hunting traits that were valued by the people living on the shores of the great bay.

Chessies and Duck Hunting

In the 1800s, duck hunting clubs dotted the shores of the Chesapeake Bay. These clubs catered to both the serious outdoorsmen and the wealthy elite from nearby New York City and other urban areas. Duck club owners, of course, wanted to create the most positive experience for their patrons to keep them coming back. A team of hardy, well-trained duck retrievers was

> **FUN FACT**
> **American Chesapeake Club (ACC)**
>
> The American Chesapeake Club (ACC) is the American Kennel Club (AKC) Parent Club for the Chesapeake Bay Retriever breed. This club is a nonprofit organization dedicated to bettering and supporting the breed. Members adhere to a code of ethics and participate in events across the nation. Membership to the club includes a subscription to a bimonthly bulletin, access to a members' only chat list, and the ability to vote on the standard for the breed. For more information, visit the ACC website at www.amchessieclub.org.

part of the business model. The hunters could be assured that every duck they shot could be retrieved and added to their cache.

The offspring of Sailor and Canton displayed exceptional duck-retrieving talents. They were bred with other water dogs, possibly curly-coated retrievers, to further improve their skills. By 1877, the Chesapeake Bay Ducking Dog was officially recognized by the American Kennel Club then renamed the Chesapeake Bay Retriever in 1918. Since then, the Chessie's breed standard hasn't significantly changed.

The waters of the Chesapeake Bay can be quite cold, even in late spring and early summer. The ideal 1800s duck retriever needed to be able to tolerate the icy temperatures. Enter the Chessie. Chessies have a double coat of thick, naturally oily fur that repels water and acts as an insulator. They are tireless swimmers, with webbed paws and strong legs. Their broad barrel chests can break up the ice on the bay to give the Chessie an open-water route to his quarry. The Chessie breed has a 'soft mouth,' or bite inhibition, meaning that the dogs can be more easily trained to gently hold their quarry in their mouths—a sought-after characteristic for hunting dogs. Chessies

Photo Courtesy of Benjamin Morgan

can retrieve downed ducks and bring them back to shore while resisting the urge to tear them apart.

A good Chessie that has been trained well will even be able to carry an egg in his mouth without cracking it. Since we don't take Hank duck hunting, he wasn't training in the fine art of the soft mouth carry, especially the part about seeing the task through to completion. I can still recall the time I saw him softly and sweetly carry my daughter's beloved teddy bear in his mouth, only to drop the toy at my feet, then rip its head off. My daughter is still traumatized by that incident.

According to Ducks Unlimited, there are about 87,000 duck hunters in the United States, but those numbers have been on a steady decline in the last few decades as hunting has fallen out of favor with many people. Nevertheless, the Chesapeake Bay Retriever remains one of the top dog breeds of choice for today's duck hunters. In fact, Ducks Unlimited consistently lists the Chessie in their lists of Top Five duck hunting dogs.

All that said, the Chesapeake Bay Retriever is not a one-trick dog. This breed of dog has plenty of positive attributes beyond its ability to find and retrieve waterfowl. People who have never considered duck hunting, like me, have discovered that the Chessie is also a great family dog.

Cousins to Labrador Retrievers?

With their brown coat and droopy triangle ears, it is easy to see why Chessies are often mistaken for Chocolate Labs. I refer to Chessies and Chocolates as cousins, but these breeds are not related at all. They have totally different family trees. Chessies and Chocolates are, however, both members of the Retriever group within the American Kennel Club. There are six members of the Retriever group – the Chesapeake Bay Retriever, Golden Retriever, Curly-Coated Retriever, Flat-Coated Retriever, Nova Scotia Duck Tolling Retriever, and the Labrador Retriever. Of this group, the Chesapeake Bay Retriever is the largest member.

The members of the Retriever group have more in common than their strong urge to fetch downed waterfowl and bring them back to their handler. This collection of dog breeds is energetic, intelligent, and great with families. There are some notable differences, however. Not every breed of Retriever is an ideal choice for first-time dog owners or apartment dwellers, for example. The chart below provides an at-a-glance comparison of the six Retriever dogs on several key categories. Each dog breed is giving a score for each category on a scale of one to five, with one being the least positive and five being the most positive.

A Charter Member of the AKC

	Chesapeake Bay Retriever	Nova Scotia Duck Tolling Dog	Labrador Retriever	Golden Retriever	Curly-Coated Retriever	Flat-Coated Retriever
Friendliness	5	5	5	5	4	5
Good for Novice Dog Owners	1	3	3	3	3	2
Adapts to Apartment Living	1	5	1	2	1	1
Good with Families	5	5	5	5	5	5
Intelligence	4	4	5	5	5	5
Trainability	3	4	5	5	4	4
Exercise Needs	5	5	5	5	4	5
Wanderlust Potential	4	3	3	2	4	4

The Chesapeake Bay Retriever is also the member of another prestigious group; this breed was one of the "charter breeds," or original nine dog breeds recognized by the American Kennel Club upon this organization's founding in 1878. In September of that year, Major James M. Taylor, a decorated Civil War veteran, called together a dozen sportsmen representing hunting and dog clubs across the country for a meeting in Philadelphia. There, Major Taylor proposed a "club of clubs" for dog enthusiasts. At that meeting, the newly formed American Kennel Club recognized nine breeds as original members of the organization. They included the Pointer, Irish Setter, Gordon Setter, Clumber Spaniel, Cocker Spaniel, Irish Water Spaniel, English Setter, Sussex Spaniel, and the Chesapeake Bay Retriever. Of these nine dog breeds, the Chessie is the only one that originated in the United States.

CHAPTER 1 The All-American Chessie

Today, the American Kennel Club recognizes 196 breeds of dog. On the list of these nearly 200 dog breeds by popularity, the Chessie comes in at a respectable 46th -- in the top 25 percent. The popularity of the Chesapeake Bay Retriever is slowly improving. Just 10 years ago, Chessies ranked at number 48 and the decade before that, they were at 51. Even as duck hunting has lost some of its luster, the Chesapeake Bay Retriever has found a new group of admirers.

Photo Courtesy of Aastin Curtis-Atkins

An Underappreciated Breed

In the dog world – even in the retriever circle – the Chesapeake Bay Retriever is an underappreciated breed. It could be that Chessies are overshadowed by their more outgoing and affable counterparts, the Golden Retriever and Labrador Retrievers. Perhaps it is because Chessies are known as duck-hunting dogs, so people who are not avid waterfowl hunters may overlook this breed in favor of one with a more family-friendly reputation. If this is the case, these people are missing out. I have never been duck hunting a day in my life, yet I have discovered that Chessies fit in well with my family and our lifestyle. Hank enjoys an afternoon at the lake or a weekend spent cutting firewood in the woods, but he also likes to cuddle on the couch watching a good football game and listening to oldies music as we barbecue on the back deck.

Thankfully, I am not alone in my appreciation for the Chessie breed and all they have to offer. Chessies are intuitive, sensitive, and gentle which makes them wonderful therapy dogs. They also have a highly developed sense of smell and can be trained to work with law enforcement sniffing out illegal drugs or detecting explosives.

Chessies are hardy, solidly built dogs that thrive on challenging work, making them an ideal breed for search-and-rescue work. They also make wonderful companion for hikes, hunts, and camping. President Theodore Roosevelt, an avid outdoorsman, adventurer, and camper, owned several Chesapeake Bay Retrievers. So did General George Armstrong Custer and Senator John McCain. Actor Tom Felton, perhaps best known for playing Draco Malfoy in the *Harry Potter* film franchise, is a loyal Chessie owner. Chessies were also the favorite breed of the late actor, Paul Walker, from the *Fast & Furious* movies.

Only 13 states in the U.S. have official state dogs as part of their collection of state symbols. Maryland started this trend in 1964 when legislation declared the Chesapeake Bay Retriever the official state dog. It was a fitting tribute to the breed that originated on the banks of Maryland's signature bay.

In a nod to its origins, the University of Maryland, Baltimore County named the Chesapeake Bay Retriever as its school mascot in 1964. The university uses both a costumed mascot, called Fever the Retriever, and a live Chessie to represent the school. One of these dogs, named Campus Sam, was the inspiration for the school's True Grit statue.

The Chesapeake Bay Retriever is a true all-American dog breed. Its origin story is befitting of its reputation as an able-bodied hunter that is robust enough to brave the frigid waters of the Chesapeake Bay or sensitive enough to lay his head on your lap when you are having a rough day.

CHAPTER 1　The All-American Chessie

Photo Courtesy of
Danielle Gaffney

CHAPTER 2:
Physical and Personality Traits of the Chesapeake Bay Retriever

Physical Characteristics

Hank is a large and imposing boy that strikes fear into the Amazon delivery driver, but his bark is worse than his bite. He is a gentle giant who is more of a lover than a fighter. But I understand why the Amazon driver is afraid to get out of the truck. Chesapeake Bay Retrievers are sweet, friendly family dogs wrapped in a somewhat intimidating façade.

Photo Courtesy of Lori Stine

Chessies are large, muscular dogs. Males can be as tall as 26 inches at the shoulder, with females just an inch or two shorter. Hank is exactly 26 inches. Male Chessies range in weight from 75 to 100 pounds and females are typically between 65 and 80 pounds. Here is where Hank overachieves. He is a bit on the heavy side because he really likes his treats. Plus, he sneaks the cat's food when we aren't looking. He has no self-control.

The head of the Chessie is broad and well-proportioned, like that of a Lab. The triangle shaped ears hang

CHAPTER 2 Physical and Personality Traits of the Chesapeake Bay Retriever

down from the sides of the skull. The Chessie's ears can be quite expressive. We can always tell when Hank is excited, annoyed, or concerned by the position of his "worried ears," as we call it. Chessies have beautiful eyes. They are usually golden or amber in color and just as expressive as his ears. The eyes of the Chessie are wise and soulful; they can peer deeply into your heart.

The coat of the Chesapeake Bay Retriever is a wonder of canine technology. Chessies have a double coat. The undercoat is thick, wooly, and full of natural oils that give the dog another layer of protection from the icy waters. The outer coat is coarse and wavy to repel water. This combination gives the Chessie an advantage in colder temperatures. This breed seems undeterred by cold and snow and will plunge right in the water, even if there is a sheet of ice on the surface. Hank accompanied us on a mini family getaway in late November and happily swam in the frigid, choppy waters of Lake Superior as if we were in sunny Florida.

If you were to ask me, I would tell you that Hank is brown. All Chessies are brown, in fact, but there are six acceptable shades of brown that the AKC allows for in the breed standard of the Chesapeake Bay Retriever: brown, dark brown, light brown, tan, sedge, and deadgrass. What exactly is sedge and deadgrass, you ask? Sedge is a brown color that has a slight reddish tinge to it, like a dark mahogany, but not a red as auburn. Deadgrass is a rather unromantic description for a brown coat with a dull grayish tan mixed in. The purpose of the shade of brown is so that the Chessie blends into its surroundings when he is working in the field.

To be strong enough to retrieve waterfowl and rugged enough to bust through the ice, the Chessie is built like a muscle-bound wrestler. His shoulders and hindquarters help give the Chessie the brawn he needs to swim through strong waves, currents, and tides to reach his quarry, and the fortitude to climb out of the surf and onto the shore with a waterfowl in his mouth. The Chesapeake Bay Retriever has one other asset that makes this breed one of the top swimming dogs -- webbed paws. A tough membrane of skin connects the dog's toes, enabling it to displace water more efficiently as the Chessie swims.

A well-proportioned Chessie may look, to the unknowing eye, to be slightly out of proportion. The hindquarters of this breed should be slightly higher than their shoulders, giving these dogs the appearance that they are walking downhill. This prepares Chessies to dive right in the water and propel their bodies through the waves with their powerful back legs. The shoulders should taper to the neck and the Chessies' trademark barrel chest.

Behavioral Characteristics

"A Chessie is a very active breed. By active, I don't mean it needs a walk around the block once a day. Rather, it needs to run and play and be stimulated both mentally and physically. If you don't give them a job to do, they will find something to do and get into trouble. If you love to hunt, camp, hike, and run and be outdoors, this is your breed. If you want a dog to lay around on the couch most of the time, I'd say choose a different breed."

SHARON POTTER
Red Branch Kennels

Of course, every dog is different, but there are some collective traits that are common to the Chesapeake Bay Retriever breed as a whole. Chessies are friendly dogs, like all Retrievers, but they are not as outgoing and gregarious as Golden Retrievers and Labrador Retrievers. A Chessie has unconditional love for his family. Everyone else, however, needs to earn his affection.

As a whole, Chesapeake Bay Retrievers are protective of their families and their property. You can expect some healthy warning barks if a stranger knocks on your door. They can be somewhat territorial, too. A few times a day, Hank asks to go outside to do a perimeter check. From my observations, it looks as though he is walking the property line, stopping to sniff the ground here and there, and marking his territory. Once he seems satisfied that the perimeter is safe, he happily trots back to the door, secure in his knowledge that all is clear.

Hank has a fairly good understanding of where our property lines are, but he also thinks that we own the road in front of the house. Any car that drives too slowly on our road will trigger the Hank alert. I can only assume that he thinks the slow-moving car is turning into the driveway and that his menacing bark has scared the intruder off, thus saving the whole family from the clear and present danger. He also goes on high alert if someone actually does pull into our driveway, but he no longer behaves like he is going to maul the Amazon prime driver or the poor high school kid delivering our pizza. Regular drivers now know Hank by name and often bring him a doggie biscuit. Hank can be bought!

I often hear people say that a Chessie can be a "one person" dog and that they tend to form a stronger bond with one family member. I would agree with this tendency, based on my own experience with the breed. Maizie, our first Chessie, was my husband's constant companion. She sometimes

CHAPTER 2   Physical and Personality Traits of the Chesapeake Bay Retriever

Photo Courtesy of
Sherri Golec

ignored my commands but hung on my husband's every word. She curled up at his feet every night and joined him outside every time he did yard work. Hank, on the other hand, is a mama's boy. He follows me from room to room, sleeps on the floor next to my side of the bed, and rests his head on my lap on the couch. This isn't to say that Chessies don't form special bonds with other family members. It is just that they seem to only view one person as their master.

Chessies are highly intelligent dogs and once they are properly trained, they are obedient. But they have a mind of their own. Sometimes, they abandon their training and follow their own wishes. They can become so focused on their quarry that they ignore their handers and their commands. Because of this, they have gotten a reputation for being stubborn. It is really just the result of their strong prey drive.

Chessies have terrific memories. When working in the field, this is an extremely helpful trait. Using his keen eyesight and observation ability, the Chesapeake Bay Retriever on the hunt takes note of where the ducks fall and remembers these locations when it is time to fetch the fowls. No ducks get left behind! Hank has several favorite balls and toys. Many times, he comes back inside after we've played in the yard then suddenly remembers that he left his ball outside. He always knows exactly where he left it, even if it is out of sight.

That soft-mouth trait of the Chessie breed doesn't excuse them from engaging in inappropriate chewing, especially when they are young puppies. As you can tell from my earlier Hank vs. teddy bear story, they can be quite destructive, so you may have to work diligently to eliminate this behavior in your Chessie. I remember when Maizie was really young, we had to leave her home alone for most of the day one weekend. Instead of keeping her in her crate, my husband decided to put her in the garage so she could go out the doggie door and into our fenced yard if she needed to. It sounded like a great plan at the time.

Maizie must have become bored. Really bored. She passed the time by chewing apart my husband's new riding lawnmower. She chewed off the foot pedals, ate the seat, and ripped off the steering wheel. She even punctured one of the tires. When we got home, Maizie greeted us enthusiastically, eager to show us all she had accomplished while we were gone. I thought my husband was going to explode when he saw his mower. Let's just say, it was a good thing that Maizie was so cute. After that, my husband worked with Maizie to overcome her chewing habit.

CHAPTER 2   Physical and Personality Traits of the Chesapeake Bay Retriever

Personality Characteristics

In general, Chessies are sweet dogs with a happy, energetic disposition, even as they are more reserved than Labs and Goldens. As a puppy, Hank had his share of the zoomies. He even got so wound up, he jumped onto the dining room table in his glee. The older he got, fortunately, the calmer he became.

Chessies are sensitive and intuitive, so much so that they make excellent therapy and support dogs. They are generally good with children, though children and all dogs should always be supervised together. The same is true with other pets. A Chessie will most likely get along well with other pets, but dogs typically need to establish their hierarchy and order of dominance with other dogs in the household. Both Maizie and Hank always had a healthy respect for cats, despite the tremendous size difference. One or two swipes across the nose from razor-sharp cat claws were enough for our big, powerful Chesapeake Bay Retrievers to give the cats a wide berth.

Photo Courtesy of Emma Totten = @daisy.the.chessie on IG

Is the Chesapeake Bay Retriever the Right Dog for You?

> *"A Chesapeake is best suited to an active family. Lots of outdoor activity is a plus. The Chesapeake can be protective of their family and must be trained to know the difference between wanted and unwanted visitors. These are not dogs that will do well with no boundaries or limits. A Chesapeake will be happy to be the boss of the family if you do not want to be."*
>
> **JOANN COLVIN**
> *Cal-I-Co Chesapeakes*

If you are looking for a dog breed that will be the ideal fit for your lifestyle and your family, how do you know if the Chesapeake Bay Retriever is the right dog for you? I would first advise you to do plenty of research on the breed. Reading this book is a great start. Learn all you can about the Chessie so you can make an informed decision before you jump in with a lively and rambunctious Chessie puppy. With your research in hand, take a close look at your own lifestyles so you can realistically determine if you can provide the type of life for your Chessie that he deserves.

Chessies need a dominant and firm owner to tame their strong will. This is not the right breed for a first-time dog owner. A novice dog owner, even one with the best intentions, runs the risk of being inconsistent with their training or accidentally reinforcing bad habits.

Chessies are large, active dogs that need open spaces. They do not adapt well to apartment living. Instead, they thrive in more rural or suburban settings, ideally in a home with a large, fenced yard. These dogs are athletes and they need to keep their muscular bodies in shape. Even if you live near a dog park or are committed to frequent walks, you may not be able to provide your Chessie with the daily workouts that he needs unless he has a sizable yard of his own.

Of course, Chesapeake Bay Retrievers love to swim, but that doesn't mean you need to install a swimming pool or build a pond for your Chessie. If you live near a public lake or river with a dog beach, you may want to plan some outings there to let your Chessie get in some laps. In the summer months, we take Hank to a park at a nearby lake that has a dog beach and let him paddle around. He has even had the opportunity to go swimming in a few of the Great Lakes. As much as he enjoys swimming, he loves to play fetch in the water most of all. There is always a tennis ball or two in

CHAPTER 2 Physical and Personality Traits of the Chesapeake Bay Retriever

Photo Courtesy of
Brad and Meghan Phillips

FUN FACT
The Camouflaged Coat

Chesapeake Bay Retrievers are traditionally hunting dogs, so it should come as no surprise that the dominant shade for these dogs is brown. According to the breed standard, Chessies come in brown, sedge, and dead grass. Sedge can range from a reddish yellow to brighter red shades, while dead grass is light brown with no red tones.

his doggie backpack and he will spend hours retrieving the ball that we throw out into the water. This is how he gets in touch with his duck-hunting heritage, I guess.

The Chessie may not be the dog for you if your work takes you away from home for most of the day. Chessies are not content to wait quietly for their people to return. When they get bored, they may act out (see my defunct lawnmower as proof). If you work from home, like I do, the Chessie may be a good choice.

If you have young children, you may want to hold off a few years before you get a Chessie. Although Chessies are good family dogs and are protective of children, young kids can be unpredictable. Little ones make sudden moves, cry shrilly, and could fall on your dog, which could startle him so much that he nips. Chessies are gentle dogs, but they are also big dogs. They could inadvertently injure a youngster. It is better to wait until your kids are older before you bring a Chessie into your life.

As hunting dogs, Chessies love to be outdoors. They make great hiking and camping buddies. More and more people today are embracing the outdoor adventurer lifestyles and spend their weekends on the nature trails. If you are one of these people, you may find that a Chesapeake Bay Retriever fits nicely into this hobby. A Chessie is strong enough to carry a doggie backpack with his own water and food and rugged enough to ford a creek, scramble over jagged boulders, and spend all day on the trail. He will happily sleep in your tent as long as he is by your side.

Like other large dog breeds, the Chesapeake Bay Retriever is predisposed to certain genetic disorders, including hip dysplasia. They can also develop progressive retinal atrophy, gastric torsion, and hypothyroidism. Before committing to bringing a Chessie into your family, you should be aware of potential health concerns that may pop up as your dog ages. Awareness of these genetic problems can help you be proactive about them.

Lastly, you need to make sure that you are fully prepared to financially care for your Chesapeake Bay Retriever. They are eating machines and need a lot of top-quality food to fuel their large, muscular bodies, so you need

CHAPTER 2   Physical and Personality Traits of the Chesapeake Bay Retriever

to have room in your budget for dog food. You will also need to plan for regular veterinary visits, medication, toys, treats, and any other supplies you may need. Hank is a bandana connoisseur, which is fortunately, a fairly inexpensive hobby.

Chessies are terrific dogs. Admittedly, I am biased but I know that these are not the ideal dog for everyone. You will be doing a great disservice to a dog if you try to mold a Chesapeake Bay Retriever into your lifestyle when it is not a compatible fit. However, if you check many of the boxes we've discussed, it could be that a Chessie would make a wonderful addition to your home. If so, read on. Let the adventure begin!

CHAPTER 3:
Finding Your Perfect Chesapeake Bay Retriever

Photo Courtesy of Chris Levey

Congratulations! If you have made it this far into this book, that probably means that you have decided that the Chesapeake Bay Retriever is the right dog for you. So, what is your next step? You need to find your perfect dog. This is a big and important step and one that should not be taken lightly. I know you are excited, but take your time, do your research, and ask the right questions. You will be rewarded in due time with a happy, healthy dog.

People may automatically think the only way to obtain a Chessie is to find a Chesapeake Bay Retriever breeder and purchase a puppy. There are, however, alternatives to this route. You could adopt a Chessie from a shelter or a rescue organization. We will discuss these options, as well as some options to avoid, in this chapter.

CHAPTER 3   Finding Your Perfect Chesapeake Bay Retriever

How to Find a Chesapeake Bay Retriever Breeder

"First and foremost: Look for breeders that do health clearances and testing. The parents should have both hips and elbows x-rayed and scored by OFA and show no signs of dysplasia. Genetic testing includes DM (degenerative myelopathy) EIC (exercise induced collapse) and PRA (progressive retinal atrophy). Run away from any breeder that simply says they've never had a problem and their vet says the dogs are healthy. That is not proof of health testing. Any reputable breeder will be able to give you the official results on both OFA (Orthopedic Foundation for Animals) and genetic results. None of this testing has anything to do with competitions, it has to do with you getting a healthy pet that can be a good family member for many years without worry of these preventable diseases."

SHARON POTTER
Red Branch Kennels

The Chesapeake Bay Retriever is not one of the most popular dog breeds in the United States, which is both good news and bad news for people looking to find a Chessie breeder. It is bad news because you may not be able to easily find someone who breeds Chessies in your area. It may take some work to track down a breeder and you may have to drive outside your region to visit the breeder's kennel. The good news is that when you do find a Chessie breeder, you may find that the breeder genuinely loves the dogs and is committed to producing top-quality pups. Since Goldens and Labs are more popular and there is a larger market for these breeds, there are more less-than-reputable Golden and Lab breeders that are more interested in making money than they are in helping to maintain the integrity of the breed.

You can start your search for a Chessie breeder by talking to your veterinarian. He or she may know of a local breeder they would recommend. You can also talk to other Chessie owners. If you happen to know someone who has a Chesapeake Bay Retriever, or you encounter someone with a Chessie at the dog park, ask them for advice on finding a breeder.

Chesapeake Bay Retrievers are popular with duck hunters so consider contacting a duck-hunting club near you. Likely someone in the club has a Chessie or knows someone who does. They may be able to point you in the right direction.

You can also contact a Chesapeake Bay Retriever club. Every dog breed has a club for advocates and supporters of that breed. Your state probably has a Chesapeake Bay Retriever club. They keep records of Chessie breeders and can supply you with the names and contact information for reputable breeders.

How to NOT Find a Chesapeake Bay Retriever Breeder

Your goal should be to find a healthy Chessie pup with a solid lineage. To accomplish this goal, you need to locate a dog breeder with a good reputation. If you happen across an ad in a newspaper, a flyer on a community bulletin board, or a post online, be sure to decode the information carefully. Often there are clues to tell you valuable information about the breeder.

Don't be dazzled by phrases like "with papers," "pedigree," "full-blooded," "licensed," or "USDA-certified." Often, backyard breeders and puppy mills toss these terms around to inflate their own reputation. They are counting on customers who are not familiar with the breeding process. Terms like "USDA-certified" and "pedigree" sound impressive on the surface, but they are actually red flags to avoid. Back in the years after the Second World War, the USDA launched a campaign to encourage farmers to breed and sell dogs as another revenue stream, essentially kickstarting the puppy mill industry. Be leery of the term "full-blooded," too. In the world of legitimate dog breeding, this word has no real meaning. The preferred term is "purebred." This is yet another ploy that puppy mill breeders use to attract unknowing customers.

By definition, a puppy mill is a dog-breeding operation that focuses more on the quantity of the puppies they put on the market than on the quality. According to the Humane Society of the United States, a puppy mill prioritizes profit over the health and well-being of the dogs. Dogs are not bred to improve the breed but are arbitrarily mated with no regard for lineage and genetic traits. Since the goal of puppy mills is to turn quick profits, overhead is kept as low as possible. The dogs are kept in poor housing, not socialized with people, receive little to no veterinary care, and are fed a low-grade diet. The females are forced to churn out litter after litter of pups before their bodies have time to fully recover and puppies are often removed from their mother and sold before they are ready.

A word of warning to keep in mind when you are dog shopping -- nearly all puppies sold in pet stores come from puppy mills. Naturally, the employees at the pet store have been trained to tell you otherwise. To be fair, most of them are not out and out lying to you. Management does a great job of masking the true source of their puppy inventory so that their employees sound sincere when they tell you that their dogs only come from quality breeders. The puppies in pet stores are terribly cute but remind yourself that nearly all the puppies have come from puppy mills. And, no, you haven't stumbled upon the only pet store that sells ethically sourced pups, no

CHAPTER 3 Finding Your Perfect Chesapeake Bay Retriever

matter what the salesperson tells you. Puppy mill breeders stay in business because enough people purchase from them. If more people were aware of the dangers of puppy mills, they would stop supporting them and their business would eventually end.

Photo Courtesy of Robert Evans

How to Differentiate Between a Reputable Chessie Breeder and a Backyard Breeder

On the spectrum of ethical and unethical dog breeders, backyard breeders are somewhere in the middle. They are not as unethical as puppy mills, but they are also not the type of breeder that has the best interest of the Chesapeake Bay Retriever breed at the forefront. A puppy from a backyard breeder may seem happy and healthy at first but he has an increased likelihood of developing a genetic disorder later in life.

Here's how it usually goes. Someone gets a Chessie and their friend, neighbor, co-worker, or brother-in-law says something like, "I have a buddy with a Chesapeake Bay Retriever. We should mate them. You can each keep a puppy and sell the rest of the litter." It sounds innocent enough. But the problem is the breeders are inexperienced and mate their dogs without considering the genetic traits of the parents that they want to bring out in the litter.

Unlike puppy mill breeders, backyard breeders are not churning out litter after litter of pups as a major source of their income. The breeding of their Chessie is usually a one-time thing. They do it because their own dog is just so stinking cute that they want to replicate it.

Often, a backyard breeder will offer puppies for sale that they claim are purebred, but not registered. The breeder may spin it so you think you are getting a bargain on a purebred Chesapeake Bay Retriever. This should serve as a red flag. An ethical breeder wouldn't purposely not register a litter of puppies just to offer you a discount dog.

One of the best ways to determine if you are dealing with a quality Chessie breeder or a backyard breeder is to ask a lot of questions. The key is that you must be able to walk away if you hear answers that you don't like, no matter how cute the puppy is. As hard as it is, you should make your Chessie puppy decision based on your head, not your heart.

FUN FACT
How Popular Are They?

In 2020, according to the AKC, Chesapeake Bay Retrievers were ranked 45th most popular breed out of 196 breeds. The AKC breed popularity ranking is based on registration statistics each year. In 2019 Chessies were ranked 46th, and in 2018 they were ranked 45th.

CHAPTER 3 Finding Your Perfect Chesapeake Bay Retriever

Questions to Ask a Breeder During a Phone Interview

"Spend some time talking with breeders you're considering, in person if you live close enough or at the very least, on the phone. Don't be surprised if you're asked a lot of questions as well. Breeders put their hearts into every puppy they produce and they want to know you'll be a great home. A good breeder will be a support system for you for the life of your dog and can answer questions and help you along the way."

SHARON POTTER
Red Branch Kennels

Ideally, your research has led you to a few Chesapeake Bay Retriever breeders in your area. Your next step is to contact each breeder and ask a series of questions over the phone. I know that we live in the digital age and people much prefer to text or email, but in this case, there are some advantages to speaking to another human on the telephone. You should be able to gauge the honesty and passion of their responses, for example. A breeder who is passionate about the Chesapeake Bay Retriever breed will be eager to discuss the breed with you and tell you about the puppies they have available. They should not make you feel like you are pestering them with all your questions. After all, their goal is to place their puppies in great homes. Prepare your questions ahead of time, so you get the information that you need when conducting your phone interview.

- **ARE THE CHESSIE PUPPIES AKC REGISTERED?**

Dogs are registered upon their birth. You cannot get an unregistered puppy and register it later on. You should also be aware that, in order for a litter to be AKC registered, both parents must also have been registered, so be sure to ask the breeder about the registration status of the parents, too.

- **CAN YOU MEET THE PARENTS?**

Ask if both parents are on site and available for you to meet them. Find out about the health of the parents. Many larger breed dogs like Chesapeake Bay Retrievers are prone to some genetic disorders, such as hip dysplasia. Ask the breeder if the parents have been health tested to screen for illnesses and disorders that are common in purebred dogs. In addition to the health of the parents, you should ask specific questions about the personality and temperament.

- **HOW LONG HAS THE BREEDER BEEN IN BUSINESS?**

Ask plenty of questions about the breeder's business. Have they been breeding Chessies for a long time or are they fairly new to the industry? About how many litters have they bred? On average, how many litters do they breed per year? Ask them why they chose to breed Chesapeake Bay Retrievers. What attracted them to this breed? Do they breed other dog breeds as well? In general, reputable dog breeders focus only on one or two breeds, whereas puppy mill breeders handle many different breeds at the same time.

- **DO YOU HAVE REFERENCES?**

Ask the breeder if he or she can give you the names and contact information for a few people who have recently purchased Chesapeake Bay Retrievers from them. Don't be afraid to call these people and ask a few questions. Find out if they are happy with the overall health and quality of the puppy they bought, if they have had any health or behavioral issues with the animal, and if they had a satisfactory experience working with that breeder. Ask if they would go back to that breeder for another puppy or if they would recommend that breeder to their best friends. If they had an issue with the breeder, ask a few more questions to determine if the problem was the fault of the breeder or if the person simply had unreasonable expectations.

- **WHEN CAN THE PUPPIES LEAVE THEIR MOTHER?**

Eight weeks is the recommended time that all breeds of dogs, including the Chesapeake Bay Retriever, remain with their mother. There is solid science behind this number. Puppies that are separated from their mothers and littermates earlier than eight weeks old have been shown to have appetite issues and growth delays, to be more anxious, clingy, and/or aggressive, and to have a higher probability of illness.

Any breeder of merit will know this. If the breeder is willing and eager to sell you a Chesapeake Bay Retriever puppy that is younger than eight weeks old, this should be a red flag. Are they trying to avoid the cost of another vet visit and round of vaccines? Are they anxious for your money? Do they need to move out a litter of pups to make room for another one? A Chesapeake Bay Retriever breeder who sells their puppies when they are too young to safely leave their mother does not have the best interest of the dogs at heart.

- **HOW ARE YOU SOCIALIZING THE PUPPIES?**

Instead of asking if the puppies have been socialized when you speak to a Chesapeake Bay Retriever breeder, ask how they are being socialized. The

CHAPTER 3 Finding Your Perfect Chesapeake Bay Retriever

answer will give you more information about the breeder, their facility, and their approach to breeding. Where are the puppies kept? Are the puppies living near the family? Are there children or other family members who play with them often? Are they readily accessible for playtime and socialization? Ask if the puppies are around other animals, be it other dogs, cats, chickens, or goats. The more people and animals the puppies encounter while they are young, the more socialized and well-adjusted they will be.

If the Chessie breeder has not been working with the litter on socialization, this may be an indicator that he or she does not know much about puppies or does not care about the type of family pets their puppies will make. Puppies have a short window for socialization and once they reach about nine or ten weeks of age, that window closes.

- **WHAT VACCINES HAVE THE PUPPIES HAD?**

A good Chessie breeder is concerned about the lifelong health of the puppies they produce and will want to give them the best start possible. That includes vaccines. A responsible breeder will take their puppies for their first veterinary visit and get them their first round of vaccines. Find out what vaccines the puppies have received, if any, and when they need to get their second round of immunizations. If the breeder tells you that the puppies have not been vaccinated and that it is your responsibility to do so, this should cause you some concern. It could be that the breeder is more concerned about making money – or saving money – than they are about the health and well-being of their pups.

- **HOW OFTEN DO YOU DEWORM THE PUPPIES?**

Chesapeake Bay Retriever puppies should be dewormed every two weeks from birth, so you are looking for this answer from the breeder you are talking to. If, instead, the breeder says that the puppies are too young to be dewormed or that they will deworm them before they are sold, ask yourself why. Perhaps the breeder is trying to cut corners and save some money. This could indicate an unscrupulous breeder.

- **CAN I COME MEET THE PUPPIES?**

If you are happy with the information you have received during your telephone interview with the Chesapeake Bay Retriever breeder, ask to set up a time to come to their kennel and see the puppies in person. A good, quality breeder is proud of their kennel and will be happy to have you come visit the facility and meet the puppies. A breeder who is hesitant about you coming for a visit or who suggests meeting at a neutral site might be hiding something. This should be a red flag to you that something is amiss.

Questions to Ask a Breeder During a Visit

After you weed through your list of potential Chesapeake Bay Retriever breeders based on the information you gleaned from phone interviews, the next step is to visit your top few choices. When you are visiting the breeders' facilities, there are a few things to look for and a few questions to ask. It is always a good idea to write down the questions ahead of time. Once you see the adorable puppies, you may forget what you wanted to ask.

- **LOOK AT WHERE THE PUPPIES LIVE**

Are the puppies in a kennel, in a house, or somewhere else? Wherever they are housed, check the overall cleanliness of their space. Is it drafty and leaky? Is it well-ventilated? Of course, puppies make messes but look to see if the space appears to have been regularly cleaned, isn't overrun with flies, and is readily accessible to the people living there. The puppies should not appear to be isolated from human contact.

You should also note the other animals at the facility. Are there several litters of puppies or different breeds? If so, this is often a sign that you are at a puppy mill.

- **INTERACT WITH THE PARENTS**

The mother will certainly be on site and, from your phone interview, you will know if the father is also there. Take a few moments to greet either parent. See how friendly they are and how they react to your gestures. Do they appear overly timid or somewhat aggressive? Remember that the temperament of the parents is often an indicator of the temperament of the puppies.

Also, see how healthy the parents seem. The mother will be thin as she is nursing a litter of hungry pups but run your hand along her spine. You should be able to feel her backbone, but it shouldn't stick out too much. Do the same with the father if you can. You will be able to tell if the dogs are well fed and well cared for.

You can also note how large the parents are which will give you a reasonable idea of how big your Chesapeake Bay Retriever puppy will grow to be. When we visited the breeder before we got our first Chessie, Maizie, I remember being stunned and terrified about how large Maizie's father was. He was an intimidating dog! But we quickly found out how friendly he was. Fortunately, Maizie took after her mother and was an average size for the Chesapeake Bay Retriever breed.

- **DO YOU OFFER SUPPORT AFTER THE PUPPY LEAVES YOUR KENNEL?**

The goal of any good Chesapeake Bay Retriever breeder is to give their customers a top-quality pup. Most breeders welcome the opportunity to

CHAPTER 3   Finding Your Perfect Chesapeake Bay Retriever

Photo Courtesy of Maria Okolita

stay in touch with their puppies' new owners and will happily answer any questions you have after you bring your new Chessie home. If you have a basic question or just want to find out if your puppy is hitting all his milestones, you should be able to give the breeder a quick call or text. Although most breeders are open to your calls and questions, the majority of them will not reach out to you to see how the pup is doing. They will respect your privacy, but they will always have a special place in their heart for your pup. You will make your breeder's day by sending a few pics now and then so they can see how your pup is growing and thriving.

- **WHAT DO THE PUPPIES EAT?**

Be sure to ask plenty of questions about the Chesapeake Bay Retriever puppies' diet. First of all, make sure that the breeder is offering the puppies a top-quality dog food and not a cheap, unhealthy alternative. It is also important for you to know what the dogs are being fed so that you can have the same food on hand for the puppy's homecoming. Puppies have sensitive digestive systems and can't tolerate abrupt changes in their diets. If you plan to feed the same type and brand of puppy food, there should be no problem. However, if you want to switch to a different dog food, you should mix the new food into the old food in increasing amounts each day to ease your pup into the new diet without causing a gastrointestinal upset.

Guarantees, Health Certifications, and Breeder's Contracts

"Chose from a breeder whose breeding stock has all the required health certifications and preferably has some competition titles on their dogs. A pedigree with known working dogs is preferable."

KATHY MILLER
Sandy Oak Chesapeakes

On the business side of dog breeding, there are several important documents that are part of the process. As a consumer, you should be aware of these and know the right questions to ask about them. These include guarantees, health certifications, certificate of sale, and breeder's contracts.

WHAT IS A GUARANTEE?

A guarantee is a document that is designed to protect both the breeder and the buyer. The guarantee states that the puppy is healthy, does not have an infectious disease, and has received the necessary vaccines. Typically, there is a clause in the guarantee that requires the new owner to take the puppy for a veterinary check-up within a specified time frame, such as within 72 hours. As per the guarantee, if the veterinarian discovers an illness or underlying health concern at this initial visit, the buyer can return the puppy to the breeder. This document protects the buyer by guaranteeing that they will be receiving a health puppy, but it also protects the breeder from deceitful owners who seek to get a refund after mistreating or neglecting their new puppy.

WHAT IS A HEALTH CERTIFICATION?

A health certification is a document issued by a veterinarian. The information on this certified veterinary inspection (CVI) is compiled after an examination of the puppy. Not only will it show that the dog is free of various illnesses and disorders, but it will note all the vaccines that Chessie puppy has received so far. In some states and municipalities, the health certification is required by law.

WHAT IS A CERTIFICATE OF SALE?

A certificate of sale from your Chesapeake Bay Retriever breeder is your receipt for the sale. This document outlines the terms and conditions of the sale and provides proof that the ownership of the puppy has transferred from the breeder to you. You will need this document if you need to return the Chessie puppy to the breeder for any reason.

What Is a Breeder's Contract?

A breeder's contract is standard practice in the world of purebred dog breeding. Once you pick out the Chesapeake Bay Retriever that you want, the breeder will ask you to sign a contract. The contract will state that you agree to purchase the puppy for the agreed-upon amount, that you will properly care for the Chessie puppy throughout its life, and that you agree to spay or neuter the animal within a predetermined amount of time. It will also state that the breeder will take the dog back at any time if you can no longer care for him.

The breeder's contract could include some stipulations that may surprise you. For example, the contract could state that you will inform the breeder if the ownership of the dog changes hands. You may think that this is nosy and unnecessary, however, the goal of the breeder is to place their puppies in good, loving, forever homes. Sometimes, though, the situation changes. You may have to move or could find out that a family member is allergic to the Chessie or experience financial hardships that make it difficult to care for the dog. A good breeder will feel responsible for the puppies they produce and will want to know where the dogs are and that they are in good homes. They also want to continue to be a source of support and information, even for the dog's new owner.

Another item that may be included in the breeder's contract might be naming convention. The document will include the puppy's AKC registered name, which is usually longer than the name that you call your Chessie. Some breeders, especially ones who consistently produce top show dogs, want their kennel name to be included in the AKC registered name.

How to Pick Out the Perfect Chessie Pup

"Make sure not just the breed, but also the individual puppy or adult Chessie fits into your environment and lifestyle. Temperaments and energy levels make a difference. A timid adult Chessie will likely not thrive in a busy household with several small children. On the other hand, a spirited Chessie puppy will not likely thrive in a slower paced environment. It's like oil and water. They can exist together, but they are never truly a part of one another."

LEAH SPRADLIN
Hickory Creek Chesapeakes

Once you have talked to the Chesapeake Bay Retriever breeder over the phone and in person and you are satisfied with the experience and background of the breeder, the cleanliness of the facility, and the overall health of the puppies, it is time to pick out a pup to call your own.

Before you rush in to scoop up the cuddly Chessie puppies, sit back for a few moments and observe how each pup interacts with his littermates. You should select a puppy that is active, confident, and outgoing, but not one that is overly aggressive or extremely timid. A shy puppy is cute, and you may sympathize with it, but its submissiveness could be a sign of anxiety or a behavioral issue.

Pick up the puppies – you know you want to! Check to see that the puppies wag their tails and hold their heads high without trying to squirm away from human contact. Gently flip the pup over on his back. He won't like this, but you need to take note of his reaction. Does he respond by nipping, vocalizing, or frantically trying to right himself? Or does he relax after a few moments and show his trust for you? A well socialized dog will be used to human touch and be trusting.

CHAPTER 3 Finding Your Perfect Chesapeake Bay Retriever

Adopting a Chessie

"First you must determine if you'd rather have a dog from a breeder or rescue. In my personal opinion, a person adopting from rescue should have had a Chesapeake previously. Whether a breeder or rescue, the person offering the dog should be able to produce health certifications for hips, eyes, genetic diseases, and vet exams. The temperament of the dog is of great importance- not shy or fearful, not aggressive. Look for a confident and happy dog and if from a breeder, confident and happy mother and kennel mates."

JOANN COLVIN
Cal-I-Co Chesapeakes

Purchasing a puppy from a Chesapeake Bay Retriever breeder is certainly not the only way to acquire a Chessie. You could consider adoption. Adoption differs from buying from a breeder in that you are acquiring the dog secondhand, either from an animal shelter or from a rescue organization that specializes in the Chesapeake Bay Retriever breed. It should not be viewed as a bad thing that the Chessie has had a previous owner. There are plenty of benefits to adopting a Chessie.

Animal Shelters

Most counties and municipalities in the United States operate an animal shelter. The purpose of animal shelters is to house stray and unwanted pets, protect vulnerable dogs and cats, and to keep lost pets safe until they can be reunited with their owners. Dogs that are surrendered to the animal shelter or strays that have not been claimed are available for adoption for a nominal fee. Animal shelters can be a great source when searching for a Chessie.

- **YOU GIVE A DOG A SECOND CHANCE**

Dogs end up in shelters for all sorts of reasons and the majority of them have little to do with the dog, and more to do with the humans. Divorce, job loss, financial difficulties, and moving are the most common reasons why people surrender their animals to shelters. According to the Humane Society of the United States, about six million pets are placed in shelters every year. At the shelter, they are fed a nutritious diet, given plenty of exercise, get lots of human interactions, and receive veterinary care. What they also need is a forever home.

Shelters are designed to be temporary housing for dogs until they can be adopted. When you adopt a dog from a shelter you are giving that animal a second chance to have a great life. He may have had a sad, neglectful background or he may have had loving owners with whom he bonded. But circumstances changed and he had to go through a period of instability and confusion. When you welcome him into your home, he will sense the change and react with a grateful, loving response.

- **YOU ARE HELPING ADDRESS THE PROBLEM OF HOMELESS PETS**

When you adopt a dog from a shelter, you are not only saving that dog, but you are freeing up space in the shelter for another animal in need. In a sense, you are saving at least two dogs. Although there are plenty of no-kill shelters that remain committed to rehoming their dogs, there are still numerous shelters that, due to limited space and resources, euthanize unwanted pets.

- **SHELTERS SCREEN ADOPTERS**

Like responsible breeders, animal shelters will screen the potential adopters to make sure that they are placing their animals in loving, caring homes. The last thing these shelters want to see is the same dog returning to the shelter because his new owners decided they didn't want him or couldn't afford him. They will make sure that their adopters do not have a criminal record of animal cruelty or abuse. When buying a dog from a pet store, there is no prescreening process. Once the payment is made, the pup is sent away with his new owners.

- **SHELTERS SPAY AND NEUTER**

The mission of animal shelters is to reduce the number of homeless pets, so they proactively spay and neuter the animals that come through their doors. When you adopt from a shelter, you will receive a dog that is fully up to date on his vaccines, is under the care of a veterinarian, and has been spayed or neutered. If the dog is too young to be spayed or neutered, you may be required to sign an agreement stating that you will have this procedure done as soon as the puppy is old enough. Many times, the shelter will even provide you with a discount voucher that will pay for a portion of the procedure.

- **ADOPTION FEES ARE MINIMAL**

Adopting a dog from a shelter is less expensive than buying a dog from a breeder or pet store. Breeders emphasize quality over quantity and price their puppies accordingly. Their primary goal is to support the breed of the dog and produce litters of puppies that conform to the breed standard. Income is secondary. Pet stores and puppy mills, on the other hand, are

CHAPTER 3 Finding Your Perfect Chesapeake Bay Retriever

*Photo Courtesy of
Celia Wright*

in business to make a profit. They increase their profit margin by cutting corners whenever possible. The majority of the funding that animal shelters receive come from county and municipal budgets and donations. The adoption fee that shelters charge covers the cost of their care: food, medical care, and housing.

- **PUREBRED CHESSIES ARE AVAILABLE AT SHELTERS**

Animal shelters see dogs of all shapes and sizes and breeds coming through their doors. Some are mixed breed dogs, likely the products of unintentional mating. Others are purebred dogs that ended up in the shelter because their owners could no longer care for them. The majority of the dogs are well-behaved, socialized, and crave human interaction. If you are patient and contact several animal shelters, it is possible for you to locate a Chesapeake Bay Retriever that has been surrendered to a shelter. These days, with the popularity of dog DNA kits, it is possible to learn the lineage of a Chessie you want to adopt.

Chessie Rescue Organizations

"If your Chessie is a rescue, you should know that it takes a long time for the Chesapeake to trust again after any traumatic experience. Therefore be willing to dedicate a lot of love, patience and routines to help him to trust again."

MECHA SAILORSBAY
Sailorsbay Kennel

In the United States alone, there are several Chesapeake Bay Retriever rescue organizations whose mission it is to care for and rehome Chessies that have been forfeited to shelters. Because these groups focus solely on the Chesapeake Bay Retriever, they have a thorough understanding of the breed.

When a Chessie comes to one of these rescue groups, the dedicated workers first make sure that the dog's individual needs are met. They get them proper veterinary care and nutrition, as needed. If necessary, they will rehabilitate the Chessie to improve the chances of him finding a loving home. They then seek responsible owners who love the Chessie breed and can provide the dog with a happy, love-filled home. You can find a Chessie rescue organization by doing an internet search or by contacting a Chesapeake Bay Retriever breed club in your area. They can often direct you to a rescue group.

CHAPTER 3 Finding Your Perfect Chesapeake Bay Retriever

Rescue organizations differ from animal shelters in that the workers are all volunteers. They have a love for the Chesapeake Bay Retriever breed and a strong desire to help place homeless Chessie in forever homes. Rescue organizations are extremely careful throughout the adoption process to make sure that potential adopters meet their high standards.

- **THE APPLICATION STEP**

The first step when adopting a Chessie through a rescue organization is the application process. The application is often lengthy and all-encompassing. You will be asked to provide a brief description of everyone living in the house. The rescue group will want to know everyone's ages, personality types, occupation, education levels, work and school schedules, and previous dog experience. They will also ask a number of questions about your home, including the square footage, yard size, if the yard is fenced, the type of neighborhood you live in, and how much traffic is on your road. You will also be asked to provide the names and contact information for several references. The application is detailed so that the organization can vet potential adopters.

- **APPLICATION FEE**

When you submit your application to a Chessie rescue organization, you will be asked to pay an application fee. The exact amount varies from organization to organization, but the fee will be non-refundable. If you change your mind or the rescue group denies your application, you will not get your money back. The application fee is used to pay for the care of the Chessies. The application makes it extremely clear that submitting the application and paying the fee does not guarantee that you will be approved to adopt a Chessie.

- **REFERENCES**

A volunteer from the rescue organization will reach out to your references to glean additional information about the applicant. Your reference will be asked how they know you and for how long. They will ask about the interactions they have witnessed between you and your previous dogs. They will be asked about your integrity and character. They want to hear positive stories about you and your previous pets. Be sure to choose your references wisely and discuss the adoption process with them so they understand the importance of it.

- **VETERINARY REFERENCE**

On the application for the rescue organization, you will be asked to give the name and contact information for your veterinarian. A trained volunteer will contact the veterinarian to ask a number of questions about you.

They are trying to determine if you are diligent about routine health check-ups, the overall care that you give to your pets, how your previous dog or dogs have died, and if your previous animals ever had a serious injury accident or illness.

- **IN-HOME INTERVIEW**

Based on the information gathered in the application and reference check stages, the rescue organization may send a volunteer to do an interview with you in your home. The interviewer won't show up unannounced. He or she will set up a time for the interview and will ask that all family members be present, if possible. The purpose of the in-home interview is twofold. First, the volunteer will assess your home to see if it seems safe and spacious enough for a Chesapeake Bay Retriever. You will be asked to show the interviewer your yard so he or she can inspect the fencing. The interviewer will ask additional questions, including why you want to adopt a Chesapeake Bay Retriever, where the dog will sleep, how familiar are you with your local dog ordinances, how long the dog will be home alone, and what hobbies and activities you enjoy. The volunteer will want to meet your other pets, too. You may be asked to disclose your budget for food, vet bills, grooming, and other dog-related expenses.

- **APPLICATION APPROVAL**

The in-home interview, the information collected from your references, and the answers you wrote on your application will all be submitted to a committee of volunteers at the rescue organization for review. The committee will decide to either approve your application or decline it. You will be notified either way. If you are approved, the next step in the process is to match you with a Chessie in need of a forever home. By this time, the rescue organization probably has a good overview of your personality, commitment, and lifestyle. They will be able to select a Chessie in their possession that they believe will be an ideal fit for you. The rescue group will arrange for a meet and greet between you and the Chessie and will monitor the meeting to see how you and the dog interact with each other.

- **A DONE DEAL**

Once your application is approved and you had a meet and greet with a Chessie or two, the adoption process will be finalized, and you can bring your rescued Chesapeake Bay Retriever to his new forever home. You will be asked to sign an adoption agreement that outlines the stipulations for the adoption. In this contract, you promise to abide by the rescue organization's requirements, including routine veterinary visits and licensing as per your town's ordinances. When you sign the contract, you will also be asked to pay the adoption fee and to give a monetary donation to the rescue organization. The adoption fee is not the same thing as the application fee. Adoption fees for rescue organizations are typically higher than they are for animal shelters. Rescue groups, unlike animal shelters, are not partially funded by the government. They rely solely on donations and adoption fees. Once the adoption process is complete, you may be asked to give a donation to the rescue group to help fund their continued work.

The Perks of Adopting an Older Chessie

Puppies are just so darn cute, but they are also an awful lot of work. Plus, they don't stay little for long. Don't discount the idea of adopting an adult Chesapeake Bay Retriever instead of getting a puppy from a breeder. There are a surprising number of perks to adopting an older Chessie.

First, older Chessies are typically housebroken already and probably know a few commands. The house-training process with a puppy is not much fun. When you adopt an older dog, you and your carpet get to skip that stage. Despite what the old wives' tale says, you can teach an older dog new tricks. Adult Chessies are smart and eager to please. They enjoy keeping their minds active and relish the opportunity to learn new tricks.

Older Chesapeake Bay Retrievers are much calmer and better behaved than Chessie puppies. Puppies are energetic and excited to experience new things. Once they become familiar with all the different aspects of life, they settle down some. That doesn't mean an adult Chessie won't be playful and active. It just means they are more controlled in their play.

You can still develop a great relationship with an older Chessie. Dogs never outgrow their ability to form connections and bond with people. When treated with kindness and love, they reflect that back to you. More importantly, older dogs need our help. Too many adult dogs of all breeds end up in animal shelters or with rescue groups and are waiting for a second shot at a happy life.

CHAPTER 4:
Get Ready for your Chessie's Homecoming

"Most pups require the same type of home preparation, but the Chesapeake should have a secure crate in the house to be safe when unattended. They also need an outdoor run, with enough room to burn some energy. A Chesapeake can become easily bored, and the outside time can give him activities to observe as well as interact with his environment."

JOANN COLVIN
Cal-I-Co Chesapeakes

Photo Courtesy of Andra Collins

CHAPTER 4   Get Ready for your Chessie's Homecoming

You have done your research, located a reputable Chesapeake Bay Retriever breeder, and selected the perfect Chessie puppy for you. While you wait for the puppy to grow old enough to leave its mother and join your family, you now need to prepare to bring the puppy home. Waiting is hard, but you can help pass the days by gathering all the supplies you need, puppy proofing your home and yard, and preparing your children and other pets for the introduction of a new dog into the family dynamics.

FUN FACT
Pancho, the Fastest Paw in the West

Chesapeake Bay Retrievers made their on-screen debut on an episode of *Walt Disney's Wonderful World of Color* on February 2, 1969. The episode was titled "Pancho, the Fastest Paw in the West" and was an Old West story about a Chessie named Pancho and his owner, a Mexican boy named Manuel.

What Supplies Do I Need to Have on Hand?

The last thing you want to do is to interrupt your Chessie's happy homecoming because you need to run to the store for puppy pads. It is best to have all the supplies you need already at your house. So, what exactly do you need?

PUPPY PADS – Do your floor a favor and purchase a few packs of puppy training pads before you bring your little Chesapeake Bay Retriever home. Spread a few on the floor. Anytime you catch your Chessie pup assuming the position, you can whisk him up and plop him on the puppy pad. Until he can be trained to let you know when he needs to go outside, he will figure out where you want him to conduct his business.

PUPPY FOOD – Ideally, you have found out what puppy food your Chessie puppy was fed at the breeder's and you purchased some of that same food. If you have decided that this is the food you want to feed your Chesapeake Bay Retriever, then you are all set. But if you want to use a different food, you will need to purchase some of both kinds of food. To avoid giving your Chessie pup an upset stomach, you will want to slowly introduce the new food by mixing small amounts of it into the food he is used to eating. Every few days, increase the ratio so that the puppy is getting more and more of the new food without stressing his digestive system.

FOOD AND WATER BOWLS – You will need to have a food bowl and water bowl for your pup. There are a lot of different food and water bowls on the market today. Some of them tout their all-natural, chemical-free, lead-free composition while others claim to reduce the mess made by exuberant eaters and drinkers. It is really a personal preference which kind you want to use. What really matters is that the bowls be washable so that you can clean them regularly.

PUPPY TREATS – Treats are more than the goodies with which you spoil your dog because he is just so stinkin' cute. They are important training tools that you will use to reinforce good behavior when you are training him. There are some extremely good, tasty, and healthy treats on the market today and an equal number of unhealthy, high-calorie treats. Be sure to read the ingredients and consult with your veterinarian to determine the best puppy treats to use that are small, soft, low in fat and calories.

A COLLAR, LEASH, AND I.D. TAG – You should always have a collar on your Chesapeake Bay Retriever with an identification tag on it when the pup is outside. If your pup runs away from you, he will carry with him your contact information for a quick reunion. Every single time you take your puppy outside, you should have him on a leash to prevent him from escaping. Look for a collar that fits snugly but isn't too tight and one that is made of soft material that won't chafe his baby skin. You may want to use a harness when you are training him to walk on a leash. As for the leash itself, look for

Photo Courtesy of JD Odell

a strong and durable one. Your Chessie puppy is small right now, but soon he will be strong and powerful.

When Hank was a young pup, we took him to the vet. Of course, he was wearing his collar and we had him on a leash. While the vet was examining him, Hank chewed the metal ring off his leash and swallowed it in just two swift bites, I swear. We were all in shock. A few moments later, Hank threw up on the exam room floor. There, in the pile of vomit, was the metal ring! The vet said she would not have believed it if she hadn't seen it herself.

DOGGIE WASTE BAGS – When you are at the pet store picking out sweet collars and fun toys, grab a few rolls of doggie waste bags, otherwise known as poop bags. Toss these in your car, your purse, your coat pocket, or get one of those little holders that clip onto the leash.

DOG CRATE – Chessie puppies only stay little for a few minutes so be sure to purchase a crate that is large enough for a growing pup. Chessies are chewers, so I would suggest getting a metal crate. We tried using a canvas travel crate, but Hank chewed right through it. There are plastic ones on the market, as well, however we opted for the metal one. Even then, it wasn't completely escape-proof. Hank bent a few wires and squeezed his little puppy body through. In just a few weeks, he was too big to repeat his escape act.

TOYS – To keep your Chessie puppy's active little brain occupied – and to distract him from chewing on your couch – offer him a supply of puppy toys. Not only are they good for mental stimulation, but the toys help you to bond. You can play fetch with a ball or tug of war with a pull toy. Chessies are chewers so look for top-quality toys that will hold up to the rigorous play of an eager puppy.

DOGGIE SHAMPOO AND GROOMING SUPPLIES – You may think that you don't need to have puppy shampoo on hand right away. Let me tell you, if you don't have dog shampoo, a brush, and other grooming supplies on hand, your new Chessie puppy will find a mud puddle to frolic in as soon as you arrive home. I speak from experience. It is better to err on the side of caution and purchase a bottle of puppy shampoo, brush, and nail clippers, just in case.

CLEANING SUPPLIES – You need to accept the fact that your Chesapeake Bay Retriever is going to make some messes. Actually, quite a few messes. Have a stock of cleaning supplies on hand so you can quickly clean up after your pup. Buy several rolls of paper towels, cleaners with enzymes that are especially formulated to remove puppy urine, and floor cleaners that are safe for puppies (they like to lick the floor). A quick mop with disposable cleaning pads is good for small clean ups. A pet hair extension on your vacuum can help get the fur off your carpets and furniture.

How Do I Puppy Proof My House?

Chesapeake Bay Retriever puppies are curious and active as they love to explore their surroundings. To keep your puppy safe and to protect your belongings, you need to thoroughly puppy proof your home before you bring your new Chessie home.

One of the best ways to puppy proof your home is to get down to your hands and knees and see the world from your puppy's point of view. When you get down close to the floor, you will better see potential hazards, such as electrical cords, tiny children's toys, ponytail rubber bands, mini-blind pulls, and eyeglasses. Move the furniture and thoroughly vacuum everywhere. There may be small objects, such as coins, thumbtacks, or broken glass, that have fallen under your end tables and behind your couch that could pose a choking hazard to a puppy.

Some common houseplants can be dangerous, even deadly, to dogs. Before your Chessie's arrival, be sure to Google the names of your houseplants so you can remove any that are toxic. If you are unsure of any plant, either remove it or put it somewhere inaccessible to your puppy. It is better to err on the side of caution. Among the more common houseplants that you should avoid in your home are aloe vera, jade, philodendron, ivy, elephant ear plant, sago palm, bird of paradise, and some varieties of lilies. Before you purchase new houseplants, always ask the experts at the garden center or nursery to direct you to houseplants that are safe for homes with dogs.

In the bathroom, make sure that everyone in the family learns to leave the toilet seat down. A thirsty little pup looking for a drink could fall in. Typically, bathroom trash cans are much smaller than kitchen ones. They are the perfect height for a curious Chessie puppy to get in to. Some of the stuff we toss into the bathroom trash can be harmful to a puppy, such as dental floss, disposable razors, discarded medicine, and those tiny rubber bands that teens wear on their braces. Make sure to move the bathroom trash to inside a cabinet or closet so your puppy won't be tempted to dive in. Be sure that the vanity doors close securely or use child safety locks to keep them closed. Bathroom cleaning chemicals are often kept under the sink, and you will want to be sure that your Chessie can't get into these.

The same holds true for the kitchen cabinets. Take steps to make sure that your new Chessie puppy can't get into the harsh cleaning supplies you have stored under your kitchen sink. And keep the kitchen trash secured. Many human foods are poisonous to dogs and can make them sick -- onions, avocados, grapes, coffee grounds, and raisins, for example. As your puppy grows taller, be mindful of items left on the counter. Chessies love to counter surf.

CHAPTER 4   Get Ready for your Chessie's Homecoming

Case in point: Hank was a lean and lanky eight-month-old puppy when this incident happened. One evening, my husband grilled a steak for dinner and set his plate on the kitchen counter when he was done. Hank jumped up and grabbed the steak knife. He held the handle in his mouth with the sharp blade sticking out. Naturally, I tried to get the knife away from Hank, but every time I reached my hand down toward his mouth, he swung his head back and forth and jumped around. I was in danger of being slashed by a knife-wielding Chessie!

This went on for several minutes and I was certain it was going to end in bloodshed, then I suddenly had an idea. I grabbed one of Hank's treats and offered it to him. Of course, he immediately dropped the knife and snatched up the treat. I know what you are thinking; by giving Hank a treat, I was reinforcing his bad behavior. Given the circumstances, however, I stand by my actions. Treats are the only way to win a knife fight with a Chesapeake Bay Retriever.

But I digress. In the bedrooms, electrical cords should be moved out of reach. Be careful what items you and your family leave on your nightstand

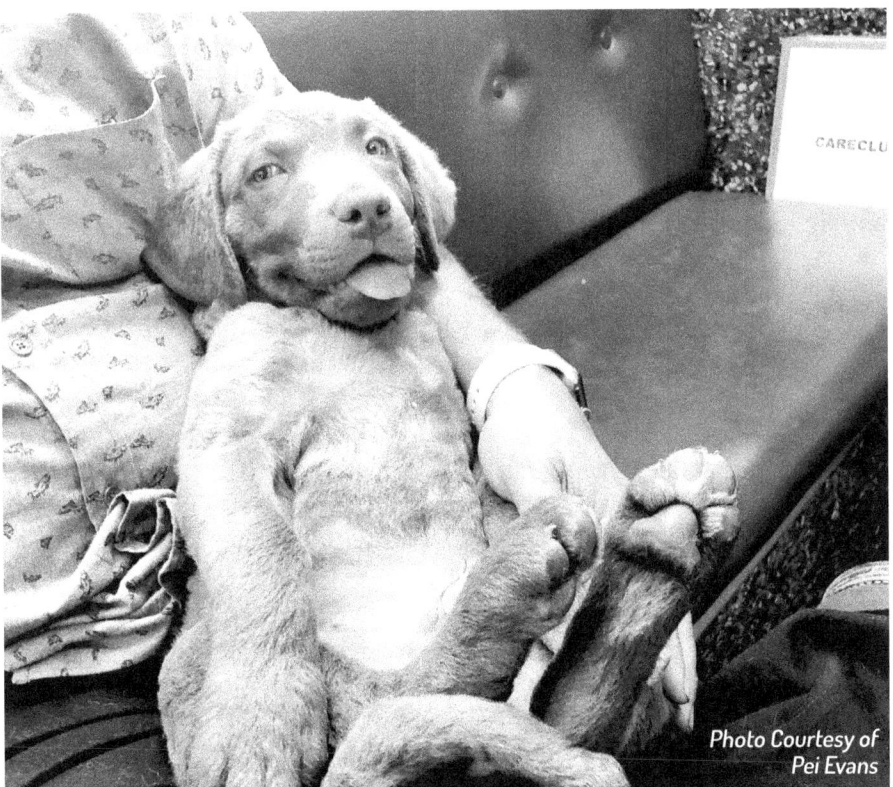

Photo Courtesy of Pei Evans

that your Chesapeake Bay Retriever could reach. This includes orthodontic retainers, eyeglasses, hearing aids, dentures, Airpods, and wedding rings.

How Do I Puppy Proof My Garage and Yard?

Chesapeake Bay Retrievers love being outside, so it is up to you to make sure that your yard and garage are safe. Let's start in the garage.

The garage is where people store a lot of our hazardous household chemicals, such as paint, fertilizers, antifreeze, and mouse poison. While some of these chemicals can make a dog sick, others are downright deadly. All of these things need to be kept in a locked cabinet. Small nails and screws, sharp tools, and fishing lures can cause a choking hazard and should also be stored safely out of way.

Before you bring your Chessie home, be sure that your fence around your yard is secure. Check to make sure there are no spots low enough for a small puppy to wiggle under the fence and no places with items stacked against the fence that the puppy can climb on to escape. Make sure that all gates latch securely as well. If you have a pool in your yard, make sure that there is a fence around the pool. Chessies love to swim, but an overconfident puppy may jump in the water and not be able to climb out.

Try to identify the plants that you have growing in your yard so you can look them up to see if they are toxic to dogs. If they are, remove the plants and replace them with more dog-friendly landscape plants. Mums, bleeding hearts, lily-of-the-valley, hostas, irises, and foxglove are all plants that could sicken your dog. In addition, English ivy, wisteria, morning glories, and clematis should be removed from your yard because that can be toxic to dogs. Landscape experts at your local garden center can help you identify the plants in your yard (bring in pictures) so you can get rid of all toxic plants and replace them with landscape plants that are dog friendly.

Many homeowners want to have a lush, green yard so they have a lawn service come to periodically treat their yard with insecticides and fertilizers. Have a conversation with your lawn service company and request pet friendly alternatives to toxic chemicals.

On your deck or patio, keep citronella candles high enough that your Chessie puppy won't be attracted to the smell and try to eat them. Likewise, be careful with your grill. Drippings from the meat fall into the racks, charcoal, or the rocks in a gas grill and the smell is irresistible for puppies. Keep the lid to the grill closed or you may find a puppy licking the grilling racks. Not that this has ever happened to me.

CHAPTER 4   Get Ready for your Chessie's Homecoming

How to Prepare Your Children for Your Chessie's Homecoming

You should strive to make your Chesapeake Bay Retriever's transition to your home as calm and stress free as possible. To accomplish this, you will need to have all your family members on board, including your children.

Before your Chessie's homecoming day, have many discussions with your children about how they should behave when you bring your puppy home. For younger children, practice by role playing so they will better understand the situation. Come up with a code word that you can give to your child if he or she starts to get too rambunctious. Set clear expectations for your children's behavior and include consequences that will happen if someone gets too excitable. Perhaps the child will need to leave the room until they calm down.

For younger kids, you need to explain to them that loud noises, like excited squeals and screams, will scare the puppy. The same goes for sudden movements, such as jumping and darting around. Toddlers and little ones should know that it is not acceptable to pull tails, yank on ears, try to ride the puppy like a pony, or hit the pup. Never leave children and dogs unsupervised, for the safety of both the kids and the puppy.

Also, make sure to talk to your children about the needs of the Chessie puppy. The pup is still a baby, after all, and needs plenty of sleep, lots of love, fresh water and food, and consistent discipline. The rules that you set need to be enforced by all family members. It is too confusing for a Chessie puppy to have to remember different sets of rules for each family member.

Older children and teens should also be prepared before the arrival of the Chessie puppy, though they are less likely to squeal and jump around. Set clear expectations for your teens so they know that they will need to help out with walking the dog. Discuss other rules regarding the new dog with your teen. Will you allow your teen to take your Chessie for car rides, for example? Can they take the Chessie to the dog park or dog beach without you?

Make sure that you teens and older children understand that it is their responsibility to keep their belongings out of reach of the puppy. When Hank was a puppy, he chewed several of my teenage daughter's dirty clothes that she left laying all over her bedroom floor. One day, she was lamenting that Hank only destroyed her items. I reminded her that the rest of the family knows how to use a laundry hamper. Many of the items that teens covet – headphones, Airpods, cell phone and laptop chargers, retainers, and eyeglasses – need to be kept out of reach of a curious puppy at all times.

Get Your Other Pets Accustomed to Other Animals

Do you have another dog at home? Or a cat? You will need to prepare your other pets for the arrival of a new puppy. You may have a picture in your head of your older dog and your new Chessie puppy as the best of friends, however it may take some time before they get to that point. Here are some pointers to help ease the transition for both animals.

IS THE TIMING RIGHT?

Assess your current dog to determine if he is ready for a new, live-in playmate. How old is your current dog? Dog experts suggest that a puppy be at least one year old before you add another dog to the household. Puppies need at least six months to adapt to their new surroundings and a full year to bond with their humans and learn all the house rules. Address any negative behavior that your current dog may have before the arrival of a new puppy. If your older dog has a barking problem, separation anxiety, or shows aggressive tendencies, these bad habits need to be corrected. A new puppy will pick up on the bad behavior of your older dog then you will have two poorly behaved dogs to deal with.

ARRANGE FOR PLAYDATES

If your dog or cat are not used to being around other animals, take the opportunity before you bring your new Chesapeake Bay Retriever puppy home to introduce your pets to other dogs. Take your older dog to the neighborhood dog park or plan a doggie play date with a friend's dog. For cats, try inviting a friend and his or her dog to come visit at your house. The more your current pets are around other animals, the more accepting they will be of your Chessie.

CONTROL THE INTRODUCTION

Instead of walking into the door with a new puppy in hand, allow your older dog to get used to the idea. Have their first encounter take place outside, either in your yard or at a nearby dog park. Your older dog won't feel quite so territorial. Enlist the help of a friend or family member to control one dog on a leash while you control the other. Allow the dogs to greet each other in typical doggie fashion, by sniffing noses and rear ends, while you observe their body language. If one dog growls, adopts a dominant stance, or shows his teeth to the other dog, separate them while you discipline the naughty one. Once they have both calmed down, try bringing them together again. If you see no worrisome signs from either dog and they seem to play well together, you can take them home.

CHAPTER 4 Get Ready for your Chessie's Homecoming

DIVIDE YOUR ATTENTION

When you welcome your new Chesapeake Bay Retriever home, be sure to share your attention with your current pets. Continue to show them love and cuddles so they don't feel like they are being replaced. Perhaps you should have a new toy or two for your current dog. Your current pets may be apprehensive about their new family member. Don't try to force their relationship. It will come in time. Until that time comes, though, watch your pets when they are together. Even a normally docile dog can act unexpectedly aggressive with a new puppy.

PREVENT FIGHTS

An older dog and a new puppy may get along great until it's dinner time. It is natural for dogs to be territorial about their food so one dog may bully

Photo Courtesy of George and Sharon Long

the other to get his food bowl, as well as his own. The bully might growl, bark, or snap at the other dog to intimidate him away from his food. To avoid this, feed the dogs in separate locations twice a day. Don't leave food bowls sitting out. The same goes for treats. Keep the dogs away from each other while they enjoy their treats, or you may have a fight on your hands.

PROVIDE PLENTY OF TOYS

Be sure to have plenty of toys for both dogs. Dogs can get territorial about their toys as well so you should monitor their play time for the first several weeks. Watch the body language of both dogs to make sure one dog isn't acting too aggressively or too timidly. If one dog holds his ears back, raises his hackles, and holds a stiff, tense body position, it may be time to separate the dogs.

WHAT ABOUT CATS?

Contrary to popular belief, dogs and cats can get along fine. As members of the hunting or sporting group, Chesapeake Bay Retrievers don't have the urge to kill small rodents (unlike the terrier group) and aren't triggered to chase running animals, like the sighthounds. Retrievers are friendly toward other animals just as they are friendly toward people. Cats, on the other hand, can be fickle. Hank doesn't seem to have any issues with our cat but the cat treats Hank like an annoying roommate he is trying to avoid.

Find a Veterinarian

As per your breeder's contract or adoption agreement, you may be required to take your Chesapeake Bay Retriever to the veterinarian within a week or two of bringing him home. If you haven't already done so, you need to find a veterinarian that you like and trust, one that shares your dog raising philosophy, offers all the services you may need, and is located close to you. Take your time and do your research before you select a veterinarian for your Chesapeake Bay Retriever. After all, this person will be your partner in managing your dog's health.

Tips for Finding a Good Veterinarian

Start your search for the ideal veterinarian by asking your dog's breeder, as well as your friends, family, and co-workers for recommendations. Find out why your friends like a certain veterinarian, but also ask if they have had any concerns or issues at the vet clinic. Are they able to get an appointment

CHAPTER 4   Get Ready for your Chessie's Homecoming

quickly if their dog is sick? Are costs clearly explained ahead of time? Do the veterinarians, office staff, and vet techs genuinely love the animals they care for?

You can do a Google search to find vets in your neighborhood. An internet search is a good start in your quest for a veterinarian because it allows you to see where the veterinary offices are on a map so you can see how close they are to your house. The internet search will also give you the option to click on each vet's website. Analyzing the website will provide you with a wealth of information about the veterinarian and the clinic as a whole. You can find out where the veterinarians went to school and when they earned their degrees. There should be a section that explains the history of the clinic. You can see what medical services they offer on site, if they offer boarding, and if you can purchase your dog food there.

Questions to Ask When Interviewing Veterinarians

From your internet search and asking for recommendations from your friends and family, you should have a list of at least a few veterinarians you are considering. You don't want to pick one sight unseen. You want to make sure that the veterinarian you choose is knowledgeable about the Chesapeake Bay Retriever breed, is someone with whom you can build a rapport, and will become a valuable source for information about raising a happy, healthy Chessie. To determine all this, you need to meet with the veterinarian in person. Relax! It is not uncommon for people to make an appointment to interview a veterinarian. When you go to the appointment, be sure to have a list of the questions that you want to ask. Here are a few you may want to ask:

- **HOW MANY VETERINARIANS ARE THERE AT THIS OFFICE?**

Some veterinarians are one-man (or woman) shows. They are the only doctor at the clinic. On one hand, this is nice because you know you will always see the same vet each time you visit and you will have the opportunity to build a relationship with that person. On the other hand, with only one doctor on staff, you may experience long waits in the waiting room or cancelled appointments if the vet is sick or is tied up with an emergency with another pet. If the clinic has multiple veterinarians on staff, you should ask a follow up question: Can you specify which vet you want to see when you call to make an appointment?

- **DO YOU HAVE OTHER CHESAPEAKE BAY RETRIEVERS AS PATIENTS?**

Chessies are unique, therefore you want to make sure that your vet has experience with this breed. How many Chessies do they currently have as patients? Have they seen Chessies in the past? What is the vet's favorite thing about the Chesapeake Bay Retriever? What common illnesses or disorders do they commonly see in Chessies? Their answers to these questions should help you determine just how much experience a vet has with the Chessie breed.

- **HOW ARE PET EMERGENCIES HANDLED?**

Unfortunately, pets sometimes get sick or injured after hours and on weekends when the veterinary office is closed. Talk to the vet about how these incidents are handled. Does the office have a 24-hour answering service to take your call? Will you be able to talk to your vet in case of emergency? Do they handle emergencies right in their office or will you be told to go to an emergency pet hospital? Does the office have its own x-ray machine, lab, and operating room on-site, for both routine visits and emergencies? It is better to know ahead of time what to expect if your dog has a medical emergency than to try to figure it all out in the midst of a crisis.

- **WHAT SERVICES DO YOU OFFER?**

Most veterinary offices cover routine care, like preventative care, wellness checks, spaying and neutering, and vaccinations, but ask what additional services are offered at the clinic. Do they take care of dental issues? Is there an on-site pharmacy? Do they have an animal nutritionist on staff? Is there a rehabilitation component to their practice? Is there a pain management specialist on staff to help animals with chronic pain? Some veterinary clinics even have dog behavioral specialists to help dogs with aggression or discipline problems, grief counselors to help you and your family through the end-of-life process, and on-site grooming facilities. It is not uncommon for veterinary clinics to also have a kennel where their patients can board their dogs when they are on vacation. You may think that these add-on services are not important, but when you need one, it is convenient to have the service right at your trusted vet's office.

Photo Courtesy of Lauren & Kevin Grace

CHAPTER 4 Get Ready for your Chessie's Homecoming

- **DO YOU HAVE EVENING OR WEEKEND HOURS?**

For people who work a nine-to-five job, it can be difficult to get time off for vet appointments. Many veterinary clinics realize this and offer extended hours one or two nights a week and on Saturdays. Find out if the veterinarian you are interviewing has evening or weekend hours. Also ask if they accept walk-in appointments or if you will need to set up an appointment time. As follow up questions, find out how long the average wait is for walk-in appointments and how far out the clinic typically schedules appointments.

- **ARE THEY AFFILIATED WITH SPECIALISTS?**

Ask if the veterinarian has an affiliation with veterinary specialists. If, for whatever reason, your Chessie needs medical care from a specialist, it will be helpful if your dog is able to be seen by a specialist that your vet has recommended and who knows your vet personally.

- **HOW MUCH DO THEY CHARGE FOR OFFICE VISITS?**

Not all veterinary clinics charge the same amount for routine office visits, wellness care check-ups, and vaccinations. Ask the vet you are interviewing to provide you with a break-down of costs. Also ask about their payment policies. Do they expect payment in full at the time of service or are they willing to set up payment arrangements with their clients when costly, unexpected vet bills arise? Do they have an online payment portal to allow you to pay your bill electronically? You should be able to compare this with the other veterinarians you interview. You shouldn't base your decision on cost alone. Instead, you should factor that in with the other information you gather and select the veterinarian that offers the services you need. They should also have a clean, friendly office, and be most closely aligned with your ideas about dog ownership.

CHAPTER 5:
Welcoming Home your Chessie

Now that the stress, anxiety, and chaos of the homecoming is over, it is time to settle into life with your Chessie. The first few days in his new home may be overwhelming and confusing for your pup, but it is also a critical time for bonding, socializing, and learning the rules of the house. You will be laying the foundation for your dog's new life in his forever home.

Photo Courtesy of Maygan Coats Lone Willow Chesapeakes

CHAPTER 5   Welcoming Home your Chessie

A Smooth Ride Home

Your Chessie's first big adventure with you will likely be the car ride home from the breeder. This may be the puppy's very first car ride. Just as you take precautions to make sure that your friends and family are safe when riding in your car, you should do the same thing with your dog. After this initial drive, your Chesapeake Bay Retriever will, undoubtedly, spend time in your car, either going to the vet, the dog park, or to join you on your exploits. It is a good idea to get him used to safety restraints in the car right from the very first voyage.

An unrestrained dog is at a much higher risk of injury or death if you are in a car accident. Even a minor fender bender could send your dog flying around the interior of your car or, worse, eject him from the vehicle. In addition, a joyful, energetic puppy may try to jump all over you as you drive, distracting you from the road. For the safety of all involved, a dog car restraint should be used.

Another benefit of using a dog car restraint system is that it prevents your Chessie from hanging his head out of the car window as you drive. This can be extremely dangerous. Insects, pebbles, tree branches, and other objects can strike the dog's head or face and cause an injury. Many dogs have lost an eye this way. It is a frightening thought.

A small puppy can even jump out of an open car window while you are speeding down the road. Even if he is sitting on your lap, an unrestrained dog is in danger in a moving vehicle. As much as you want to hold and snuggle your new puppy –easing his fears during his car ride home – it is safer for him to be in the backseat and in a dog crate. Put a soft blanket in the crate to make it more comfortable for the puppy, but don't include a food or water dish. The motion of the car may make him sick, so it is better for him to refrain from eating and drinking during this time. (For more information about dog car restraints, see Chapter 19.)

> **FUN FACT**
> **True Grit**
>
> A Chesapeake Bay Retriever became the mascot of the University of Maryland, Baltimore County (UMBC) in 1966, two years after the Chessie became the official state dog of Maryland. For the school's 20th anniversary, alumna Paulette Raye was commissioned to construct a statue of the mascot. Raye modeled the statue after a Chessie named Nitty Gritty and eventually called the statue "True Grit" in honor of Nitty Gritty's father. True Grit can still be seen on the UMBC campus today, and it's become a tradition for students to rub the statue's nose for good luck before finals.

How to Create a Stress-Free Environment
For Your Chesapeake Bay Retriever

Chessie puppies are energetic and active but, amid that play, they are keen observers. They will size up you, your family members, and the new surroundings then store the information in their intelligent brains. As sensitive

Photo Courtesy of
Courtney Oliverio

CHAPTER 5 Welcoming Home your Chessie

and intuitive as they are, Chessies will take their cues from you. If you are flustered, your puppy may show signs of anxiety. On the other hand, if you are calm, nurturing, and patient, your Chessie will feel relaxed and content.

Try to plan your Chessie's homecoming for the start of a weekend or take a day or two off work so you can spend bonding time with your puppy during those crucial first days. You can use this time to show your Chessie that he is part of the family and – more importantly – where he fits into the family structure. Chesapeake Bay Retrievers can be assertive, domineering dogs that need to be taught to obey their owners and respect the position of the master.

Always keep in mind that your Chessie is still just a baby and needs lots of love and rest. His first day in his new forever home could be scary and chaotic. He has left the security of the kennel, his mother, and his littermates to embark on a terrifying car ride to an unfamiliar place filled with unfamiliar faces. It is all exhausting and intimidating to a young puppy. Don't be alarmed if he wants to curl up in a quiet place and sleep.

How to Help your Chessie through the First Night

The excitement of his welcome to his new forever home will likely wear out your Chesapeake Bay Retriever. You may assume that he will sleep soundly through the night, but that may not be the case. Nighttime in a new place can be frightening for a young pup, especially one that is away from his mother and littermates for the first time. When the house gets dark and quiet, expect your puppy to be lonely and scared. He will cry and whine and maybe even bark. Additionally, he will need to relieve himself often. Remember that puppies have tiny bladders and are still learning how to control them. The first nights will be challenging for you and for your Chessie.

It is at this point that many Chesapeake Bay Retriever owners make a critical mistake. Instead of letting the puppy cry it out in his crate, they bring the pup into their bed and let him spend the night there. For the Chessie puppy, this is an ideal arrangement. He is no longer lonely and, in fact, he feels like he is back with his littermates. At first, you may even like this sleeping arrangement. The puppy is cute and cuddly, and he is no longer whining and crying all night. Beware, though, that allowing your dog to sleep with you in your bed is a bad habit to start and an almost impossible one to break. Take it from a person who sleeps with a 120-pound Chesapeake Bay Retriever on my feet every night.

When you try the "cry it out" approach, you are teaching your puppy to find his own method for comforting himself. You can help by putting a cozy blanket in his crate. A hot-water bottle will give your pup the feeling that he is snuggled up to one of his littermates. If you have an old-fashioned alarm clock that makes a ticking sound, you could set that outside his crate. The ticking breaks up the silence and replicates the soothing sound of a mother's heartbeat. Even

Photo Courtesy of
Cary and Amanda Petitt

though it disrupts your own sleep, you could place the Chessie's crate in your bedroom. The pup will be comforted knowing you are close.

Prior to bedtime, take your pup for a late-night walk to expend some of his energy and to allow him to relieve himself. In fact, you may even want to engage your Chessie puppy in some vigorous playtime before bedtime to wear out the little guy and help him fall asleep faster.

The first few weeks will be rough, but soon your Chessie will adapt to the new routine. He will be able to get himself to sleep and stay quiet all through the night.

Set Boundaries from Day One

Your Chesapeake Bay Retriever starts learning about you, your family, and your house from the minute you walk through the door with him. Smart and perceptive, the pup is picking up cues from you and your family that will help him figure out not only his place in the family hierarchy, but the rules and boundaries of the house. Don't confuse the poor little puppy by permitting some behavior on his first day home that you punish him for the very next day. You need to establish a routine, rules, and boundaries right from the start.

Establish Physical Boundaries

Instead of giving your Chessie puppy immediate access to the entire house, you may want to consider setting up a puppy safe zone. This should be a space that is big enough for the Chessie to explore and a spot where the family hangs out. Don't lock the scared pup in a guest bedroom, basement, or laundry room. He needs to be near people so he can form bonds and learn socialization. You could, for example, set up some baby gates to keep the Chessie puppy in just one room. Be sure to place all the things he needs – his crate, toys, food and water dishes – in that room. You and other family members should spend as much time as you can in that room with the puppy. You know you want to anyway!

Start Housetraining

Housetraining should start as soon as your Chessie arrives home. While your pup is learning how his bladder works, you will need to watch for signs that he needs to relieve himself. Squatting, cocking a leg, and hiding in a private place are all signals that his bladder is full. Immediately pick the puppy up and rush him outside. In most cases, he will be so startled that he will stop peeing until you set him on the grass. If you allow him to do his business in the house, you are, in a sense, granting him permission to pee and poo wherever he wants. Watching for your dog's cues and acting immediately on them sets the foundation for housetraining, which we will discuss in greater detail in Chapter 6. It also spares your carpet from permanent stains.

Teach Rules

Your Chesapeake Bay Retriever doesn't know your house rules yet, therefore he will push the limits from time to time. For example, if you don't want your dog to get on your furniture, gently push him down if he tries to climb onto the couch. If he begs for food at the dinner table, tell him "no" and remove him from the kitchen or dining room. The same goes for destructive behavior. If you catch your Chessie chewing on a cell phone charger, a flip flop, or table leg, stop him from what he is doing, gently scold him, and divert his attention to something else. We will address bad habits and poor behavior in more detail in Chapter 11, but you should know how important it is to prevent bad habits from becoming big issues.

Start Socializing

"Socialization can happen during the most simple, everyday tasks. Take them to the post office with you, and let them observe the people. If there is a bench in the area, just sit with them a few minutes. Take them out to meet the delivery person, but only in your arms or on the end of a short leash. They do not yet know that vehicles can be deadly."

LEAH SPRADLIN
Hickory Creek Chesapeakes

Of course, you don't want to overwhelm your Chesapeake Bay Retriever in his first few days at home, but you should start socializing your puppy right away. Pick him up often so he gets used to being touched and handled. Teach him to sit still while you fasten his collar, harness, or leash. Soothe him and quiet his barks when someone knocks on the door. Call him by his name to get him used to hearing it. Slowly introduce him to new sights, sounds, and smells. Perhaps take him with you to a dog-friendly pet store, like PetSmart or to a restaurant with a dog patio. Until he is a bit bigger, you

CHAPTER 5 Welcoming Home your Chessie

may want to avoid the dog park. Discuss socializing with your veterinarian before your outings. Your vet may suggest avoiding outings until your puppy is fully vaccinated. More information about socializing your puppy can be found in Chapter 8.

Preparing for your Chessie's First Vet Visit

Once you decide on the ideal veterinarian, you will need to set up your Chessie's first appointment right away. In fact, it may be required in your breeder's contract or adoption agreement that you take your Chesapeake Bay Retriever to the vet in the first 7 to 14 days. That initial visit with the vet may be overwhelming for your Chessie, but you can help it go smoothly by preparing ahead of time for the appointment. Here are some tips:

PLAN A MORNING APPOINTMENT

As unexpected things come up throughout the day, the veterinarian's time can get squeezed. Appointments scheduled for first thing in the morning are more likely to be on time. This means fewer minutes sitting in the waiting room with a squirmy puppy and fewer trips outside for him to relieve himself. No matter what time you schedule your appointment, be sure to arrive early so you have plenty of time to fill out paperwork.

BRING EVERYTHING YOU NEED

During that initial visit with the veterinarian, be sure to bring the paperwork from the breeder or the adoption agency so that the vet can see your Chessie's previous medical history. These documents will also list what vaccinations the dog has already received and which ones are needed. Also bring with you the brand name of the dog food you are currently feeding your Chessie, as well as your list of questions for the vet.

BRIBE YOUR CHESSIE

Does your Chesapeake Bay Retriever have a special treat that he absolutely loves? Bring along a few of them when you go for your vet visit. Sneak one each to the vet tech and to the vet and allow them to offer it to your Chessie. He will be thrilled and will remember them fondly on future visits.

DON'T LET YOUR ANXIETY RUB OFF

Some people are deathly afraid of needles, even when they aren't the ones getting the shots. If you are one of those people, you may want to step out of the room when it is time for your Chessie to get his vaccinations. Chesapeake Bay Retrievers are adept at reading people's emotions and moods and will often mirror those feelings back. If you are anxious, your Chessie will be scared too. Seeing you leave the room is far less stressful for the puppy than watching you become a nervous mess at the sight of a needle.

Photo Courtesy of Ronald Bowler

CHAPTER 5   Welcoming Home your Chessie

ASK YOUR QUESTIONS AND TAKE NOTES

You compiled a list of questions to ask the veterinarian. When the check-up is over, pull out your list and discuss your questions with the doctor. Don't feel like you are wasting the vet's time. Your vet wants to see your Chessie grow big and strong and lead a happy life, just like you do. He or she will be happy to answer your questions and give you advice to help your Chessie thrive.

Finding Puppy Training and Obedience Classes

"Once the pup has had all of his/her vaccinations enroll the pup into a puppy kindergarten class, preferably with an AKC member obedience club, and continue on thru beginning and at least intermediate training classes."

KATHY MILLER
Sandy Oak Chesapeakes

Once your Chesapeake Bay Retriever puppy is current on his vaccinations, you can begin your training and socializing in earnest. A great way to do both at the same time is to enroll your Chessie in a puppy training class or an obedience class. When you are talking with your new veterinarian, ask if he or she could recommend a class for your Chessie. Many dog trainers and obedience class teachers post their flyers in the lobbies of veterinarian offices.

Another way to find a good puppy training class is to talk to other dog owners. Your friends, family members, co-workers, and neighbors that have dogs may be able to recommend a training facility. If you strike out at your veterinary office and with your friends, you can always do an internet search to try to find obedience classes or training classes in your area.

The Benefits of Obedience Classes

We didn't take Hank to obedience class, but I wish we had. When we brought him home as a puppy, we had four active teens or pre-teens still living at home and we spent nearly every night driving to and from various practices and activities. Adding one more obligation was out of the question. Hank, although well-adjusted and fairly well trained, missed out on the opportunity for early socialization and the chance to learn in a quiet, focused environment.

Here are some of the benefits of taking your Chesapeake Bay Retriever to obedience classes or puppy training classes:

LEARN TO BE FIRM YET GENTLE

Chesapeake Bay Retrievers can be headstrong at times. They are not recommended for novice dog owners because they need a firm hand. Working with a dog-training expert during an obedience class will help you tremendously to learn tips and techniques for controlling your Chessie's willfulness.

Photo Courtesy of Bridget Kelly

CHAPTER 5   Welcoming Home your Chessie

BONDING TIME WITH YOUR CHESSIE

Spending dedicated time with your Chessie will help you develop a stronger bond with him. Away from the distractions of home, you and your dog will spend an hour or so learning more about each other. Throughout the training process, your Chessie is soaking up information. He is learning to understand your commands and the tone of your voice and what behavior makes you happy. You will also learn more about the personality and disposition of your Chessie. Equally important, you will learn to work together as a team.

SOCIALIZATION OPPORTUNITIES

There will be other dogs in the class beside your Chesapeake Bay Retriever. In fact, your dog is likely to be the only Chessie enrolled. It is important for your dog to learn how to get along with dogs of every shape and size. Dogs have an innate set of "pack rules" that dictate their interactions with each other. You cannot teach these rules to your Chessie. The only way to learn these doggie life lessons is to spend time with other dogs. For a young puppy, an obedience class provides a safe setting for these lessons.

YOU BOTH LEARN FROM AN EXPERT

Your Chessie is not the only one learning in his puppy training class. You are, too. The instructor is a trained, experienced dog expert who will provide tips to help you teach your dog to follow your commands. These tips will be useful when you work on your lessons at home with your Chessie and long after the class is over.

LEARNING PROPER BEHAVIOR

You may wonder what your Chessie will learn at obedience school. In general, you can expect the class to focus on socializing with other dogs and people. He will learn to not jump on people when he greets them. He will practice walking on a leash and learn not to pull or strain against it. Lastly, he will work on basic commands, such as "sit" and "stay."

A CHANCE TO MEET OTHERS

Puppy training classes are a great way to connect with other new dog owners. You can swap stories of puppy antics and commiserate over destroyed shoes. Your Chessie will make friends, too. It is quite common for humans and dogs to form friendships at obedience school that carry over into doggie playdates and rendezvouses at the dog park long after doggie graduation.

CHAPTER 6:
Housetraining your Chessie

"Be consistent. Little puppies eat and immediately need to go outside to eliminate. If you can, get them going through the outside door on their own feet rather than carrying them....even if you will then need to carry them down any stairs. Walking through that doorway under their own power seems to help them make the connection. Take them out more often than you think you'd need to. Each correct elimination helps create the habit. Don't scold for mistakes indoors. Just pay attention, and when you see the puppy start to circle or squat, hurry it outside."

SHARON POTTER
Red Branch Kennels

From the moment you bring your Chesapeake Bay Retriever home, you should be working with him on housetraining. It is important for you to potty train your Chessie as soon as possible so you will be done with the mess and smell of puppy accidents in your house, and to protect your carpets, rugs, and floors from permanent damage. The earlier you housetrain your dog, the less likely he will be to develop bad habits, like urinating in out-of-the way places in your home.

Housetraining a young puppy is a frustrating time for you and for him. The biggest thing to keep in mind is that you need to have patience and be consistent. Your puppy is still young and learning how to control his bodily functions. There will be times when he simply can't hold it any longer, times when he gets so excited that he dribbles, and times when he forgets his training. He will never poop or pee in the house because he is angry at you or to get back at you for something. That's just not how Chessies think. Yelling at your Chessie and punishing him for occasional accidents will only make him sad and confused, which may prolong the housetraining process.

CHAPTER 6 Housetraining your Chessie

One of the top reasons why people decide to surrender their dog to an animal shelter is because of potty training trouble. The dog has not been properly house trained and has been allowed to develop bad habits. Frustrated at the constant mess, the owner gives up on the dog, not realizing that it is not the fault of the dog. It is a sad, yet preventable situation.

Housetraining goes beyond potty training. It also involves training and teaching your Chessie how to live in your household. This includes teaching what your house rules are, rewarding good behavior, and disciplining negative behavior. It all helps your Chesapeake Bay Retriever to be a well-behaved member of your family.

Photo Courtesy of Jeremy and Mary Ann Vlasich

Take Frequent Walks

To teach your Chesapeake Bay Retriever to learn to relieve himself outside, take him on frequent walks. They can be short walks just around the backyard if that's all you can do, but you should go often. This gives your Chessie ample opportunity to empty his bowels and bladder. As he gets better at controlling his bodily functions, you can take fewer walks and rely on your Chessie to tell you when he wants to go outside.

Stay on Schedule

Observe your Chesapeake Bay Retriever and note when he goes. Most dogs end up on a reliable schedule. For example, you may notice that your Chessie needs to relieve himself when he first wakes up, shortly after he eats, after spending time in his crate, and after rigorous play. Take a cue from your dog and take him outside at these times. He may even adapt his bladder schedule to accommodate your schedule. If you go home every day for lunch, he will learn to relieve himself at that time. Once your Chessie is on a schedule, stick to it as much as possible. Try not to deviate from it or you risk your dog having accidents.

What Goes In Must Come Out

The food your Chessie eats and the water he drinks has to go somewhere. If you will be away from home and you don't want your dog to pee or poop, be mindful of what he eats and drinks in the few hours leading up to the time you leave. Of course, that doesn't mean you should ever withhold food or water.

Be Patient

Housetraining your Chesapeake Bay Retriever is a process. Go into it with realistic expectations. The training could take several weeks, therefore it is important to be patient with your puppy. Remember that he is doing his best, but he is still figuring out how his body works and how to please you. It is a lot to learn at once and sometimes, things don't go as planned. Refrain from yelling and never strike your Chessie out of anger. If an accident happens, it is not because your Chessie is being defiant or vindictive. His accidents are simply accidents. Go back to your tried-and-true methods and get your Chessie back on track to becoming potty trained.

CHAPTER 6 Housetraining your Chessie

Puppy Pads: A Temporary Solution

One of the biggest benefits to using puppy pads, or paper training your dog, is that it protects your floors from messes and stains. For the puppy, however, it should be viewed as a temporary solution and a step in the housebreaking process. When you lay out a puppy pad on the floor, you are, in a sense, giving your dog a green light to do his business inside, rather than

Photo Courtesy of Tammy Roman-White

out in the yard. When the Chessie puppy is young, watch him closely for cues that he needs to relieve himself. Squatting and lifting a leg are the biggest signs. When you observe this behavior, quickly relocate the dog to the puppy pad and allow him to finish what he started. In no time at all, he will figure out that he should go right to the paper or pad when he needs to go.

Puppy pads are a good solution if you live on an upper level of an apartment building and it takes a few minutes to get outside. They can also be beneficial if your Chessie will be home alone for long stretches of time or if you live in an area with extreme weather. During the Polar Vortex in early 2019, temperatures in my area dipped to -15° (F) with wind chills exceeding -40° (F). It was brutal out. Naturally, Hank had to go outside to relieve himself. I let him out the patio door and watched him closely. He collapsed into the snow on his way back to the door since he simply couldn't stand the frigid temperatures. We had to rush out to pick him up and carry him back inside. If we ever have another day like that, puppy pads might come in handy.

Eventually, however, you want your Chessie to go potty outside. Transitioning from puppy pads to alerting you to go out can be challenging. The best way to make housebreaking work is to incorporate traditional outside training with the puppy pads. You can do this by repeating a word or phrase when your puppy relieves himself on the puppy pad. Try something like "Let's do your business" or "potty time." When you take him outside, repeat this phrase. Your Chessie will become conditioned to relieve himself when he hears those familiar words.

The Role of Crates in Housetraining

Are you already using a crate for your Chesapeake Bay Retriever? The good news is that potty training using a crate is one of the most effective methods for housebreaking your dog. All dogs are, by nature, clean animals. They don't like urine and feces in their living quarters. They would rather hold it and alert you to their needs than to soil their bedding.

The key is to use the right sized crate for your dog. It needs to be roomy enough for your Chessie to stand up and turn around, but not big enough that he feels comfortable using one end as his personal bathroom. If you have purchased a large crate in anticipation of a full-grown Chesapeake Bay Retriever, consider adding a partition to keep the space smaller while the Chessie is still a puppy.

Your Chessie will alert you when he needs to relieve himself. He will whine and paw at the crate door to get out. As soon as he shows these signs, take him outside. Don't make him wait; his small bladder may not be able

CHAPTER 6 Housetraining your Chessie

to hold it much longer and he could have an accident. Often, your Chessie puppy will ask to go outside at inconvenient times, like right when you sit down to dinner or just as your team is about to score the winning points. It stinks to have to stop what you are doing and attend to your dog. But it stinks even more to allow accidents to happen.

Photo Courtesy of Ronald Bowler

Learning the House Rules

Potty training is just one of the house rules that your Chesapeake Bay Retriever will need to learn to help him be a good member of your household. He will also need to learn your basic house rules that you want him to follow. Do you plan to ban him from the dining room when the family is eating? Will he not be allowed on the furniture? During the crucial few weeks after you bring your Chessie home, you need to make these rules clear to your dog by being firm and consistent, rewarding positive behavior, and using proper discipline.

Ways to Reward Good Behavior

Many dog training experts agree that rewarding good behavior is a much more effective way to train a dog than punishing bad behavior. The goal is to motivate your Chesapeake Bay Retriever to repeat the good behavior. To do this, the reward needs to be adequate, you need to add praise to the reward, and your reward needs to be timely.

Treats as a Reward

While it is true that tasty treats are a great motivator for Chesapeake Bay Retrievers, there is more to rewards than just food. A word of caution about treats. There are so many different doggie treats on the market that you will find an entire shelf dedicated to them at the pet store. Not all treats are created equal, however. Some may taste delicious, but are full of unhealthy ingredients, contain too much fat, and are high in calories. Proper nutrition is so important to your Chessie; you certainly don't want to load him up with empty calories. Instead, look for treats that contain healthier ingredients, are lower in fat and calories, and are approved by your veterinarian . Even then, be careful not to overload your Chessie with too many treats or he will soon look like Hank!

Praise as a Reward

Rewards can also come in the form of praise. Chesapeake Bay Retrievers want to please you and make you happy, so you can reward good behavior by giving him extra petting, hugs, and play time. Dogs are pack animals and thrive on attention, interaction, and companionship. Show your Chessie that you approve of his good behavior by showering him with love.

Verbal Cues as a Reward

Don't underestimate the power of verbal rewards to reinforce your Chessie's positive behavior. When you are happy and pleased, your Chesapeake Bay Retriever is happy and pleased. One way he knows this is by the tone of your voice. When you are praising your Chessie, be sure to keep your voice excited, upbeat, and happy as you repeat phrases like, "Good boy!," "Good dog," or "Good job!" Don't mumble, whisper, or use a monotone. Even if you are saying the same "Good dog" phrases, it won't carry as much weight as when you speak in a clear, cheerful voice. He will understand the happiness in your voice more than the actual words. Also, don't be too loud or too high-pitched in your praise. Your Chessie may think that you are shouting at him.

Timing Is Everything

Your Chesapeake Bay Retriever needs to learn to connect his behavior with your reward, therefore the reward needs to happen immediately after the good behavior. He will assume he is being praised for the action he just did so make sure that your timing is right. For example, say you have been working with your Chessie to stop jumping up on people when he greets them. You are taking a walk with your Chessie and you run into a friend walking her dog. Your Chessie starts to jump on her, but then remembers his training and stops. Instead, he sniffs the other dog's rear end. When you praise him for his good behavior, he may think that you are rewarding him for how he greeted the dog, not the owner. Positive reinforcement works, but you have to be sure your timing is correct, so you are rewarding the right behavior.

Tips for Correcting Naughty Behavior

Chesapeake Bay Retrievers are not naughty dogs, but they are somewhat stubborn and strong willed. A negative behavior can quickly turn into a bad habit that is difficult to break. Correcting bad behavior can be a lengthy and frustrating process. Many first-time or inexperienced dog owners give up at this point and simply put up with the bad behavior or get rid of the dog. If your Chesapeake Bay Retriever is behaving badly – yanking on his leash, jumping on people, barking excessively, or counter surfing – there are ways to correct his behavior.

When addressing your dog's negative behavior, remember that your goal is to stop the bad behavior and teach your Chesapeake Bay Retriever that he should no longer act that way. You shouldn't go into this with the mindset that you are punishing your dog. Never hit your dog. This is not the way to encourage your Chessie to behave better. It will only cause him to fear you or react with aggression.

Prevent the Bad Behavior

Sometimes, your Chessie's bad behavior is triggered by actions that you can adapt. For example, your dog may counter surf because he knows he can always find food up there. Instead of leaving food on the counter to tempt him, put everything away. If your Chessie always barks and paws at the fence, trying to get at the dog that lives a few houses down, go a different way on your walks so you don't have to pass that house. As I mentioned earlier, when Hank was a puppy, he would chew on clothes that were left on bedroom floors. We soon learned to put our dirty laundry in the hamper or risk it being destroyed. Occasionally, altering your own behavior is all that is needed to correct your Chessie's bad behavior.

Adopt a Stern Tone

Chessies respond positively when you speak to them in an excited and happy tone. They also can sense your anger and disappointment when you speak in a stern, authoritative voice. Avoid yelling and screaming at your dog as this will only scare him. Instead, show your disappointment with the tone of your voice and a scolding.

For a Dog, All Attention Is Good Attention

In a dog's mind, any kind of attention, good or bad, is still attention and dogs crave attention. Let's say you have two dogs, and your Chesapeake Bay Retriever has developed the bad habit of taking toys or bones away from your other dog. If you intervene, take the toy away, and give it to the other dog, you are still giving attention to the Chessie, which is what he wants. He may think you are playing some sort of game in which you take the bone from him, give it to the other dog, and wait for the Chessie to take it back. Sometimes, ignoring the bad behavior and not giving the Chessie your negative attention is enough for him to stop the behavior all together.

Again, Pay Attention to Timing

When you scold your Chesapeake Bay Retriever for bad behavior, keep in mind that he will think he is being punished for the last thing that he did. If you are gone at work all day and come home to find your favorite sneakers in shreds, don't immediately scold your dog. He will start to connect your arrival home with being disciplined. Instead, take a few moments to greet your Chessie as you normally would, take him outside to relieve himself, then take him to the shoes. Show them to him and tell him this was naughty in a stern, firm voice.

Timing is especially important in other circumstances. Say you are at the dog park and your Chessie bolts away from you. You call his name several times and beckon him to return to you. When he does, don't scold him for running off. In his mind, he is being scolded for returning to you. In a case like this, it is better to reward his return as good behavior than to punish him for running off.

To Crate or Not to Crate, That Is the Question

One of the rules of the house may involve crating your Chesapeake Bay Retriever. I know people who think that it is cruel to use a dog crate. They liken the crate to a cage. But honestly, crate training your puppy is not cruel. As long as you don't use it as punishment, the crate becomes a safe haven for your Chessie pup. It is his own quiet place where he can go when life becomes too overwhelming. It is instinctual. All dogs naturally seek out quiet, secure places when they feel stressed by their surroundings. If you don't use a crate, your Chesapeake Bay Retriever will still look for a safe place. It may be under a bed or in a closet. By providing a crate to your dog, you are granting him permission to step away from the household chaos from time to time, which is just what he needs.

A crate will also keep your Chessie out of trouble when you are away. A bored and anxious Chessie puppy will find some way to occupy himself. Unfortunately, it might be by gnawing on your chair legs, or as Hank loved to do, eating an iPhone charger or two. Chesapeake Bay Retrievers grow fast, so be sure to get a crate that is large enough for a growing dog. And make it as comfy and cozy as possible. A washable dog bed will do the trick. Be sure to toss in a few toys to keep your dog entertained when you have to leave him in his crate.

As soon as you arrive home and let your Chessie out of the crate, take him outside to relieve himself.

Creating Safe Zones

One way to physically show your Chesapeake Bay Retriever that he is not allowed in certain areas of the house is to set up gates to block off some of your rooms. If you don't want him to go in the dining room or your child's bedroom, for example, set up gates to restrict his access to these areas. Chessies grow fast and have long legs. Look for a doggie gate that is taller than an ordinary baby gate. Hank jumped the gate that we used to keep him out of the kitchen when we were cooking. The gate we had did not screw into the wall. It worked, instead, like a spring tension. We moved the gate up about six inches. Hank could no longer leap over it and it never dawned on him to crawl under it.

An alternative to a dog crate is a dog pen. These are free-standing pens, usually circular or hexagonal in shape, that you can set up in one of your rooms. You can find them in a durable plastic or a metal wire material. Dog pens are roomier than crates while still keeping your Chessie confined. He will be able to move around more in a dog pen, have more toys to keep him occupied, and have room for a food and water dish. There are a few drawbacks, however. Chesapeake Bay Retrievers can escape easily from dog pens. Also, dog pens are not ideal for potty training. There is so much room in them that your Chessie may feel comfortable relieving himself at one end of the pen, far away from his bedding.

Tips for Leaving your Chessie Home Alone

Unfortunately, you will have to leave your Chesapeake Bay Retriever home alone from time to time. Depending on where you work, your boss may not welcome your dog at the office. When you go out with friends, to attend a wedding, to see a movie, or to work, your Chessie will have to stay at home. You may worry that your Chessie will be sad when you leave, bark all night, or chew up your belongings, but if you try a few expert tips, you will be able to trust your Chessie to chill at home for a while.

FIND THE BEST LOCATION FOR YOUR CHESSIE

Depending on your Chessie's age, level of training, and personality, you should be able to determine the best location for your Chessie while you are away from home. This might be a crate, a dog pen, a room in your home

CHAPTER 6 Housetraining your Chessie

Photo Courtesy of Alan and Donna Wright

such as a mudroom, or you may allow your Chesapeake Bay Retriever to have free run of your house when you're gone. You may even opt to leave your Chessie outside in an outdoor dog kennel or in your fenced-in yard, if the weather is agreeable. When making your decision, you should factor in how long you will be gone, how long your dog can contain his bladder, and if there are any potential hazards or valuable items that could be chewed. When Maizie was a puppy, we thought the garage with access to the yard was a good option, but we failed to look for items that could be damaged by a bored puppy.

Here's a word of warning if you decide to leave your Chessie outside. In your yard, even protected by a secure fence or outdoor dog kennel, your dog is at risk. Criminals have been known to steal dogs right out of the backyard. In addition, your dog will be at the mercy of the elements. If an unexpected rain shower blows through, your Chessie will be unprotected. He will need shade to protect him from the harsh summer sun and plenty of water. Lastly, he will be more prone to fleas and ticks if he is spending long hours outside.

KEEP TO A SCHEDULE

If your work allows it, try to keep to a set schedule so your Chessie learns when he can expect you home. This will be easy if you work a typical eight-to-five job, but it will be more challenging if you work in healthcare, retail, or the service industry. My daughter, a 911 dispatcher, and her husband, a police officer, both switched to the night shift and it caused their dog all sorts of stress and anxiety. They solved the issue by crating their dog overnight and hiring a neighbor to take him for walks during the day while my daughter and her husband sleep. That brings us to our next point.

HIRE A DOG WALKER

If your schedule keeps you away from home for long periods of time, consider hiring someone to stop by, let your dog out, and take him for a walk. You may find a neighborhood kid or college student that can help you out. If not, there are a few apps, like Rover, that connect you with dog walkers and dog sitters in your area. The gig workers are vetted and go through a background check so you can have peace of mind that your dog will be well cared for. The dog walker may be a stranger at first but will soon be one of your Chessie's best friends.

PROVIDE MENTAL STIMULATION

Spending the entire day stuck in a crate can be boring. To help keep your Chesapeake Bay Retriever's mind active and stave off boredom, you need to provide as much mental stimulation as you can. Before you leave for the day, take your Chessie on a long walk. It will help expend some of his energy, give him a chance to empty his bowels and bladder, and stimulate his mind. It is good for you, too. If you must feed your dog before you go to work, consider purchasing a puzzle feeder or dog food dispenser toy like the kind that Kong makes. It will be more challenging to get to his food, which will occupy his mind and fill his time by giving him a project to work on. Look for other toys and chews that are designed to stimulate a dog's brain and are durable enough to last for hours in a crate.

CHAPTER 7:
Keeping your Chessie Fit and Happy

The Chesapeake Bay Retriever was bred to be a working dog, helping duck hunters retrieve waterfowl from the icy water. As a breed, Chessies are active, energetic, and athletic. To stay in good shape and to maintain their happy disposition, Chessies need plenty of exercise. You may not think there is a connection between exercise and the happiness level of your Chessie, but there really is. A dog that doesn't get enough movement can experience a form of doggie depression. For his physical and emotional health, be sure that your Chessie gets plenty of exercise. Just how much activity your Chessie needs depends greatly on his age.

Photo Courtesy of
Shawn and Joan Casement

CHAPTER 7   Keeping your Chessie Fit and Happy

Exercise Requirements of Young Chessies

"With young Chessies you need to be aware that their growth plates haven't fully closed, and won't until they are between 18-24 months. Walking your puppy is fine, but do not jog or run long distances until the growth plates have closed. Moderation is the key: moderate swimming, walking and retrieving."

JOANNE SILVER
Silvercreek Chesapeakes

A young Chesapeake Bay Retriever puppy gets an adequate amount of exercise by just playing and running around the house. Until his bones and muscles get stronger, your Chessie puppy shouldn't engage in activities that are too rigorous. He is not ready for an all-day hiking trip or an eight-mile run at this point in his life.

When your Chessie puppy reaches his three-month birthday, he is ready to start his workouts. Start small. Walks should last about 15 minutes or so. As your pup grows, you can increase the duration of his walks by five-minute increments. When your Chesapeake Bay Retriever is five or six months old, you can play fetch with your puppy. He will naturally chase after a ball when you throw it and bring it back to you to throw again. Playing fetch in the yard is a great way for your puppy to get the exercise he needs while honing his natural retrieving skills.

Chesapeake Bay Retrievers are natural-born swimmers. To keep your puppy safe, however, you should wait until he is at least nine months old before you take him to the dog beach. By this time, he will be strong enough to handle the waves. About this time, you can increase the intensity of his walks, too. He should be able to go on long distance runs with you, enjoy lengthy hikes, and climb up rocky boulders.

FUN FACT
World-Champion Dock Jumper

Smoke, a Chesapeake Bay Retriever from Ramona, California, near San Diego, is a world champion in dock jumping. Dock jumping, sometimes called dock diving, is a sport where dogs compete for distance jumped from a dock. Smoke's record is 29 feet and 1 inch, which is nearly as far as the human record for long jumping, which is 29 feet and 4.5 inches. The San Diego area has produced several dock-jumping champions, including another Chessie named Henry, who was the world dock-jumping champion in 2009.

Exercise Requirements of Adult Chessies

When your Chessie reaches adulthood at about 15 months, you should plan to provide him with at least one hour of rigorous exercise every day. Chesapeake Bay Retrievers are muscle-bound athletes that need intense workouts to keep them in great shape. Chessies that don't get enough regular exercise, can become restless, anxious, and bored. They may develop behavioral issues, such as defiance, disobedience, and destructiveness. Physical activity is the best way to improve the emotional and mental health of your Chessie, as well as his overall vitality.

Photo Courtesy of
Ronald Bowler

CHAPTER 7 Keeping your Chessie Fit and Happy

You can break up that one hour of exercise per day by taking your Chessie for a half-hour walk in the morning before you go to work and another one in the evening. You could even combine your morning workout with your Chessie and take him along on your morning jog. Swimming, playing fetch, catching a Frisbee, and playing tug-of-war are all terrific ways for your Chessie to get in his exercise time while having fun and bonding with you.

As always, it is a good idea to establish a routine with your Chesapeake Bay Retriever so he can anticipate when exercise time will be. Walking or jogging before and after work is an easy routine to follow. Or you could ask your teenage son or daughter to spend some time playing fetch with your Chessie every day when they get home from school. If you work odd hours or if your work schedule changes from week to week, consider hiring a dog walker so that at least one of your Chessie's daily workouts will follow a routine.

The Benefits of Walking

While many Chessie owners may regard their dogs' walks as simply potty breaks, there are much more than that. Going for a brisk walk is a great way for your Chesapeake Bay Retriever to stretch his legs and work his muscles. When you take your Chesapeake Bay Retriever for a walk, he is releasing his pent-up energy, which will make him happier and better behaved. Walking is a way for your Chessie to get his heart rate pumping, breathe in fresh air, and burn excess calories. As well as the physical benefits, going for walks is an ideal way to keep your Chessie mentally stimulated.

The Benefits of Running

A Chesapeake Bay Retriever can easily join you on your runs if you are a running enthusiast. Running with your dog appeals to his need to run with his pack. If your Chessie is a bit overweight, like Hank, jogging can help him shed the extra pounds.

In addition to the physical benefits of running, your Chesapeake Bay Retriever will experience lowered anxiety, relieved stress, and increased mental sharpness. The mental stimulation from jogging reduces boredom and improves your Chessie's disposition.

Running can be hard on your Chessie, though. If he is an older dog or recovering from an illness or injury, the jarring motion could be damaging to your dog's joints and muscles. If he starts to limp or lag, shorten the distance or go for walks instead.

The Benefits of Swimming

Chesapeake Bay Retrievers love to swim. It is what they were bred to do. The webbed toes and oily coat of the Chessie make them terrific swimmers. As a form of exercise, swimming offers many excellent benefits. It gives Chessies a great cardiovascular workout, strengthening the dog's heart and lungs. And your Chessie will thoroughly enjoy himself. When we go to the dog beach with Hank, we always make sure to bring a few tennis balls. He loves when we throw a ball into the waves for him to swim out and retrieve. Hank gets a good workout, but he thinks we are playing a game.

I think one of the best parts of swimming for Hank is that it cools him down. In the heat of the summer, Hank loves to run into the cool lake water. I recall one particularly hot day when we had gone for a long walk that ended at a dog beach at Lake Michigan. When we reached the shore, Hank ran into the water

Photo Courtesy of Amy Houston

CHAPTER 7 Keeping your Chessie Fit and Happy

until it covered most of his body. We could almost see how content he was to let the cool water wash over him. If you live in an area that experiences hot summer days and you are lucky enough to have a dog beach nearby, skip the long walks and runs and let your Chessie swim to get his exercise.

Since swimming is such an instinctive part of the Chesapeake Bay Retriever breed, the more you interact with your Chessie in the water – swimming with him or playing fetch – the more mental stimulation your dog will enjoy. It is a great way to bond with him and to keep his mind active and engaged.

The Importance of Mental Stimulation

"Join a club, whether it's simple obedience classes or hunting, rally, dock diving, hunt tests or trials. This is great for training and gets you and your dog out doing what the dog was bred to do."

SHARON POTTER
Red Branch Kennels

Keeping your Chessie's mind fit and active is just as important as his physical fitness. Staying in a crate or alone at home all day is boring. Your Chessie needs stimulation to keep his keen mind engaged and to stave off boredom. Mental stimulation reduces separation anxiety, lowers aggression, lessens hyperactivity, and gives your dog a happier and more fulfilling life. Mental stimulation can also be a tool for teaching your puppy how to properly behave. Fortunately, there are techniques you can employ to keep your Chesapeake Bay Retriever occupied.

Outdoor Exercise

"Choose exercise that you can provide for them regularly. Chessies are 'duck dogs' but that doesn't mean that if you live in a neighborhood without open areas that your dog cannot get enough exercise. Walk them often. Let them meet the neighbors and learn appropriate behaviors. Do not try to wait until you can get to a rural area to exercise them. They love you. They love to move. It's hard to go wrong when you combine the two in an appropriate setting."

LEAH SPRADLIN
Hickory Creek Chesapeakes

Karen HARRIS | The Complete Guide To Chesapeake Bay Retrievers

Photo Courtesy of
Jessica Richmond

CHAPTER 7 Keeping your Chessie Fit and Happy

Spending time outside, going on walks or playing fetch in the yard, provides your Chessie with fresh experiences and situations that get the wheels in his brain turning. Routine walks and runs are ideal. If you and your family members are not available to take your Chessie on regular walks, consider hiring a professional dog walker to stop by every day to engage in outdoor play with your dog. Another option is to take your Chessie to a doggie daycare. He will be able to play with other dogs, run outside, and keep his mind engaged.

Puzzle Feeders and Treat Toys

We bought Hank a puzzle feeder because he gulped down his food so fast. He enjoyed working out the best way to get his kibble pieces from the maze pattern in the dish. There are several different puzzle feeders on the market and one great suggestion is to purchase several different feeders. You can rotate these feeders on a day-by-day basis to keep your Chesapeake Bay Retriever guessing at each meal. You will also find a wide variety of treat toys to choose from. To use these toys, you insert a treat or two inside it. It takes some work to release the treat and stimulates his mind. Like the puzzle feeder, it is a good idea to buy several different treat toys so your smart Chessie doesn't learn the trick to removing the treat too quickly.

Stay Connected with Technology

The technological age, with all its fun gadgets, extends to the dog world, too. You will find several products on the market that allow you to stay in contact with your Chessie even while you are at work. We have a basic doggie cam for Hank. Everyone in the family has the app associated with the doggie cam on their phones. At any time, we can log on and see what Hank is doing. It has a feature that allows us to talk to Hank through the camera, but we don't use this option very much. It confuses Hank and causes him to run around barking. There are some doggie cams that you can mount on the wall at eye level for your dog. There is a screen so that when you log on to check in with our Chessie, he can see you just as you can see him. Some of them even have a feature that lets you release a treat when you are video chatting with your dog. I have also seen freestanding dog-treat dispensers on the market that periodically releases treats.

CHAPTER 7   Keeping your Chessie Fit and Happy

Doggie TV

If your Chessie is a bit of a couch potato, you can help him stay entertained by leaving your TV on when you are gone. There are DVDs and YouTube videos that offer visual and audio stimulation for your dog. There are some with flying birds, some with farm animals, and some with other dogs. Set your TV to play some of these doggie videos for an hour or two while you are at work.

Chew Toys

Chessies are chewers. When they get bored, they might entertain themselves by chewing on things. Hank has apparently been very bored in his lifetime. He has chewed on the drywall, his crate, chair legs, and throw pillows. We learned that we had to give him the tools he needed to occupy himself when he was home alone. We give him a chew toy or treat now when we are leaving him for a few hours. He spends a good deal of his time working on the chew toy, which keeps him out of mischief.

A Chessie who is not struggling with boredom and who gets plenty of exercise will be a happy, well-adjusted, well-behaved dog.

CHAPTER 8: Socializing your Chessie

The difference between a well-socialized Chesapeake Bay Retriever and one that has had little to no socialization is significant. If your Chessie has been properly socialized, he is a dog that your friends and family want to spend time with. He is friendly, obedient, loving, and well mannered. But a dog's good manners and happy disposition have a great deal to do with socialization.

Photo Courtesy of Sarah Hyde

CHAPTER 8 Socializing your Chessie

Photo Courtesy of Shelby Ethier

Why Socializing Is So Important

It is a sad fact that many dogs are left at animal shelters because of a behavioral problem. In the overwhelming majority of cases, the behavioral issue is not something that has been bred into the animal. The dog simply hasn't been properly socialized and therefore doesn't know how to handle unfamiliar situations. As a result, he had learned a behavior or a response to stimuli that are negative, like barking or nipping. It is not the dog's fault, but the owner's.

Your Chessie puppy has a number of teachers. He learns first from his mother and littermates, then from you, his obedience school instructor, and all the other dogs he encounters. When we invite a dog into our homes, we expect them to learn human rules along with dog ones. To do so, he needs to spend as much time as he can, particularly when he is young, with other dogs and other people.

Dogs have their own set of rules, therefore it is important that your Chesapeake Bay Retriever learns proper doggie protocol. Your Chessie will lose these skills if he doesn't spend a lot of time with other dogs. An unsocialized dog behaves in a timid and fearful manner when he is around other dogs. Or he acts aggressively toward the other dog, which he perceives as a threat. Either way, he is anxious and stressed, and this shows in his stance, behavior, and mannerisms. A well-socialized dog will know how to greet other dogs and will have positive experiences from interacting with other dogs. An unsocialized dog will have a negative experience meeting other dogs because he has not been taught how to engage with other animals.

The world is full of strange, new experiences. The more your Chessie encounters unfamiliar situations and places, the better prepared he will be to handle new sights, smells, and sounds with confidence. He will be less fearful and apprehensive. He won't react defensively or aggressively because he will have learned that there is no threat. Socialization will help your Chesapeake Bay Retriever to embrace new experiences as an opportunity to learn and stimulate his curious mind. An unsocialized Chessie may cower or take an aggressive stance with his hackles up because these are the only ways he knows to react to the unknown.

Socialize Early and Often

"Start young, as soon as the full series of vaccinations is completed. Take them to places where there are other SAFE dogs that you personally know are dog-friendly. And steer clear of dog parks, which tend to be filled with untrained dogs that have owners who think their dog would never attack...until it does. Puppy classes are also good places to socialize, as are some doggie day cares."

SHARON POTTER
Red Branch Kennels

Your Chesapeake Bay Retriever's learning begins at birth so that's when socialization should start. In the early weeks of his life, your Chessie will learn social skills from his mother. She will teach him how to be a dog. As he becomes more active, he will learn to socialize with his littermates.

Ideally, your dog's breeder will work on socialization with the puppies. Picking them up, playing with them, and handling them all teach the pups about human interaction, trust, and proper behavior. When the litter is a bit older, the breeder should let them play outside and continue giving them plenty of attention.

After you bring your Chesapeake Bay Retriever home, it is time to ramp up the socialization training. Going for walks, visiting friends, stopping at the

CHAPTER 8 Socializing your Chessie

dog park, joining you for lunch at a dog-friendly restaurant, and going for car rides are all great ways to introduce the big, wide world to your Chessie puppy. Good, effective socialization appeals to all the senses. Unfamiliar smells, new noises, strange smells, and different terrain can all stimulate your puppy's eager brain. You can also enroll your puppy in an obedience class or puppy training course. The experts teaching the class will make sure the dogs get plenty of social time and will also give you pointers on how to socialize your Chessie.

Socializing with New People

Your Chesapeake Bay Retriever needs to learn how to interact with new people. You don't want your dog to view every stranger he meets as a potential threat. Your dog also needs to know not to jump on people as he greets them. Fortunately, it is easy to get your Chessie used to other people. Invite some friends over to hang out or have a backyard cookout and allow your Chessie to be part of the action. You could also take your Chessie along when visiting friends, as long as they allow it.

Introduce your Chessie to different kinds of people. Often, you will hear a dog owner claim that their dog "doesn't like men". What they are really saying is that their dog hasn't been socialized with various types of people. Your Chessie should be introduced to men – especially large men with deep voices—in addition to women, older people, people with disabilities, people of various ethnicities, and young children. When you are at the dog park, out for a walk, at the veterinarian, or at the pet supply store, allow your Chessie to meet the people you encounter. The majority of people will greet your Chessie, call him by name, and pet his head. They will speak in an upbeat and friendly manner. This shows your Chesapeake Bay Retriever that people are nice and can be trusted therefore he will respond in a positive, appropriate way.

HELPFUL TIP
CBR R&R

Chesapeake Bay Retriever Relief and Rescue (CBRR&R) is a nationwide 501(C)3 nonprofit rescue organization. Run entirely by volunteers, CBRR&R evaluates and treats rescues for medical conditions, provides socialization and fostering, and thoroughly screens potential homes before placing Chessies out for adoption. To find your regional chapter of CBRR&R, visit www.cbrrescue.org.

Socializing Your Chessie with Children

If you have children in your home, your Chesapeake Bay Retriever will have ample opportunity to interact with them. Just be sure to supervise your children when they are playing with all dogs. Children are unpredictable. They will make sudden, loud, or high-pitched noises that could frighten a dog. Kids also make unexpected movements, like jumping, running, and falling. These can also startle a dog, especially a hunting dog with a sharp prey instinct like a Chesapeake Bay Retriever. The more your Chessie spends time with youngsters, the more he will understand and anticipate children's behavior.

There are ways to help your Chessie socialize with children if you don't have young ones in your immediate family. Take your Chessie along, with prior permission of course, to family gatherings and introduce him to your young cousins, nieces, or nephews. Do your friends or neighbors have children? You could arrange supervised play times with them if their parents are willing to help you in your socialization lessons.

When we brought Hank home eight years ago, all four of our daughters still lived at home. They were teenagers, so we hosted lots of weekend sleepovers, late-night bonfires, and birthday parties with their friends. Hank fit right in because he learned early on that teen and pre-teen girls scream, squeal, and shout.

Meeting Other Dogs

Dogs are pack animals, and therefore, very social. There is an instinctual doggie code of conduct that dictates the pecking order of dogs. Every time your Chessie meets another dog, he sizes it up to determine if this new dog is higher or lower than him on the doggie hierarchy. Once this is established, the dogs will act accordingly. Often, it is clearly evident which dog is the dominant one, but other times, the clues are more subtle.

A few years back, my sister-in-law adopted an older dog from the local animal shelter, a commendable thing to do. The day after she brought him home from the shelter, we had a backyard cookout at our house. When my sister-in-law asked if she could bring her new dog, we naturally said yes. This dog, a 10-year-old German Shepherd/Pitbull mix, attacked Hank within minutes of their arrival while he was still on the leash. My sister-in-law is petite and couldn't control him and the dog would not listen to her. It took my husband and father-in-law to separate the dogs. Poor Hank suffered bloody bites on one leg and on his ear and had to go see the vet the next morning. As for my sister-in-law's dog, she never brought him to another family function. The dog had never learned how to socialize with other dogs.

CHAPTER 8   Socializing your Chessie

You want to encourage your Chessie to have positive interactions with all the dogs he meets. When you are going for a walk or visiting the dog park, bring along some treats. If your Chessie shows off his best behavior when he meets a new dog, reward him. He will associate this positive reinforcement with his behavior and remember it for next time.

In order for your Chesapeake Bay Retriever to learn how to socialize with other dogs, you need to go where the dogs are. The dog park, the dog beach, or a dog-friendly pet store are great places for your Chessie to meet other canines. You don't have to force the encounters. The dogs will naturally gravitate to each other. Let them interact but watch them closely. Soon, your Chessie will make new friends with confidence.

Doggie Social Rules

"I recommend introducing your Chessie to new dogs using a 6' leash, and be in a neutral yard. Only introduce to one other dog at first, and watch their body posturing for signs of fear or anxiety. I use treats for both dogs to help make them feel comfortable. Slowly add another dog only after they have been introduced individually. Use lots of praise and treats during these first meetings."

CAT WEIL
Timbercreek Acres

Dogs have their own set of social rules that they need to learn on their own. These rules are passed from older dogs to puppies and ensure that dogs get along and understand how to interact with each other. As pack animals, dogs are social. Wild dogs of the past had to know the rules for getting along and working together as a group. These rules also let dogs know how they should behave, based on their position in the doggie chain of command. Once your Chessie knows the basic dog social rules, he is less likely to get into a fight with another dog.

Personal Space

Part of these dog rules pertains to personal space. Like humans, dogs don't like it when other dogs violate their personal space. If you pay attention, you will notice that dogs approach each other slowly and with caution. They will sniff the ground in front of them, walk alongside each other, and yes, even sniff each other's butts. The dog that is lower on the doggie hierarchy may even adopt a submissive stance, like rolling on his back to show his belly. The dominant dog may take a dominant stance, like humping.

Mounting

Humping is not just about over-zealous hormones for dogs. One dog may hump or mount another to show his superiority and dominance. Eager puppies that try to mount older dogs are usually put in their place with a growl and a nip. The pups learn quickly that this behavior is not to be tolerated. Your handling of your Chesapeake Bay Retriever reinforces this. If your Chessie has a habit of humping, separate the pets and scold your dog. He will learn from other dogs and you that this is not acceptable behavior. Of course, there is a sexual component to mounting, but once your dog is spayed or neutered, this urge greatly decreases.

Doggie Body Language

Dogs learn how to read the body language and mannerisms of other dogs as part of the doggie social rules. Take, for example, a dog's posture. How a dog stands says much about his mood. A dog that is crouched down or cowering is fearful or anxious. The stance is the animal's way of trying to appear smaller and less threatening. On the other hand, a dog that stands stiffly and alert with his weight slightly forward and his tail held high is adopting an aggressive stance. When a dog lays his chest on the ground and keeps his rear end in the air, he is indicating that he is happy and eager to play.

The Eyes

Your Chessie's eyes will also give you a cue to his feelings when he meets another dog. Most of the time, Chessie's have kind, gentle eyes with relaxed eyelids. This tells us that the dog is happy and unstressed. But when his eyes become cold, fixated, and hard, the dog is feeling aggressive and threatened. Note your Chessie's amount of eye contact, as this also indicates his mood. A nervous or anxious dog will avoid eye contact and look away. A dog that stares intently is just waiting for one more trigger to attack. Sometimes, you will notice your Chessie's eyes are so wide that you can see the whites of his eyes. This is a sign that your dog is uncomfortable and worried.

The Hackles

Chessies, as well as other dog breeds, have hair on their back, called hackles, that stands up depending on the dog's mood. When your dog is on high alert to a perceived threat, his hackles will be up. It is your dog's

CHAPTER 8 Socializing your Chessie

way of trying to appear bigger and more opposing than he really is. If the threat turns out to be real, your dog wants to seem as intimidating as possible. When your Chessie meets a strange dog for the first time, pay attention to both dogs' hackles. Raised hackles could be a clue that the dogs might act aggressively toward each other. You may want to keep them apart.

The Smile

You probably notice that your Chessie seems to smile at you when he is happy and excited. When he smiles, he is displaying his front

Photo Courtesy of Kali and Billy Bissell

teeth to you, but not in a menacing way. Watch your Chessie when he meets a new dog. If he shows his teeth, it may not be a happy smile. If the corners of your dog's mouth are arc-shaped and the front teeth are exposed, it could be an aggressive expression. Dogs will bare their teeth as a warning to other dogs. Often this expression is coupled with a snarl or growl. If either dog displays this behavior, keep them away from each other.

The Tail

One of the most expressive parts of your Chessie's body is his tail. We often assume that when a dog wags his tail, it means he is happy, but this isn't always the case. You need to look at the position of the tail, how fast he is wagging it, and the direction of the wag to really interpret your Chessie's mood. Typically, the higher the dog's tail in the air, the more assertive and confident the dog is. You have seen a dog tuck his tail between his legs when he is scared or being scolded. That's because he is no longer feeling confident at that time. A tail wag could mean that your Chessie is aroused. The faster the wag, the more intense the feelings are. At the end of the workday when you return home to your dog, your Chessie is so happy to see you that he wags his tail so vigorously that his whole backside wiggles. When your Chessie is on alert, his tail won't wag as much as it will twitch. Researchers have also noticed that the direction of the dog's wag is also telling. When a tail wag is predominantly to the left, the dog is experiencing negative feelings, but wags to the right are positive.

Chessies and Other Pets

Chesapeake Bay Retrievers need to be around other dogs to learn the "dog code," but what about other animals? More than a third of all households have cats and cats don't follow "dog code." Cats are so independent and aloof that they do their own thing. Your Chessie should spend some time with cats if you don't have a cat at your house. It is important for your dog to learn that cats are pets and not prey. Chessies have a strong prey drive and will instinctively chase a running cat.

The same holds true for other pets you may have, such as rabbits, hamsters, and snakes. When Hank was young, one of my daughters had a pet hamster, Humphrey. She often put Humphrey in his ball and let him roll around the house. On more than one occasion, we found Hank holding the ball in his mouth. For his part, Humphrey seemed oblivious to his brush with death and happily rolled away.

Chessies and Livestock

For Chessie lovers living in rural areas, it might be likely that they are bringing their Chesapeake Bay Retriever home to a hobby farm or full-scale farm. If this is the case, your Chessie will need to learn that farm animals are not to be chased.

We live on a hobby farm. One of our goats is a brown Nubian named Brown Sugar. She is exactly the same color as Hank. A few days after we brought Hank home from the breeder, my husband took him out to the pasture with him to introduce him to the goats. Poor Hank must have though Brown Sugar was his mother. Excited, he ran to her. The goat, however, perceived this as a threat. She defended herself the only way she knows how – she head-butted Hank. Hank went somersaulting backwards, a little dazed and confused. Soon, he learned that goats are not his mother, but he still occasionally gets head-butted when he gets too close or tries to chase a goat.

Hank has gotten in trouble a few times for chasing the chickens, but thankfully, he has never killed one. Just as you would do with household pets, monitor the interactions between your Chesapeake Bay Retriever and livestock closely. A dog as large as a Chessie could harm an animal -- intentionally or unintentionally. Likewise, horses, cattle, and hogs could hurt a dog if they wanted to. Err on the side of caution and always keep your eye on your Chessie on the farm.

The world is a big place, full of new sensations. Unless your Chesapeake Bay Retriever has learned how to handle unfamiliar stimulation, he will be

CHAPTER 8 Socializing your Chessie

overwhelmed. An anxious and stressed dog may react with aggression and be defensive, or he may cower and act shy. Neither reaction is ideal. You want your Chessie to be happy and confident when encountering new experiences. He can only do this if he has been properly socialized from an early age and routinely practices his social skills. Your Chessie will be happier and you will be happier with your Chessie.

Photo Courtesy of
Maygan Coats
Lone Willow Chesapeakes

CHAPTER 9:
Training your Chessie

You may have heard that Chesapeake Bay Retrievers are stubborn and strong-willed. Some of that is true, but that doesn't mean Chessies are difficult to train. On the contrary, they are intelligent, intuitive, and eager to please -- all traits that help make training easier. Chessies like to be top dog. They want to be as high on the social hierarchy of the household as possible so they will assert their dominance as much as you allow them too. It requires an experienced dog owner to handle a Chessie, to teach him to respect his owners, and to provide him with consistent training. It is well worth the effort you put in for you will be rewarded with a well-behaved, obedient, happy dog that is a welcomed member of your family.

Photo Courtesy of Sarah Pope

CHAPTER 9 Training your Chessie

Why Is Good Training So Important?

"A Chesapeake is a very soft dog and learns very quickly, but the owner must also be able to understand their dog as Chessies can be difficult to train in the hands of an inexperienced owner. You must be able to control their energy without deflating their attitude. Commands must be clear without double meanings. If you are not clearly communicating with your dog you can expect to have problems. Often times you need to negotiate with your Chessie, but generally once they learn something they never forget it."

KATHY MILLER
Sandy Oak Chesapeakes

A Chessie that has been properly trained is a joy to be around. And the dog will be much happier, too. He will have respect for you and clearly know his place in the family chain of command. Once you have helped your Chesapeake Bay Retriever accomplish these two things, he will no longer need to compete with you and other family members for his position in the pecking order. Imagine the relief he will feel. As a result, he will experience less stress and anxiety.

Training sessions provide mental and physical stimulation for your Chessie. Long after he has been trained, his brain will still rev up when he is asked to follow an order or obey a command. Sometimes, your commands may even require your Chessie to use some creative problem solving. When you toss a ball, for example, and it lands in the bushes, your Chessie will have to use his skills to locate it. Or if you call your dog to come to you and there is an obstacle in the way, your Chessie will need to figure out how to maneuver his way around it to get to you. It is especially important to combine training with mental stimulation when your Chesapeake Bay Retriever is a puppy. The mental workout he gets will keep his agile mind so occupied that he won't have time for mischief.

When you spend time training your Chesapeake Bay Retriever, you are reinforcing the bond you have with each other. Training sessions provide an opportunity for you to get to better understand your dog's personality and for your dog to learn more about you. The more time you spend together in focused training, the more your dog will respect you as his pack leader.

A dog that has been properly trained can tag along with you on more of your outings. He will know how to behave around other people and other dogs in unfamiliar situations. His training will help him feel at ease in new surroundings. Your Chessie will find these adventures to be mentally stimulating, positive, learning experiences.

Safety is another reason for properly training your Chesapeake Bay Retriever. Through consistent, on-going training, your Chessie will learn to respond to your voice commands. Then, if he pulls the leash out of your hand to bolt after a squirrel or zips out the front door as soon as you open it, you will be able to call him back to you before he runs into the road or around the neighborhood. His training will decrease the chances that this will happen but, still, squirrels can be tempting.

Sometimes it is necessary to leave your dogs at home when you go on vacation or a business trip. Things will go much smoother in your absence if your Chessie has been trained. Whether you hire a dog sitter to stay at your home or board your Chessie a t a kennel, your Chesapeake Bay Retriever's training will pay off. He will understand the commands given to him by other people and will know how to get along with other dogs.

Be Consistent

"I came from SeaWorld and the Cincinnati Zoo cat ambassador program, so I only know clicker (positive reinforcement) training. It might take a little longer, but you'll develop a dog that will 'offer' behaviors. And the training will be more solid. Consistency is the key to training. Chessie's are smart!"

CAT WEIL
Timbercreek Acres

The majority of the time, dogs live with more than one person. When we brought Hank home from the breeders, there were six of us living in the house. With six different people with their own set of boundaries and rules, it had to be so confusing for Hank to know what he should and shouldn't do. No wonder he went through a naughty stage as a puppy. The poor guy was just trying to figure out where the line in the sand was drawn. Admittedly, my family was not all on the same page in regard to Hank's training. We lacked consistency.

Chesapeake Bay Retrievers in particular prefer to have just one master. When other members of the family start giving your Chessie commands and expectations, it forces the dog to reevaluate his place in the pecking order. This alone is enough to create confusion. Add to this the inconsistencies of each person and you end up with a dog that may appear to be stubborn,

CHAPTER 9 Training your Chessie

Photo Courtesy of JP and Annia Hargon

defiant, or hard to train, but who is really just trying to figure out all the rules and boundaries.

Chessies are happier when they know what they are supposed to do. For your Chessie's sake as well as your own, you and the rest of the people living in your household need to all be on the same page when it comes to your Chessie's training, rules, and expectations.

Tips for Clear, Consistent Training

We know that it is important to be consistent when training your Chesapeake Bay Retriever, but often, this is easier said than done. Being consistent – and making sure the rest of the family follows suit – is hard work. Even when you are tired or stressed or rushed for time, though, you still need to enforce the same rules with your dog. Here are some pointers to help you maintain consistency.

USE THE SAME WORDS

In his lifetime, your Chesapeake Bay Retriever will learn to recognize and understand about 165 words. When training a Chessie puppy, however, it is important that everyone uses the same words as commands. Remember that your Chessie doesn't know English. He doesn't know that "come" and "come here" mean the same thing. Talk to your family to make sure everyone is using the same word for commands. For example, you should all decide if you will use "sit" versus "sit down" or "siddown" (they sound different to dogs), "come" versus "here," or "give" versus "drop."

USE THE SAME GESTURES

Chesapeake Bay Retrievers carefully observe the world around them. In addition to learning a large vocabulary of words, they will also learn to understand your gestures. It is equally important that you and the others living in your home adopt the same gestures when training and giving commands to your Chessie. If your Chessie is barking at a knock on the door, for example, do you hold up the palm of your hand in a "stop" gesture, or do you point your index finger at him? Pick one gesture that your whole family uses.

FOLLOW THE HOUSE RULES

You can unwittingly teach your Chessie some bad behaviors just because you are not consistent in enforcing basic house rules. Let's say one of your house rules is that your Chessie should not beg for food when you eat. To accomplish this, you know you should never feed your Chessie from your dinner plate when you are sitting at the table. If you never give your Chessie a morsel under the table and no one in your household does, your dog will learn that begging is a waste of his time because it never ends in a tasty morsel of human food.

FUN FACT — Maryland State Dog

Chesapeake Bay Retrievers, named after the same-named bay region in Maryland, became the official state dogs of Maryland in 1964.

You also need to be consistent in other situations involving food, too. Your Chessie may learn not to beg at the dinner table, but if your daughter slips him the crust of her toast every morning, your Chessie will learn he can beg at the breakfast bar. Likewise, if you have the guys over every Sunday to watch football in your family room, and you always order pizza for everyone, don't allow one of your buddies to give your Chessie a crust of pizza from his plate. And if you regularly invite the neighbors over for a backyard cookout, ask everyone to refrain from giving your Chessie a piece of their hot dog. You want your Chesapeake Bay Retriever to understand that he is not to beg for food anywhere, no matter the location, person, or situation. To do this, you need to be consistent.

KIDS NEED TO BE CONSISTENT TOO

When Hank was a puppy, we quickly discovered that our children are all suckers for big brown puppy dog eyes! We set rules like no jumping up on people and not allowing Hank to sleep in our children's beds. Then we found out that one daughter was "dancing" with Hank, allowing him to jump up as she held his front legs. I think all of our children were guilty of letting Hank hop up on their beds. They claim that he just showed up in the night but, a few times, I caught them inviting him to snuggle in bed with them. In our situation, it wasn't that Hank was poorly trained and couldn't follow orders. It was that our children were poorly trained and couldn't follow orders!

BE CONSISTENT, EVEN WHEN YOU'RE TIRED

Being consistent is hard work and, from time to time, we feel like it would be easier to let the rules slip than to enforce them. But if you allow your Chessie to break the rules, even just once, he will remember this and push the boundaries with you again and again.

Positive Versus Negative Reinforcement Training

"We have found that training methods have certainly changed over the years. The old way of training (popping and jerking the dogs) did not work with a Chessie. We encourage positive reinforcement style training with praise and treats. They will work for anything positive."

JOANNE SILVER
Silvercreek Chesapeakes

When we train our dogs, we can either use a positive approach, in which we reward good behavior, or a negative approach, in which we punish bad behavior. Basically, when using a positive reinforcement method, you are adding some sort of happy, exciting aspect – like a treat, belly rub, or enthusiastic "good boy!" – to increase the likelihood that your dog will repeat that good behavior in the future. The opposite is true for negative reinforcement training. You attach some sort of unpleasant aspect – like a stern scolding – to the behavior in hopes that it deters your Chessie from doing it again in the future. To put it simply, you are teaching your dog that there are consequences, both good and bad, for his behavior.

Positive Reinforcement Training

Also called reward-based training, positive reinforcement is the preferred method of training among professional dog trainers because it strengthens the bond of trust between a Chessie and his owner. Positive reinforcement training, however, is more than just rewarding your Chesapeake Bay Retriever with a treat, scratching his ears, and offering him a hearty, happy "good dog!" compliment. It also involves ignoring the negative behavior altogether.

Dogs want to please their owners. According to proponents of positive reinforcement training methods, if a dog is engaging in a bad behavior and he is ignored by his owner, he will stop doing the behavior. The behavior did not result in a positive aspect, like a treat, so the dog will abandon that activity in favor of one that will result in positive attention from his owner.

What if the dog is engaging in destructive behavior, like chewing on your shoe? You cannot simply ignore the behavior, or the result will be a ruined

CHAPTER 9 Training your Chessie

Photo Courtesy of
Maygan Coats
Lone Willow Chesapeakes

sneaker. How can the bad behavior be addressed while you are ignoring the dog? Dog-training experts suggest that you redirect the dog's focus away from the negative activity and engage him in a positive activity. In the shoe example, the experts advise you to remove the shoe from your dog and replace it with something the Chessie is allowed to chew on, like one of his toys. Once he diverts his attention to the toy and not the shoe, reward his good behavior. He will learn very quickly that good behavior gets him treats and praise, while bad behavior gets him nothing.

Negative Reinforcement Training

Negative reinforcement training often gets a bad rap because people associate it with animal cruelty and abuse, but when done right and in conjunction with positive reinforcement training, it can be an effective training tool. Negative reinforcement training is sometimes called aversion training. It works by associating an unpleasant consequence with an unwanted behavior. It is important that the unpleasant consequence is not harmful to the Chessie. You should never hit or strike your dog, even if the dog is misbehaving. Examples of negative reinforcement training are using a spray bottle full of water to remind your dog of his inappropriate behavior or scolding the dog with a stern voice, but not yelling and screaming at him.

When using negative reinforcement training, never use your Chessie's name in a negative manner. You want your dog to associate his name with happiness and love. If you do have to scold your Chessie, mind your words carefully. Instead of using his name, replace it with a nonsense word that can serve as your go-to bad boy word. It sounds silly, but we used "Bobo" in place of Hank's name on occasion. When he knocks over the trash or digs a hole in the yard, we remind him that he is being a "bad Bobo."

Timing is key when using negative reinforcement training. Your Chessie won't be able to connect the bad behavior he did at 8 a.m., as soon as you left for work, with the punishment you give him at 5:30 p.m. when you get home. Too much time has passed. Even if you show your Chessie the uprooted houseplant or the chewed flip flop, he won't understand that he is being punished for something he did eight hours ago. If you cannot immediately punish your Chessie for misbehaving, it might not be worth punishing him at all.

Pitfalls of Punishment-Based Training

"Never raise your voice or hand when scolding a Chessie. This will destroy a Chessie faster than anything. All they want is unconditional love and to please you."

ANDREA HURT
Chessies R Us

Used incorrectly, negative reinforcement training can be detrimental to a dog. Excessive punishing, yelling, and threatening a dog with physical harm can all harm the dog's psyche. He may become more aggressive and engage in more negative behavior. After all, negative attention is still attention. Or your Chessie may become timid, shy, and nervous. No animal should live in fear. Training methods must be humane, effective, and designed to enhance the dog-owner bond, not tear it down.

Many new puppy owners opt to sign up for a puppy-training class or obedience school. Often, they are under the mistaken belief that these classes will take the place of in-home training sessions. In truth, nothing can replace consistent training on a daily basis, however there are benefits to obedience classes, and some drawbacks as well.

Pros of Obedience Classes

- **THE TEACHER IS AN EXPERT**

Obedience-school teachers are expert, experienced dog trainers. They have worked with so many dogs over the years that they have an instinctual understanding of dog behavior. They are a gold mine of knowledge and can offer you tips and tricks to improve your training sessions with your dog. You will learn as much as your Chessie does.

- **YOUR CHESSIE WILL BE AROUND OTHER DOGS**

Because the classes are held in a group setting, they serve as an opportunity for socializing as well as education. Your Chesapeake Bay Retriever will have the chance to interact with other dogs in a safe, controlled setting. He will love it. Dogs enjoy being around other dogs and it is good for them, too. They learn how to politely greet other dogs, which will help them feel more confident the next time they meet other dogs, be it on a walk, at the dog park, or visiting a friend.

- **YOU'RE ALL IN THIS TOGETHER**

As a new puppy owner, you are probably experiencing some stress, frustration, and worry. In a puppy obedience class, you will be surrounded by other new puppy owners who are all feeling the exact same way. This is a good opportunity to discuss your concerns with other people who are in the same situation. You can bounce ideas off each other to find new approaches to puppy rearing. If your Chessie is going through a phase that has you frustrated, the chances are good that another puppy in the class is doing the same thing and its owner would love to talk to you about it. Who knows? You may even make some friends.

- **HANDS-ON EXPERIENCE**

A good obedience class will give you real-world, hands-on experience that is guided by the instructor. For example, the instructor may have everyone walk their dogs around the block to get used to walking on a leash and walking with other dogs. You may have a field trip to a dog park so the students can practice interacting with other dogs. I have even heard of training classes that have a "final exam" when the whole class meets for dinner at a restaurant with an outdoor, pet-friendly patio. All of these activities help your Chessie to learn how to behave in various settings.

Cons of Obedience Classes

- **THE CLASSROOM IS DISTRACTING**

A half dozen hyper, over-exuberant puppies -- what can be distracting about that? Joking aside, there are benefits to learning in a group setting, but there are also plenty of distractions that may prevent your Chesapeake Bay Retriever from learning. First, your puppy will be in an unfamiliar place, full of new sights and smells to explore and investigate. Second, there will be other puppies there. The dogs may just want to play together and ignore their lessons. Lastly, there will be strangers there – the instructor and the other dog owners. With so much to see, it is difficult for many dogs to focus on the instructions they are given.

- **IT'S NOT HOME**

Home is a familiar place for your Chessie. He feels safe and relaxed there, which puts him in a better mindset to learn his training. You may find that your Chesapeake Bay Retriever embarrasses you in class because he won't listen to you, but he will perform beautifully at home. That's because he feels far less anxious in a familiar setting.

CHAPTER 9   Training your Chessie

- **DOG BULLIES**

With so many dogs in one room, there may be one or two puppies that try to be the top dog. Even though the obedience class instructor is well versed in breaking up dog fights, it is possible that an aggressive-acting dog will cause the rest of the puppies to feel stressed and tense during class time.

- **YOU MAY IGNORE YOUR DOG**

During the obedience class, you and the rest of the humans may be so tuned in to what the instructor is explaining, that you stop paying attention to your Chessie. Your dog will be giving you nonverbal cues to let you know how he is feeling about the situation. But you have been taught to be a good student and listen intently to your teacher. Doing so, however, means you shift your focus from your Chessie to the instructor and you may miss out on the bonding experience with your dog.

Working with an expert dog trainer is an excellent idea. They can help you avoid pitfalls and to be more consistent in your training. You will have to evaluate your own circumstances to determine if you think a puppy obedience class is a good choice for you and your Chesapeake Bay Retriever. Did Hank go to puppy school? No, he didn't because we live in a rural area. There are no classes offered near us. Had there been, I believe Hank would have benefited from the expert instruction.

CHAPTER 10:
Teaching your Chessie Basic Commands

"There is a myth that the Chesapeake is hard headed and stubborn to train. I do not find that to be the case. The Chesapeake is a very sensitive dog. They respond to positive reinforcement and turn off to harsh or heavy handed training. It's important that the dog understands what is being asked. Avoid confusion and mixed messages."

JOANN COLVIN
Cal-I-Co Chesapeakes

When you teach your Chesapeake Bay Retriever basic commands like sit, stay, and come, you are doing much more than teaching him tricks to show off to others. You are giving him instructions and skills so that he knows what to do in unfamiliar settings. And since these basic commands are almost universal, you will be providing your Chessie with the tools he needs to be a well-trained, well-adjusted, well-socialized dog that is a happy member of your family.

Tips for Making Training Fun for your Chessie

Training time should be a fun time for your Chessie. You should begin training your puppy as soon as he is old enough for you to bring him home. But keep the training sessions short while he is still young. Typically, five to ten minutes will be long enough to practice the lesson and keep your puppy's attention. If you keep the focus on fun, your dog will have a positive training experience and will be more receptive to the lesson and to future lessons.

You know that you need to be consistent in your training but repeating the lessons over and over again will be just as boring for your Chessie as it is

CHAPTER 10 Teaching your Chessie Basic Commands

for you. Here are some tips for keeping the focus on fun and positivity when you are training your Chesapeake Bay Retriever:

- **SWITCH UP LOCATIONS**

Say you always have your training sessions in the family room or the backyard. For a change of pace, go to a different location to work on your Chessie's basic commands. Sure, he can sit on command in the living room;

Photo Courtesy of Abigail Hughes

he's done it a hundred times. But will he understand that you want him to sit in the bedroom or the kitchen or on the sidewalk out front? Go find out. Find a quiet corner at the local dog park and spend a few moments running through commands with your Chessie. The combination of a new location and the familiar lesson will get the wheels turning in your Chessie's active brain.

- **PRESENT A NEW LESSON**

Sit. Stay. Come. These commands are necessary, but they can get tiring after a while. Your Chessie needs to be challenged. From time to time, throw in a "trick" lesson as part of his training. Work on giving high-fives or balancing a treat on his snout until you give him the command. You can even work on tricks like fetching your slippers or catching a Frisbee. Nothing staves off boredom and complacency like a new challenge.

- **TAKE A BREAK**

It is true that consistency and repetition are important, but sometimes your Chesapeake Bay Retriever just needs a break. You may notice that your Chessie's training has hit a plateau. Taking a few days or even a whole week off from lessons will allow you both to come back refreshed and renewed. During your break, you still need to enforce the rules with your dog, just skip the focused training sessions.

- **STAY POSITIVE**

Your mood and attitude are an important part of the training. When you are in a foul mood, impatient, or frustrated, your Chesapeake Bay Retriever will sense it and it can have a negative impact on the training session. If you recognize that you aren't in the best mood, postpone the training session until your spirits lift. You don't want your mood to cause you to speak harshly to your Chessie. You will break his trust and may undo weeks of training.

Basic Training Commands

"Chessies are extremely smart. Once they learn a task, they do not forget it. If they do not respond to your command, it's not because they do not remember. Much like with children, misbehavior occurs because they are choosing to ignore you or they are upset with you."

LEAH SPRADLIN
Hickory Creek Chesapeakes

CHAPTER 10   Teaching your Chessie Basic Commands

We teach our dogs the basic commands like sit and stay so that we can use these commands when needed and our dogs will know what to do. For example, if your Chesapeake Bay Retriever becomes over-excited when guests arrive at your home and wants to greet them by jumping up on them, you can redirect his behavior by telling him to sit. Because he's been trained, he will understand what you are expecting of him. The basic commands should be taught to all dogs.

HOW TO TEACH YOUR CHESSIE TO SIT

When we taught Hank to sit on command, we did what dog training experts say not to do. We repeated the word "sit" as we gently pushed on his rump until he sat down then we rewarded him for it. He learned to master the command, but experts now advise dog owners to refrain from forcing the dog into a sitting position. This is confusing and upsetting to many dogs. Instead, they recommend either the lure or capture method.

With the lure method, the goal is to get your Chessie to sit without physically putting him in the sitting position. You do this by luring him with a treat.

1. Hold the treat right in front of your Chessie's nose so he becomes interested in it.
2. Slowly raise the treat above the Chessie's head.
3. Your dog will instinctively sit and raise his nose higher. Give him the treat only when his rump is on the ground.
4. Do this a few times then try it without the treat, just using your hand.
5. When your dog sits, still reward him with a treat. Soon he will connect your hand signal to the action of sitting. Once he does, start saying "sit" right before you use the hand signal. Your Chessie will learn to sit on command, whether that command is a hand signal or the verbal command.

The other method for teaching your dog to sit is often referred to as the capture method. In this technique, you essentially wait for your dog to sit on his own, then reward him for it.

1. You do this by standing in front of him with a treat and calmly waiting. The dog will eventually sit.
2. When he does, praise him and give him the treat.
3. Move your position. This will make your Chessie stand back up.
4. Repeat the technique with another treat.
5. Once he seems to get the hang of it, add in the verbal "sit" command. He will associate his movement with your command and the treat.

HOW TO TEACH YOUR CHESSIE TO STAY

When your Chessie masters the "stay" command, he will know that he needs to remain seated until you give him the command to move. Therefore, this basic command is really two commands in one. Your Chesapeake Bay Retriever needs to learn the command to remain in place and the command to get up and move. Teaching your Chessie to stay requires a two-pronged approach.

In this case, you need to start backwards.

1. First, teach your Chessie the release word. Pick something simple, like "go," "okay," or "now."
2. Stand next to your Chessie and throw a treat out in front of him.
3. When he moves forward to get the treat, say your release word.
4. Repeat this several times, then try saying the release word before you toss the treat.
5. When your Chessie moves on your command, and not just when the treat is thrown, reward him. He is understanding that you want him to move when you give him the release word.

Once this skill is mastered, you can move on to the first part, the sitting and staying part.

1. To teach this skill, have your Chessie sit and move to a spot facing him.
2. Give him a treat so he knows what his reward will be.
3. Next, tell your dog to stay as you hesitate, then offer the treat.
4. Do this several times, increasing the wait time a few seconds longer each time.
5. Each time you do it, give your dog the "sit" command, then the release command as he gets up to get the treat.
6. When your Chessie can sit patiently for several seconds and only gets up when you give him the release command, start adding more distance between the two of you. Take a step back and repeat the lesson.
7. When you practice this lesson the next day, start closer to your Chessie, but then move a bit further away. The goal is to work up to longer distances.

The "stay" command is a useful skill for a dog, as we discovered with Hank. Often, especially in the summer months, we will all be outside with Hank, doing yard work or having dinner on the deck. When the Amazon Prime van pulls in, as it does often, Hank wants to run full speed toward it. He is so large that most people are terrified. Since we want the Amazon

CHAPTER 10 Teaching your Chessie Basic Commands

driver to keep coming back with our goodies, we give Hank the "stay" command until one of us can approach the driver, get the package, and assure the driver that our dog won't rip a leg off. Most of the time, we will give Hank the release command while we are chatting with the driver. We want Hank to know that delivery drivers are not the enemy.

HOW TO TEACH YOUR CHESSIE TO LIE DOWN

When you are teaching your Chesapeake Bay Retriever to lie down, you can use the same approach you used when teaching him how to sit.

1. Wait until your Chessie lies down on his own and begin reinforcing this positive behavior with treats.
2. Give him the release command from your sit/stay lessons, rewarding him when he gets up.
3. When you see your dog start to lie down, give him the command word -- usually "down" or "lie down" -- as you offer a reward.

You can also lure your Chessie into a lying position using another method.

1. Hold a treat in front of him and slowly lower it to the floor, so your dog follows the goodie.
2. When your Chessie's elbows hit the floor, reward him with the treat.
3. Once he seems to get the hang of this, use just your hand without a treat to encourage your dog to lie down. He should soon lie down on your hand signal.
4. Then you can start to add in the command word. As your Chessie sits, tell him "down."
5. When he is completely down, reward him with a treat.

Just like teaching the sitting command, do not force your Chesapeake Bay Retriever to lie down when you are working on this command. It will only confuse your dog and make the lesson counterproductive.

How to Teach your Chessie to Roll Over

Once your Chesapeake Bay Retriever has mastered the lie down command, you can move on to the "roll over" command. You may think this is an unnecessary command – that it is more like a trick than a useful command. There are times, however, when it is useful for your Chessie to know how to roll over on command. I recall one time when Hank wandered out behind the barn and came back with lots of burrs stuck in his fur. Most of them were on his underside, which must have been extremely uncomfortable.

CHAPTER 10 Teaching your Chessie Basic Commands

Photo Courtesy of
Jay Garrity and Molly Welch-L1

We removed all the burrs from his back then gave him the command to roll over. This made it easier for us to pick off the burrs from his belly.

Teaching your Chesapeake Bay Retriever to roll over should be done after he knows the lie down command.

1. Start the lesson by telling your Chessie to lie down.
2. Get down on the floor next to your dog and hold a treat near his nose to get his attention.
3. Slowly, move your hand away from his nose and toward his shoulder.
4. As your dog follows the treat with his nose, he will naturally end up on his side with his head on the ground. This is what you want.
5. Reward him with the treat.

For the next lesson, don't stop moving the treat when your Chessie is lying on his side. If you continue moving it, he will roll onto his back. Go a little bit further and he will keep rolling, too. Offer him the treat as his reward. Your Chessie should quickly learn that he will get a treat when he rolls. When he can roll over on a consistent basis with the treat as his incentive, start adding in the "roll over" verbal command. Try it without the treat while just using the hand gesture and the verbal command. Still praise your Chessie when he successfully rolls over. Soon, he will be able to roll over on your command, without the treat or hand gesture.

How to Teach your Chessie to Come

You should start training your Chesapeake Bay Retriever on the "come" command from an early age. It is an important skill to master, for your dog's safety. Excited, distracted puppies can run off, intent on chasing a butterfly or a bicyclist. Your Chessie could run right into traffic or encounter other dangers. Start training him early and he will know to return to you as soon as you call him.

It is best to hold the first several training sessions inside and in a room that is quiet and free of distracting noises.

1. Begin your training by sitting on the floor with your Chessie puppy.
2. Repeat whatever your "come" command will be – "come," "here," or your dog's name. When you say the command, give your Chessie a small treat. He will love it! He is getting rewarded for doing nothing.
3. For the next step, toss the treat on the floor in front of your Chessie. He will, of course, eat it.

CHAPTER 10   Teaching your Chessie Basic Commands

④ When he is done, say his name. He should look up at you.

⑤ When he does, give him another treat. He is learning his name!

⑥ Start tossing the treat further and further away as your Chessie becomes better at looking at you when he hears his name.

⑦ By this time, your Chessie and the treat should be several feet away from you.

⑧ In the next step, toss the treat out as usual and say your dog's name as he finishes again, to get him to look at you.

⑨ Now, show the dog another treat that you have in your hand.

⑩ When he trots back to you, say the command word, "here" or "come."

⑪ When he comes to you, present him with the treat.

When he masters this, you can begin challenging your Chessie more. Take the lesson outside or move to another room in the house. The goal of the lesson should be the same -- to get your Chessie's attention when you say his name and to get him to return to you when you give the "come" command.

A few words of caution. You want your Chessie to know his name and respond to it but take care that you don't inadvertently assign too many meanings or commands to his name. This will only confuse him. When using the "come" command, remember to keep the tone of your voice happy and upbeat. Why would your dog want to return to you if you are angrily shouting the "come" command at him?

Also, remember that timing is important with praising or reprimanding your dog. If your Chessie darts away from you, for example, and you call out his name to get his attention then give the "come" command, so he returns to you, your Chessie has successfully done everything you taught him. He will not understand why you would scold him. To him, the action of darting away was in the past and long forgotten. He will think he is being scolded for returning to you when called. Next time, he may think twice about heeding your "come" command since it did not result in a positive outcome for him.

How to Teach your Chessie to Give or Drop the Ball

Although retrievers are naturals at chasing after a ball or Frisbee and bringing it back to you, they can sometimes seem unwilling to part with the ball. They want you to throw it again, but they don't want to give you the ball so you can. You can keep the game of fetch going with your Chesapeake Bay Retriever by teaching him the "drop" or "give" command.

1. For starters, you will need to decide which word you are going to use when you want your Chessie to give you the ball. Share this with the rest of the family. It will only confuse your Chessie if you teach him "give" but someone else expects him to "drop."
2. The next step is extremely easy. Just play fetch with your Chessie. Throw the ball or Frisbee and allow him to run after it.
3. After he picks up the ball, he should instinctively return to you. If he doesn't, use the "come" command.
4. If he is unwilling to drop the ball for you, bribe him with a treat.
5. As soon as he sees the treat, he will gladly give up the ball. As he does, say the "give" or "drop" command.
6. Each time your Chessie brings the ball back to you, say the "give" or "drop" command as he releases the ball to get a treat. He will quickly learn the command for giving you the ball.

Learning the "give" or "drop" command is useful for other applications, as well. Take, for instance, the time Hank snatched my daughter's favorite stuffed animal and pranced around the house with it. My daughter tried chasing him to get her toy back, but Hank thought it was all part of the game. Then she remembered his training. She said Hank's name to get his attention and then firmly said, "Give." It worked like a charm. Hank dropped Mr. Fluff, and my daughter got her toy back unscathed.

Tips for Leash Training your Chessie

Every time you are out in public with your Chesapeake Bay Retriever, he will need to be on a leash. There are some off-leash dog parks and dog beaches, but you should plan on having your Chessie leashed when he is out with you. Straining and pulling on the leash will just make every outing miserable for you and for him. Knowing how to properly walk while leashed is an important skill every dog should learn.

- **START EARLY**

From the time you bring your Chesapeake Bay Retriever home from the breeders, get him used to wearing a collar or harness. Let him wear these around the house so he gets accustomed to the feel of them. Once he seems content wearing a harness and collar, add the leash. Start with just short periods of time on the leash and reward your Chessie with treats and praise. Pretty soon, he will associate the leash with the positive experience of attention, food, and fun.

CHAPTER 10   Teaching your Chessie Basic Commands

● BABY STEPS

1. When your Chessie is comfortable with the leash, stand next to him, holding the leash.
2. Get your puppy's attention by saying his name.
3. Show him a treat in your hand and hold your hand out in front of the dog's nose.
4. Once he is focused on the treat, take a few steps forward. He will step forward as well, to move closer to the treat. This is what you want him to do, so reward him for it.
5. Practice this a few times then try it without using a treat, just your hand. Still reward him with a treat when he successfully walks with you.

Keep the lessons short while your Chessie is still young but work up to longer lessons and longer steps forward before you reward him. When he can confidently walk next to you on the leash across a room, it is time to move your lessons outside.

Holding leash lessons outside increases the challenge for your Chessie. There are so many distractions he needs to learn to block out – birds, squirrels, butterflies, random neighbor kids, other dogs, and other people. So much to see. So much to smell. So much to hear. Being outside also gives you more space for longer leash walks but start small. Reward your Chessie for remembering proper leash behavior, even if it is just a few steps. Longer leash lessons will follow.

With so many distractions outside, your Chesapeake Bay Retriever will probably test his limits on the leash. He may pull or lunge. It may be tempting to pull back on the leash if your Chessie starts pulling. This is counterproductive. Instead, you should stop walking and stand still, holding firmly on the leash. Your Chessie wants to move. He will give up going his way and come back to your side. You can refocus his attention and continue walking.

Your Chessie may try to bolt after a squirrel, a bicyclist or another dog. It is a natural response to seeing something unfamiliar and exciting. Your task is to scan the surroundings for potential triggers so you can keep your Chessie's focus on the leash lesson. You can offer a treat or say the dog's name to keep his focus on you instead of the distraction.

If your Chessie does try to lunge after something, hold your ground. Stand in place and firmly hold the leash without pulling at it. Once the target of his fascination moves on or your dog realizes he can't get it, he will stop lunging. Bring his attention back to you, then reward this positive behavior with a treat.

Tips for Off-Leash Training your Chessie

"Come and stay are two of the most important commands for a Chessie. If there is a danger present, you need for them to come on command so that you can prevent injury. Stay is important because if there is a distraction, you need for them to listen to your command, not to other people or distractions that may be present."

LEAH SPRADLIN
Hickory Creek Chesapeakes

Your Chesapeake Bay Retriever has a natural urge to run around and explore his surroundings. The leash is holding him back. The majority of the time you are out in public with your Chessie, you will want him to be on a leash for his safety. It's also good dog owner etiquette. There are, however, sometimes when it is perfectly fine for your dog to go off leash. Before you unclip the leash, be sure to check the surroundings and be sure your Chessie is ready. He should have already mastered commands like "come" and "stay."

Hank is allowed off leash in a few places. The dog beach we frequent permits dogs to swim off leash as long as their owner has them under control. Hank can also go off leash at Grandpa's cabin in the woods. Hank has been there so many times that he knows his way around if he were to wander away from us. The majority of the time, though, he stays within sight of us when we walk the trails through the woods. He is trained well enough that he comes when we call him. Everywhere else we go, Hank stays on his leash.

FUN FACT
Sporting Group

Chesapeake Bay Retrievers belong to the Sporting Group of dogs, according to the AKC. This group consists of active dogs who serve as excellent companions. Most of these dogs excel at hunting as well as other field sports. The four main types of Sporting dogs are Pointers, Retrievers, Spaniels, and Setters. As of 2020, a Chessie has yet to win the Sporting Group at the annual Westminster Kennel Club Dog Show.

Thoroughly assess your Chessie before you try going off leash. Every Chessie is different, and you know your dog better than anyone. Does he have a tendency to wander off or chase after things? Is he aggressive? Is he in good health and up to date on his vaccines? Is he friendly toward strange people and dogs? Does he always return to you when you give the "come" command?

If you think your dog is ready to try an off-leash outing, do a few trial runs in a controlled environment. Go to a place that has a large, fenced area, like a dog park. There are a couple off-leash dog parks near me that are about an acre in size with a fence surrounding the whole area. A site like this is ideal to test your Chessie's behavior when you unclip the leash. You can determine if your Chesapeake Bay Retriever can be trusted unleashed.

When your Chesapeake Bay Retriever masters the basic training commands, like "sit," "stay," and "come," he has learned much more than fun tricks to show off when you have friends over. He now has the skills he needs to obey you, even when he is in an unfamiliar situation. These basic commands help your Chessie feel confident and less anxious because he understands what you want him to do, no matter the surroundings. It is also important for your Chessie's safety that he understands that he needs to listen to you and follow your commands.

Chesapeake Bay Retrievers are intelligent dogs. They enjoy the mental exercise that training provides. It is well worth the effort on your part to train your Chessie as you will end up with a confident, well-mannered dog.

CHAPTER 11:
Nipping Bad Behavior in the Bud

"Chessies tend to be soft as far as handling pressure, compared to other retriever breeds. Their feelings are easily hurt, and while they will accept fair corrections, if you lose your temper they can also hold a grudge and will not take kindly to being unfairly treated. They are not stubborn, and believing they are stubborn is not a good mindset to have. They are highly intelligent with a level of canine instinct far more primitive and strong than most other dogs, and learn fast. This means they won't like doing the same thing over and over for an hour at a time when training a new skill. Do it a few times, have success, then stop and come back and repeat it later on."

SHARON POTTER
Red Branch Kennels

Photo Courtesy of Cheryl Glang

CHAPTER 11 Nipping Bad Behavior in the Bud

We welcome dogs into our lives to bring us joy, love, and companionship. You didn't sign up for destruction, naughtiness, and aggression. It is important that you prevent bad habits from starting and nip naughty behavior in the bud before it becomes a major problem. The vast majority of dogs that end up at animal shelters are left there because their owners were fed up with the dogs' bad behavior. Sadly, the humans are the ones to blame. Dogs are creatures of habit. Once they learn a bad behavior, especially if their owner inadvertently reinforces it, it is difficult to unlearn it. The key is to start early and be consistent. If you do that, you can nip bad behavior before it blossoms.

Bad Behavior Isn't Cute

Chesapeake Bay Retriever puppies are incredibly cute. These adorable little fluff balls are so curious about the world that they often get into mischief as they explore. We laugh at their funny little antics and gush over their escapades. When they play-fight with our hand or trot around with a shoe in their mouths, we find it humorous and adorable. What we are doing, though, without even realizing it, is reinforcing their naughtiness by rewarding it with our praise and attention.

Sometimes your Chessie may misbehave because he thinks it pleases you. It is a difficult thing to do, but you must be aware of how you react to your Chesapeake Bay Retriever's actions, right from day one. If your Chessie puppy pulls one of your throw pillows off the couch and tries to drag it around, you might exclaim, "What a big puppy you are!" in an excited tone. This tells your Chessie that he is doing something that makes you happy. He will do it again because he wants to continue to make you happy.

It's all fun and games until your pillow gets shredded into a million pieces. When that happens and you reprimand your Chessie, he will be so confused. All along, he thought he was doing a good thing and now, suddenly, it is bad? He should have been taught from the beginning that pillows are off limits.

Try to think about how things are perceived from your Chessie's point of view. When Hank was a puppy, we gave him an old sneaker to play with. It was one of the kids' shoes that had paint spilled on its mate. We threw that one away and let Hank have the other shoe to play with. He had lots of fun playing with it, but one day he couldn't find it. No problem, he thought. He marched over to the door, picked up another sneaker to chew on and ruined a perfectly good pair of Nikes. Although it would have been easy to be mad at Hank and scold him for his naughtiness, we knew we were at fault. By giving him a shoe that was destined for the trash bin, we sent the message to him that all shoes make good chew toys.

Tips for Correcting Problem Behaviors

There are some effective, general strategies for preventing behavior issues with your Chessie. As we said, starting early and staying consistent are two of the best ways to ensure success. By starting early, you can prevent your Chessie from developing bad habits to begin with. And if you remain consistent about enforcing the rules, your Chesapeake Bay Retriever will quickly figure out that he can't push the limits. However, if you allow him to break the rules on occasion, he will not know for certain where your line in the sand is. He will push the limits because he remembers that it worked a few times in the past. There are other overall strategies to use as well.

- **ELIMINATE TEMPTATIONS**

Do your best to keep your home free of temptations that may lead your Chesapeake Bay Retriever astray. As we discussed earlier in the book, periodically you should thoroughly puppy proof your space. Put shoes in a closet, remove throw pillows from your couch, hide electrical cords, put houseplants on a shelf, keep children's toys out of reach, and don't leave homework sitting out. Follow your Chessie puppy as he wanders about. If he shows an interest in some item that you don't want destroyed, move it out of his reach. The fewer temptations he has, the less likely he will be to chew up your belongings.

- **PROVIDE GOOD TRAINING**

Learning the basic commands, like "sit" and "stay" can reduce bad behavior in your Chesapeake Bay Retriever. First, the training sessions will keep his mind engaged so he's not bored. The lessons will also increase the bond between you and your Chessie. He will learn to love, trust, respect, and obey you. Second, you can use the commands if you catch your Chessie starting to misbehave. You can say his name to refocus his attention back to you. You can use the "come" command if he is going where he is not allowed to go. More importantly, you can use the "give" or "drop" command if your Chessie has something in his mouth that he is not supposed to have, like your wallet or the TV remote.

- **OFFER PLENTY OF EXERCISE**

Most Chessies get into mischief when they are bored. They need a lot of physical and mental stimulation to keep boredom at bay. If you work outside the home, your Chesapeake Bay Retriever may be spending long stretches of time home alone or in his crate. He is eager to see you and to exercise his legs, no matter how tired you may be. When your Chessie doesn't get enough exercise, he will channel his pent-up energy into extracurricular

CHAPTER 11 Nipping Bad Behavior in the Bud

activities, like digging up your houseplants, chewing on your table legs, and eating your earbuds.

Even if you are exhausted after a long day at work, it is still important for you to take your Chesapeake Bay Retriever on a long walk or a jog through the neighborhood to burn off his excess energy. If you can afford it, hire a dog walker to come during the day to exercise your Chessie. A dog that has plenty of exercise will be happier and less likely to get into mischief.

Let's look at some specific types of puppy naughtiness and discuss ways to correct the bad behavior.

Photo Courtesy of Lorraine Robinson

Chewing and Destroying Property

Chewing is a natural and instinctive behavior for Chesapeake Bay Retrievers. This is especially true during the puppy stage when the dogs are teething. The best way to save your valuables is to keep them well out of the way of your curious Chessie. Provide him with alternative things to chew on. Just make sure that the chew toys you give your Chessie are safe for him. Don't do what we did and offer your Chessie an old shoe. Your local pet store is filled with safe and appropriate toys that are designed to hold up to the vigorous chewing of a determined Chessie.

If your Chessie does get a hold of something he is not allowed to have, give him the "drop" or "give" command. When your Chessie drops the object, replace it with one of his chew toys. When he is happily chewing on his toy – and not the random household object – reward him with a treat so he understands that what he is doing is the positive behavior that you want.

Barking and Growling

Barking is another instinctive dog behavior. It is your Chessie's way of communicating. Dogs bark when they are happy and excited, when they are warning you about a perceived threat, or when they want something. Hank occasionally barks when he is playing with his Golden Retriever friend, Marlowe. These are happy barks. He also barks to let me know when the mail goes by, someone jogs past the house, or the Door Dash delivery has arrived. These are his warning barks because he worries that mail carrier, jogger, and delivery person all appear threatening. He will also bark to let us know his water bowl is empty or he needs to go outside. These are just little woofs to get our attention.

Excessive barking can quickly turn into a real problem. Unfortunately, some Chessies fall into the bad habit of unfounded barking. It is a terribly annoying habit. Your neighbors will complain. The barking can wake your children. And it will interrupt your Zoom meetings. Start working with your dog when he is still a puppy and train him to control his barking and to stop barking on your command.

You should try to determine why your Chesapeake Bay Retriever is barking. Does he need to go outside? Is he bored and looking for attention? Is there a suspicious person in your neighborhood? Or is there a deer in the front yard? Sometimes all it takes is to take care of his needs or divert his attention away from his bark trigger.

Keep in mind that your Chessie is probably barking as a natural response to something he views as a danger. If you become agitated and yell, your

CHAPTER 11 Nipping Bad Behavior in the Bud

Chessie will mimic your response. He will think, "This is not a drill!" Be sure to keep your voice and your demeanor calm, no matter how excited you are for your Door Dash delivery. Your Chesapeake Bay Retriever picks up his cues from you, so you need to model the behavior you want to see in your dog.

Training to control excessive barking is also important and should start at an early age.

1. When your Chessie puppy is barking, wait for him to stop.
2. When he does, offer him a treat and give him a command word, like "quiet," "shhhh," or "that's enough."
3. Be careful to only reward him when he stops barking. He will learn that he will be rewarded when he stops his barking and is silent. It takes a lot of practice, but he will also learn to connect the treat with the command word. In time, he will know what to do when you say, "that's enough" or "shhhh."

Photo Courtesy of Celia Wright

Digging

Chesapeake Bay Retrievers are not natural-born diggers, but that doesn't automatically mean that your flowerbeds are safe. You may still find that your backyard has craters here and there, your lawn has massive divots, and your perennials have been uprooted. Digging is a bad habit for some dogs, but there are ways to prevent it from starting.

First, you should look for the cause of the digging and address that problem. Is your Chessie digging because he is bored? Play with him when he is outside. Don't just expect him to entertain himself. Toss the ball, throw the Frisbee, or play some tug of war. It's great exercise, and he will enjoy the bonding time with you. More importantly, it will keep his mind stimulated, so he won't have time for digging.

One summer, we noticed that Hank dug long trenches in the yard, not the typical big hole we would have expected. It turned out that we had a mole problem. Hank could either smell or hear them under the ground and dug to try to reach them. A few mole traps took care of the problem. If your Chessie is digging, especially if it is out of character for him, it could be because you have a rodent problem.

There have been a few other times that we caught Hank digging. There is a patch of dirt under the walnut tree and we can never get grass to grow there. In the heat of the summer, Hank will sometimes dig a wide shallow area there, then lay down in the dirt. It cools him off. We haven't given up hope that one day grass will finally grow there, so we strongly discourage Hank from digging there. Besides, we don't want him to think he can just dig wherever he wants. We have done a couple things to prevent him from digging in that area. First, we fill up his little kiddie wading pool and let him cool off in that. Second, we have sprayed vinegar around the area to act as a deterrent.

If your Chessie has picked up a digging habit, you can break it by distracting him from digging and reward him for refocusing his attention elsewhere. Let's say you catch your Chessie in the act of digging a hole in your yard. Get his attention by calling his name, then use the "here" or "come" command to get him to come to you. Give him a toy or some other activity then reward him for playing with that toy. Digging doesn't get him a treat so he will stop doing it.

CHAPTER 11   Nipping Bad Behavior in the Bud

Begging

It is really hard to enjoy a nice, home cooked meal when your Chesapeake Bay Retriever is staring intently at you, drool dripping from his mouth, just waiting for a tasty morsel. In his defense, the food must smell amazing to your Chessie's super-nose. But begging for food when you are eating is a terrible habit that most dog owners find very aggravating. It is even more annoying and embarrassing when you have guests over for dinner. You can approach the bad behavior of begging by preventing the habit from starting or by distracting your Chessie and retraining him to break the bad habit.

You can prevent your Chesapeake Bay Retriever from developing a begging habit by never feeding him people food from the table. Ever. This means all family members. Your Chessie will display a remarkably long memory of the one time he was able to convince someone to give him a bite. So certain is he that this will happen again that he will beg his little heart out. It is best to never start so he knows that begging is futile. If you do want to give him a treat off your plate – and we will discuss the dangers of giving your Chessie people food in Chapter 14 – do so after you are done eating and away from the table. Maybe put the morsel in his dog dish so he knows that is the only place he gets fed.

If your Chessie has already developed a begging habit, you can crate your dog during mealtimes, or put up a baby gate to keep your Chessie out of the dining room. Once he is well-trained, you can use the basic commands of "sit" and "stay" to keep him away from the table.

There are a few things you can do to make this easier. First, make sure to feed your Chesapeake Bay Retriever before you eat. If your Chessie is hungry, he will be more tempted to want the delicious-smelling food you are enjoying. You can try offering him his food in a puzzle feeder to keep him occupied longer. Or you can use one of the dog toys in which you can hide a treat or two, like a Kong toy. He will be so busy trying to retrieve the treat that you can enjoy your meal in peace.

You can also use positive reinforcement to retrain your Chessie. When he starts begging at the table, lead him into another room and give him the "sit" or "lie down" command, followed by the "stay" command. Leave him and go back to the dining table. If your Chessie minds his training and remains there, after a few minutes go a reward him with a small treat and a pat on the head. He will soon learn that he won't get fed if he loiters around the table or begs, but he will if he is a good dog, obeys your commands, and remains away from the table when you are eating.

Photo Courtesy of Kim Florich

CHAPTER 11   Nipping Bad Behavior in the Bud

Jumping Up on People

It is so embarrassing to have guests come over and your Chessie greets them by jumping up on them. Jumping is naughty dog behavior no matter the breed, but for a dog as large as a Chesapeake Bay Retriever, it can be dangerous as well. You definitely want to stop your Chessie from jumping on people before he knocks Grandma to the ground.

Start by acting calm when guests arrive. This goes for all members of the family. I know you have outgrown the urge to squeal and run outside when friends come over, but your children may still act like this. Explain to your kids that your Chessie is mimicking their behavior. Since they are running out to give Grandma and Grandpa big hugs, your Chessie will want to run out and greet them with the same level of enthusiasm. It is much better for your guests and for your Chessie to remain calm and keep the excitement level to a minimum.

The reason why your Chessie is jumping up is to get attention. He will stop when he finds out it doesn't work. When your dog tries to jump on you, simply turn your back to him and stand still, bracing yourself for impact. Only give him attention when he settles down and sits.

Your Chessie will jump up on your friends for the same reason. Warn your guests ahead of time that you are trying to break your Chesapeake Bay Retriever of the bad habit of jumping and tell them that they can help with the lesson by ignoring your dog when he jumps and turning their backs on him. Too many times, guests are delighted to see dogs and will reinforce the naughty behavior by allowing them to jump up.

With your guests on board, you can also fall back on the basic commands that your Chesapeake Bay Retriever already knows to stop the jumping behavior. Get his attention by saying his name. Call him to you by giving him the "come" or "here" command. Ask him to "sit" and "stay" and only release him once everything has settled down. You can also try keeping your Chessie on a leash or in his crate until he is calm enough to greet your guests like a well-behaved dog.

Aggression Toward Children

Children and dogs should never be left together unsupervised. Both parties are unpredictable, therefore a responsible adult should always observe the interaction between children and dogs for the safety of everyone involved. A child may act aggressively toward the dog and, likewise, the dog may act aggressively toward the child. The Chesapeake Bay Retriever breed has a reputation for being good family dogs, but individual dogs behave their own way. If you observe your Chessie acting in an aggressive manner toward children, you need to address the problem immediately and work with your dog to break this bad behavior.

During your Chessie puppy's socialization training, be sure to spend time with children. In general, a dog that has been raised with children will learn how to interact with them. He will become used to the sudden squeals and shouts, the erratic movements, and the jumping around that kids do. He will get plenty of this type of socialization if you have children in your household, but if you don't, look for ways to familiarize your Chessie with kids. Allow the neighbor kids to play with your dog (with their parents' permission, of course, and with proper supervision). Invite your nieces, nephews, cousins, and friends with kids over. When you are taking walks and your Chessie is leashed, allow children to pet him if their parents say it's okay.

Have your Chesapeake Bay Retriever spayed or neutered. An unaltered dog, in general, is more aggressive and more easily agitated. Chessies that have been spayed or neutered are calmer and more laidback and not as easily provoked. Spaying or neutering also reduces the urge to hump or mount, though don't expect this to never happen. Humping or mounting is often a sign that a dog is exerting dominance over something or someone else. Your Chessie may not know where small children fall on the dog hierarchy, but he wants to be sure he is as high up the ladder as possible.

HELPFUL TIP
Chessies and Young Child

Chessies are intensely loyal dogs and can make excellent family pets. Though these dogs are great companion dogs, they may tend to be possessive of toys and food. Because of this, Chessie puppies might be better suited to a family without very small children. Older Chessies who are accustomed to small children may be a better fit for your family if you have children younger than eight years old. Always teach children how to approach and handle dogs, and be sure to curb overly possessive behavior in your Chessie before it becomes a serious problem.

Talk to children about how to behave around dogs. Let them know that sudden movement and noises can startle your Chessie and he may react defensively. Explain to kids that they need to avoid getting overly excited and wound up. They should be taught not to roughhouse or wrestle with your dog. The same goes for ear pulling, tail yanking, and trying to ride the dog like a

CHAPTER 11 Nipping Bad Behavior in the Bud

horse. Kids need to know to never attempt to take food, treats, or toys away from your Chessie. If he is chewing on something he is not supposed to have, the child should alert you or another adult. Your Chessie may feel provoked if a small child is reaching for his food.

Consider calling a professional if your Chesapeake Bay Retriever acts aggressively toward children. For the safety of others, you cannot let this problem go. It is also not fair to your Chessie to give up on him. Too many dogs are surrendered to animal shelters because their owners have labeled them as aggressive. Instead of working to resolve the problem and retrain the dog, they give up.

Pets are not disposable toys to be discarded when they appear 'broken." You are betraying the trust and bond you have with the dog. You owe it to your Chessie to find a solution to his aggression, even if it requires you to seek the help of an expert dog trainer with experience dealing with dog aggression. We will go into more details about professional dog trainers later in this chapter.

Aggression Toward Other Animals

It is always shocking and disheartening when our dogs act like animals. We expect them to be sweet and well-behaved all the time, but sometimes, they can be triggered by another dog and react aggressively. Aggression is a major problem, yet it is one that can be addressed with consistent training and socialization. It is a tough bad behavior to correct and you may need to call in a professional dog trainer, but it is worth the investment in time and money. In the end, you will have a Chesapeake Bay Retriever that is more trustworthy, happy, and docile.

Always monitor your Chesapeake Bay Retriever's interaction with dogs and other animals. As pack animals, dogs are always trying to vie for a higher position in the social hierarchy. When they encounter another dog, they will size it up to figure out which one is dominant. One or both dogs will act aggressively to show their dominance. When your Chessie meets a strange dog or another animal, watch for body language that indicates the potential for aggressive behavior.

If your Chessie stands with a stiff body posture and seems to be leaning slightly forward with his ears pinned back, you may want to move him away from the other animal. This is a good indication that aggressive behavior may follow. Also watch for growling, baring of teeth, and snarling as these are also signs of aggression. Does your dog appear nervous or timid? It could be that your Chessie is picking up signs of aggression in the other dog that is making him anxious.

Early socialization is one of the best preventative measures for curbing aggressive behavior. Often, the reason why your Chessie acts in a menacing manner is because he doesn't know any other way to act when he encounters an unfamiliar dog. You can help your Chessie to learn how he should behave by introducing him to other dogs and different kinds of animals as many times as possible during the puppy stage. The encounters need to be supervised and with animals you know and trust. Proper socialization will mean you are familiarizing your Chessie with other animals and giving him the tools he needs to understand how he should act when other dogs are present.

Dogs don't suddenly lash out with aggression. Something triggers or provokes this behavior. Perhaps your Chessie is hurt and is reacting instinctively to the pain. Maybe your dog is scared or being protective. If your Chessie is very territorial and engages in resource guarding, he may act aggressively if another dog tries to eat his food or play with his toy. Look for the underlying causes of the aggressive behavior. You may be able to eliminate the aggression simply by addressing the cause.

Correcting aggressive behavior in dogs can be done, but don't expect a quick fix. It requires diligence and consistency on your part to retrain your Chessie's brain. You can use positive reinforcement training to break your dog of the bad habit of displaying dominance and resource guarding. For example, reward your Chesapeake Bay Retriever with a treat when he allows another dog to nibble from his food bowl.

Try to catch your Chessie and reward him before he has a chance to react aggressively. First of all, distract him from his aggression and focus his concentration elsewhere. Speak to him calmly, yet firmly, and give a command word, such as "share" or "be nice." Try to catch your Chessie every time he tries to exert his dominance over another dog and reward him with a treat before he can hump or growl. Again, reinforce the lesson with the command word. In time, your Chesapeake Bay Retriever will understand that "be nice" means he needs to keep his aggression in check.

Any sort of aggressive behavior needs to be dealt with immediately before a small bad habit turns into a big one. Scheduling a few sessions with an experienced dog trainer can help, as we will see later.

CHAPTER 11   Nipping Bad Behavior in the Bud

Biting, Nipping, and Mouthing

Chesapeake Bay Retrievers use their mouths to explore the world. They will pick things up with their mouths, taste things, and chew on things, as a way to learn more. As duck-hunting dogs, Chessie have been bred for their mouthing tendencies. They are bred to hold the fallen bird gently in their mouths without damaging the meat. This doesn't mean that Chessie are immune to the bad habit of biting, nipping, and mouthing. This is a bad behavior that can start by accident when we actually reward and reinforce the nipping behavior in puppies. Once the bad habit starts, it can be challenging, but not impossible, to correct the problem.

It is so adorable when your little Chessie puppy attacks your hand and bites you with his tiny puppy teeth. It is not so adorable when he is six or eight months old and nearly drawing blood when he nips your hand. The best way to stop the bad habit of nipping, biting, and mouthing is to not start the habit in the first place. As cute as you think your puppy's play fighting is, remember that you are inadvertently rewarding your pup's bad biting behavior every time you laugh and praise him when he nips at you. This is a lesson that the whole family needs to participate in. If everyone in the family discourages play biting except your daughter, your Chesapeake Bay Retriever is learning that it is okay to bite and nip at her, but not others. When he gets bigger – and he will – it could become a real issue.

Your goal is to teach your Chessie puppy to not bite or nip, but the first step is to train them to understand bite inhibition. Bite inhibition is the Chessie's ability to recognize how hard he is biting and to tailor the strength of his bite to the circumstance. Young Chessie puppies that have been taught bite inhibition will know not to bite down hard, even when acting defensively or in pain.

When puppies play together, they learn bite inhibition from each other. If you watch a litter of pups play, you will notice that they nip and bite at each other. You will also hear a little yelp when one puppy bites a bit too hard on another puppy. The sound startles the offending puppy and brings the play to a screeching, albeit temporary, halt. This is how they learn about bite inhibition. It is totally instinctual. You can mimic this response by giving your Chessie puppy a high-pitched yip, followed by a command word, like "gentle" or "enough." Once he understands this, try yipping every time he bites or nips at you. He will learn that this is behavior you don't want him to do.

Another effective tool is to stop playing with your Chessie puppy for a few minutes every time he nips or bites you. Your Chessie wants to play with you and he relishes the attention he gets from you. This is positive attention, and he wants it to continue. If he bites or nips too hard, give him the command word, "enough," then walk away from him. After a minute or two, you can return to your play with him. You can even incorporate positive reinforcement by giving your Chessie a treat when you return to play with him, and he licks you instead of nipping at you. He will figure out that you don't want him to bite and nip.

You can also try to distract your Chessie from nipping and substitute your skin for another object. When your puppy gets wound up and tries to bite at you, pull your hand away and replace it with one of your Chessie's toys. When he bites and plays with the toy instead of your hand, reward this positive behavior with a treat. This will tell him that he can bite and mouth his toys, but not you.

If biting and nipping continue to be a problem, or if these bad habits come on in adulthood, you may want to consult with a dog training expert.

Do You Need Training Help from a Professional?

Chesapeake Bay Retrievers can be a challenge to train. Training a Chessie is best left to an experienced dog trainer rather than a novice dog owner. You must be firm and consistent at all times, even when you are tired or busy. And you must keep your cool. Getting angry and frustrated at your Chessie only complicates the training process. Training sessions should always be positive, fun experiences. Knowing all this, you should consider hiring a professional dog trainer if you are an inexperienced dog owner or if you know you are not up to the task. Training your dog is just so important that you shouldn't chance it.

The vast majority of bad habits can be corrected using proper training techniques. Never give up on a dog because of a behavioral issue. Hire an expert instead. Too many dogs are abandoned at animal shelters because their owners are fed up with a bad habit, however the habit is usually accidentally reinforced by the owners. With diligence and commitment, the habit can be reversed. If your Chessie is misbehaving, you need to take a hard look at what you are doing. A dog training expert can help you see that your methods may be contributing to the problem.

You may want to call in a professional dog training expert if your Chesapeake Bay Retriever is exhibiting some bad behaviors, such as acting aggressively, biting, excessively barking, and destroying your belongings. For your safety, the safety of your Chessie, and the safety of other people and animals, your dog should be well-trained and well-behaved. Don't be stubborn. Ask for help if you need it.

A professional dog trainer understands how your Chessie thinks and feels. He or she can often explain to you why your Chessie is behaving the way he is. This can be eye opening. You may learn that the tactics you have been using are counterproductive. The trainer can train you as much as he or she trains the dog. You will receive information and instructions to help you better analyze your Chesapeake Bay Retriever's behavior and to use critical thinking and logic to develop ways to solve various problems.

You could join an obedience class and work with the trainer as part of a group. You may also look into private training sessions or in-home training classes. The type of lesson is up to you. You need to assess your situation, budget, time availability, and other factors to determine the best option for you and your dog. Whichever one you pick, you need to commit to the training sessions. Go into the training sessions with a good attitude and an open mind. Acknowledge that the trainer is the expert, therefore you need to listen to the advice and realize that the trainer is more knowledgeable and experienced than you are. You will get more out of the lessons and be better equipped to help your Chessie be the best dog he can be.

When your dog misbehaves or picks up a bad habit, it is up to you to address the issue as soon as possible before it becomes a bigger problem. You can often resolve the behavior problem by evaluating your own actions and training techniques to make sure you are not inadvertently reinforcing the bad habit. Then you can use positive reinforcement tactics to retrain your Chessie.

CHAPTER 12:
Chessies as Hunting Dogs

The Chesapeake is ultimately a dog bred to accompany the hunter and you can see in its expression it's always thinking ... what can I do for you? What I see as wonderful in training with them is the great effort they always put into learning and that their enjoyment and reward is working. They never expect a reward for it. They are already happy just doing it!"

MECHA SAILORSBAY
Sailorsbay Kennel

Photo Courtesy of Dennis Cox

CHAPTER 12   Chessies as Hunting Dogs

Chesapeake Bay Retrievers are bred for two things – swimming and hunting. Developed on the shores of the Chesapeake Bay, the Chessies were bred to be strong, hardy dogs that can assist duck hunters on the choppy bay in the 1800s. Today, the Chesapeake Bay Retriever is still one of the most popular hunting dogs, although most Chessies enjoy life as a family dog. If you are planning to raise your Chessie to be a hunting dog, there is additional training that you will need to do to enhance the natural, instinctive traits of this remarkable water dog.

FUN FACT
Chessie Origin Story

The history of Chesapeake Bay Retrievers is often traced back 200 years to 1807 when two Newfoundland dogs were rescued from a floundering British ship in Maryland. The two dogs, named Canton and Sailor by their rescuer, George Law, were bred with local Retrievers and are considered to be the start of the line of American dogs who would eventually become the Chessies we know today.

Chessies Are Natural Water Dogs

The waters of the Chesapeake Bay can be treacherous, but the Chessies are well-suited for it. They have a unique coat that has been adapted for swimming in cold temperatures. They have a double coat with a wooly underlayer and thick and wavy fur on the outer layer. Chessies secrete natural oils into their coats that repel water and hold in their body temperatures in frigid water. Hank has never been to the Chesapeake Bay, but he does enjoy swimming in the Great Lakes. He swam in Lake Superior in late November and seemed unaffected by the cold as we stood shivering on the shore.

Chesapeake Bay Retrievers have larger webbing between their toes than most other dog breeds. This is a trait carried over from one of their ancestors, the Newfoundlands. Like the Newfies, Chessies have large paws. With their webbed toes, the Chessie paws are like boat paddles, displacing large amounts of water as the dog propels his way through the waves.

In addition to oily coats and large webbed paws, Chesapeake Bay Retrievers have broad, powerful chests that can break through thin layers of ice on the water. The chest muscles and leg muscles are incredibly strong on a Chessie. He can power through tall waves and swim against the current. Add to this, the breed's boundless energy and fierce determination, and Chessies are no quitters. They will muscle their way through the water to get what they are after, a fallen duck.

Chessies Are Natural Hunters

Several Chesapeake Bay Retrievers' traits, in addition to their expert swimming ability, help make this breed an ideal hunting dog. They are smart, hard-working, alert, and good problem solvers. They are not afraid to get dirty or wet and they are motivated by a willingness to please. These natural characteristics can be greatly enhanced through proper training. Once fully trained, a Chessie can be an asset to hunters.

Chessies have a "soft mouth." When they are retrieving waterfowl, it is important that they don't damage the meat. A well-trained hunting Chessie can be taught to clamp down with only a slight amount of pressure -- enough to hold the bird in place, but not hard enough to damage it. It is not uncommon to hear about a Chessie that can carry a raw egg in its mouth without cracking it.

Chessies instinctively want to go after things and bring them back. It's in their DNA. A good trainer can work with this natural instinct and create a hunting companion that will work as a valuable team member on the hunt.

Chessies may have been bred for duck hunting, but they aren't a one-trick breed. They are also exceptionally good at pheasant and quail hunting. They can help flush out the birds for the hunters to shoot, then retrieve them after they land. They have a keen memory and an equally keen sense

Photo Courtesy of Alan and Donna Wright

CHAPTER 12   Chessies as Hunting Dogs

Photo Courtesy of Jena Herrick

of smell. This helps them remember where a pheasant has fallen and locate it for the hunter.

Hank has not been trained to be a hunting dog and has never been duck hunting. When he was about a year old, however, my father took Hank with him pheasant hunting. Honestly, I think it was because all his hunting buddies were bringing their dogs and my dad didn't have one to take. For an untrained dog, Hank held his own at flushing birds, but he was startled when the gun went off.

In the retrieving category, Hank was definitely overshadowed by the other hunting dogs, but he seemed to have fun playing outdoors with my dad. For some reason, though, my father never invited Hank to join him on another pheasant hunt. I don't think he passed the test. We can't blame Hank. He wasn't trained to hunt.

Tips for Training your Chessie to Hunt

If you are investing in a Chesapeake Bay Retriever to serve as a hunting dog, it is important that you devote time, energy, and maybe even money to making sure the dog is properly trained. Chessies are not the best choice for a person who has never owned or trained a sporting dog before. They can be strong-willed and need a firm and consistent owner. If you opt to hire a

Photo Courtesy of
Cortney Closman

professional hunting dog trainer, you need to be deeply involved in the process so the Chessie understands to listen to you and obey your commands.

- **START WITH SOCIALIZATION**

Before you can begin with specific hunting training, you need to give your Chesapeake Bay Retriever a good overall education. Start early and socialize your Chessie puppy. Good socialization will ensure that your Chessie has the confidence to be a good hunting companion.

- **DEVELOP A STRONG BOND**

Spend a lot of time with your Chessie from puppyhood. Another key to the success of a hunting dog is to have a good bond with its owner. If your Chessie has learned to love, trust, and respect you, he will be eager to please you on the hunt. He will also be willing to listen and obey commands, even if he is excited and eager to chase after a bird. Prior to starting your hunting training, do what you can to make sure that you and your Chessie have a strong bond.

- **MASTER COMMANDS**

Your Chessie should also have a solid knowledge of the basic commands before you begin to focus on hunting. He should have mastered "sit," "stay," and "give," along with the other basic commands so that he is a good student during his hunting lessons and a well-behaved member of your hunting team.

- **GET OUTDOORS**

When he is on the hunt, your Chesapeake Bay Retriever will be expected to cover a lot of ground. Once your Chessie is trained enough on the basic commands that you are confident he will return to you when called, take your dog into large wilderness areas, and let him run off leash. The big world can be a scary place. Learning about it by exploring and making discoveries can help your Chessie become more confident and independent. Keep your eye on your dog as you allow him to wander around and follow his nose. Periodically, call him back to you, just to remind him of his training. Be sure to give him a reward for following your command.

- **GET YOUR CHESSIE USED TO ROAD TRIPS**

Get a good-quality transportation crate for your Chessie. When you begin hunting in earnest, you will need to transport your dog in your car to the hunting grounds. If your Chesapeake Bay Retriever is not used to a transport crate, it could be a stressful experience for him, and one that affects the hunt. It is best to get a crate early and get your Chessie acclimated to it. Start with short car rides at first and work up to longer ones. Make the crate

Photo Courtesy of Matthew Creed

CHAPTER 12   Chessies as Hunting Dogs

as comfortable as possible by adding a blanket or dog bed. Have plenty of fresh water, food, and treats on hand, too.

- **INTRODUCE YOUR CHESSIE TO HIS FIRST BIRD**

You want your Chesapeake Bay Retriever to learn to retrieve birds but, chances are, your dog hasn't had any interactions with birds. Introduce him to birds by presenting him with a dead pigeon. A live bird will flap and squawk, scaring your dog. Let your dog hold the dead bird in his mouth, but don't allow him to bite down on it or shake it. If you have taught your Chessie a "gentle" command when he nips or mouths you, use this command when he is holding the bird. He will understand that he is to hold it softly and gently. Don't let him linger too long with the bird or he may be tempted to shake it.

You can start with small lessons in your backyard. Hide a dead pigeon somewhere where your Chessie can easily find it. Have your dog "sit" and "stay" until you are ready, then give the release word and allow your Chessie to find the bird and bring it back to you. Be sure to reward him for doing this correctly. As the lessons progress, hide the bird further away and in more challenging spots. Once your Chessie has mastered this lesson, you can move to more open spaces, like a hunting field.

- **SEEK THE ADVICE OF EXPERTS**

Training a Chesapeake Bay Retriever to seek out and return waterfowl takes hard work and commitment. At any stage of the training, you should feel comfortable asking for help and advice from dog training experts and people with specific experience training Chessies to hunt. If you are an avid duck hunter, chances are you probably know someone who can help. Or you can connect with someone through your hunting club. An expert will help you view your training in a fresh way and may help you overcome obstacles. You should never feel like a failure for seeking help. More experienced dog trainers are typically happy to help. After all, they were once in your shoes.

Be Alert to Outdoor Dangers

Getting outside, running through an open field, and hiking through the woods are activities that your Chesapeake Bay Retriever will absolutely love, but you have to be cautious. There are some dangers in the great outdoors. You need to take care to avoid the dangers to keep the outdoor adventure as fun, safe, and positive as possible.

SKUNKS

Skunks don't really pose much of a threat as much as a nuisance. Hank is apparently a slow learner because he has been skunked, not once, but three times in his life. It is a smell you will never forget. The first time, unfortunately, I brought Hank into the bathroom to get a bath. His normal dog shampoo didn't remove the odor and my whole house smelled like skunk. I contacted our veterinarian and got some special shampoos that are especially designed to remove the skunk odor. For his next bath, I filled up the kiddie pool outside. I have learned to keep this shampoo on hand, but I found a less expensive version on Amazon. In a pinch, you can also use a tube of toothpaste which lathers up nicely and removes the odor.

RACCOONS, COYOTES, AND BADGERS

As human housing developments encroach into natural areas, the animals that make their homes there are forced to scoot over and make room for people and their pets. This means, in many parts of the United States, wild animals like raccoons, coyotes, and badgers are frequent visitors to our neighborhoods.

CHAPTER 12 Chessies as Hunting Dogs

In general, the threat to your Chesapeake Bay Retriever is low. After all, a full grown Chessie is a large and intimidating dog. Coyotes don't often attack animals that are larger than they are. Raccoons and badgers, in general, don't attack unless provoked. All three of these animals, however, can cause nasty injuries to a Chessie if a fight were to break out. Dusk is when these animals are most active. Keep a close eye on your Chessie during this time of day. Make sure he is supervised outside.

We have coyotes, foxes, and raccoons near us. The coyotes and foxes never bother Hank, but he has had a few run-ins with raccoons. Hank has a large collection of bandanas that he wears. One day, he went outside and came back without his bandana. We searched the yard but couldn't find it. Days later, we discovered it, torn and stained, under a bush in the back corner of the property. This happened a few more times, until I decided to follow Hank to the back corner. There, I witnessed Hank flushing a raccoon out from the bushes. Hank acted menacing toward it, but the raccoon reared back on his hind legs and swung a front paw at Hank. It snagged Hank's bandana! The raccoon then ran off with the bandana. We often retell the story of how Hank got mugged by a raccoon!

SNAKES, SPIDERS, AND SCORPIONS

With the exception of Alaska and Hawaii, there is at least one type of poisonous snake in every state in the United States. The chances of one slithering into your yard are slim, but you could encounter one on a hike in a state park or wilderness area. There are a few steps you can take to protect your Chesapeake Bay Retriever from a snake bite.

Did you know that there is a vaccine for dogs that can protect them if they get bit by a rattlesnake? If you live in a region where rattlesnakes are common and you spend a lot of time hiking with your Chessie, discuss this option with your veterinarian. The vaccine, however, only offers protection against rattlesnake venom as this is the most common type of snake bite.

The best ways to prevent a snake bite are to stay on the trail with your Chessie and to keep him on a leash. In fact, consider using a retractable leash so you can keep your dog close to you if you are hiking through an area with tall grass or lots of boulders, the favorite habitat of snakes. Don't hike with headphones, earbuds, or air pods in. That way, you can keep your ears alert for the sound of a rattle. If you hear one, immediately back up and leave the area. It is best to avoid a confrontation with a snake.

If you live in the Southwest, you need to be wary of scorpions in addition to snakes. Only a few types of scorpions are venomous enough to be potentially deadly to dogs, especially one as large as a Chesapeake Bay Retriever.

Photo Courtesy of Raya Tufaro

In most cases, a scorpion sting will be more painful than life-threatening. You may hear a sharp yelp when your Chessie is initially stung.

Contact your veterinarian if your Chessie seems to have trouble breathing, is wheezing, or vomiting. Also look for signs of excessive salivation. At the vet's office, you can expect the veterinarian to carefully remove the stinger, then clean and bandage the wound. You will also be given medication to help with the pain and to reduce the allergic reaction in your Chessie. You will be advised to keep an eye on your dog and alert the vet if the conditions worsen.

There are a few varieties of spiders that can be dangerous to dogs. The brown recluse spider is one of them, as is the black widow spider. The bites from these spiders can cause pain, swelling, breathing difficulty, seizures, and paralysis. The symptoms can range from mild to severe. Take your Chessie to the veterinarian or to an emergency animal hospital if you suspect he has been bitten by a poisonous spider. Symptoms can take a turn for the worse quickly if no treated.

The veterinarian will treat your Chessie's spider bite with pain medications and antibiotics. He or she may also give your dog an antihistamine to slow the allergic reaction. Your Chesapeake Bay Retriever will be watched closely for signs of fever, muscle stiffness, arrhythmia, shallow breathing, shock, renal failure, and anxiety. With prompt treatment and proper care, your Chessie should make a full recovery from a spider bite.

We have been fortunate that Hank has not run afoul of snakes, scorpions, or spiders. At least once a summer, however, he catches a yellow jacket in his mouth and gets stung in the throat. We've had to make several trips to see the vet when this happens. Now I know the proper dosage of Benadryl to give him when he swallows his next yellow jacket.

Even though your Chessie may spend his evenings cuddled up with you on the couch, Chesapeake Bay Retrievers were bred to be hunting companions and to fetch waterfowl for duck hunters. A powerful swimmer and loyal companion, a well-trained Chessie will be an asset to your hunt.

CHAPTER 13:
Chessies and Dog Shows

You may think that dog shows are only for spoiled, pampered pups and not for rugged hunting dogs like the Chesapeake Bay Retriever, but in reality, there are dog shows for every breed. In fact, dog shows have been in existence for more than a century. The reason why these events started

Photo Courtesy of Carla Daniels

CHAPTER 13   Chessies and Dog Shows

in the first place is the same reason why they are still prevalent today – to give dog owners and breeders an opportunity to see how their dogs stack up against other dogs of the same breed. It is important to note that, in dog shows, the dogs are not being judged against each other. Instead, they are judged against a set of breed standards that each dog breed's governing body has established.

If you are considering using your Chesapeake Bay Retriever as a show dog, there are several things to consider. While you may have seen things like the Westminster Dog Show on TV, there are also local and state dog shows, as well as competitions that showcase a dog's agility and hunting prowess.

The Pros and Cons of Dog Shows

Before you commit to showing your Chesapeake Bay Retriever, you should consider the pros and cons of dog shows. Educate yourself about the realities of dog shows and evaluate your lifestyle to determine whether you think showing your Chessie is the pastime for you.

THE PROS

Certainly, one of the main reasons why we participate in any type of competition is to win. It feels good to bring home a trophy or a ribbon. Winning shouldn't be the only reason for entering your Chessie in a dog show, though. Participating in dog shows is a great way for you to meet other people who share your love of the Chesapeake Bay Retriever breed. Furthermore, dog shows provide a chance for you to spend time with Chessie owners and breeders. Ideally, you can build a network of Chessie lovers that you can rely on to help you if you have questions or concerns.

When you participate in dog shows, you will become more familiar with the breed standards for the Chesapeake Bay Retriever. Familiarity with the requirements of the breed will help you to identify the best traits when selecting a Chessie puppy.

Your Chessie will probably love competing in dog shows. You will spend a lot of time with your dog during the training and preparation aspect of dog shows. It's a great bonding time. And your Chessie will gain some valuable socialization experience with you, other people, and other dogs.

THE CONS

Participating in dog shows is an expensive hobby. You will need to have the funds for travel, entry fees, grooming and medical costs, and more.

To be competitive, especially in state or national-level dog shows, you will need to purchase a Chessie puppy of the highest quality from a top breeder. Breeders with a reputation for producing champions will charge a premium price for their Chesapeake Bay Retriever puppies. One thing to be aware of is that, in the majority of dog shows, spayed and neutered animals are generally not permitted to compete.

Agility Shows with your Chessie

Instead of a traditional dog show, you may want to think about entering your Chesapeake Bay Retriever in an agility show. Agility shows are less about the appearance and conformity of the dog and more about how well trained and smart the dog is. In this type of competition, the handler

Photo Courtesy of Kathy Miller Sandy Oak Chesapeakes

CHAPTER 13   Chessies and Dog Shows

guides the dog through a series of obstacles, such as stairs, tunnels, teeter-totters, and hurdles. Each dog runs the course and is scored on both accuracy and time.

Training your Chessie to be successful in agility shows takes time, patience, and lots of repetition. When the dogs compete, they are off leash and are guided through the course with just the handler's voice or hand gestures. In fact, it is against the rules for the handler to touch the animal or an obstacle and to use treats as an incentive.

> **FUN FACT**
> **First American-Registered Breeds**
>
> The Chesapeake Bay Retriever was among the first nine breeds to be registered in America in 1878, along with the Pointer, Clumber Spaniel, Cocker Spaniel, Sussex Spaniel, Irish Water Spaniel, English Setter, Irish Setter, and Gordon Setter. Chessies were recognized by the AKC when it was founded in 1884.

The agility courses are designed to be so challenging that dogs cannot run the course without help from their human handlers. Sometimes, the obstacles are numbered and the handlers must direct the dogs to each obstacle in the right order. This is where Chessies shine. Chesapeake Bay Retrievers are naturally smart, inquisitive, focused, and good at problem solving. They won't back down from an unfamiliar obstacle but will throw their keen minds into figuring out the best way to conquer the obstacle. Chessies are also hard-working dogs with strength and endurance and can handle the physical demands of an agility course.

Competing in dog agility contests with your Chesapeake Bay Retriever can be fun and rewarding, but it also requires a higher level of training. Your Chessie must be skilled and experienced off-leash. He must also be well-trained in the verbal and hand gesture commands that you will need to use when directing him through the course. Ideally, you should have some of the more common obstacles – like the teeter totter and the tunnel – set up in your backyard for practice. It would be even better if there was an agility training course near you. Some dog parks have them.

If you have never trained a dog, especially a Chesapeake Bay Retriever, to run agility courses, you should seek expert help. Chessies can be hard-headed at times and you will want to make sure you are training your dog correctly. You don't want to reinforce bad habits that will need to be corrected later. Training your Chessie to compete in dog agility contests will help strengthen the bond of trust and respect between you and your dog.

Field Trials with your Chessie

Chesapeake Bay Retrievers were bred to help hunters and there are dog competitions where your Chessie can show off his ancestral retrieving chops. In field trials, or sporting dog trials, which are often organized by hunting dog clubs, dogs compete against other dogs to show their skills as pointers, flushing dogs, or retrievers. As you can guess, Chessies are usually entered in the retrieving events.

First, a little background on field trials. These competitions have been around since 1866 when the first such event was held in England. It served as a way for dog breeders to validate the superiority of their dogs over their fellow breeders. In those days, having a great hunting dog was a necessity since it meant food on the table. People were eager to find the best breeders that could give them the hunting dog they needed and to watch the field trials to see which dogs performed the best.

Today's field trials are similar to the original ones held 150 years ago, but the focus has shifted a bit. Now, field trials are designed to highlight the skill and training of the dogs, and how well they work in partnership with

CHAPTER 13 Chessies and Dog Shows

their human handlers. The events are structured to resemble an actual hunt. They take place outdoors, in fields, near ponds, or wooded areas. In most cases, the hunters shoot real guns. Real prey animals, like ducks, rabbits, and pheasants, may be used. The dogs are scored on their ability to track and find prey, retrieve it, and follow the commands of their handler.

If you are already a hunter and you are experienced in training your Chessie to assist you on the hunt, you may want to enter a field trial dog competition near you. Not only will you have the opportunity to bring home a trophy or two, but you could also meet other Chesapeake Bay Retriever enthusiasts and learn from their techniques and experiences. Your Chessie will enjoy the chance to dust off his instinctual hunting traits. Just be aware that, to be competitive in field trials, you need to start training your Chessie from puppyhood and devote plenty of time to daily and weekly training sessions.

CHAPTER 14:
Your Chessie's Nutrition

Chesapeake Bay Retrievers are large, powerful dogs. They require the proper fuel to keep their athletic muscles in tip-top shape. Choosing the best nutrition plan for your Chessie, however, can be a daunting task. Just stroll down the dog food aisle at the pet store and you will know what I mean. It can be overwhelming. Both sides of the aisle are packed with different food options for your dog. In this chapter, we will discuss many of these options and give you tips on picking the right nutrition plan for your Chessie.

CHAPTER 14 Your Chessie's Nutrition

Why Is Nutrition So Important?

A proper, nutritious diet is the difference between a happy, healthy, active Chessie and a sluggish, paunchy dog with numerous health issues and a diminished lifespan. Food is what powers your Chesapeake Bay Retriever. The nutrients help his bones, skin, muscles, organs, and brain to grow and develop. A good diet of nutritious dog food, in the proper portions, will stave off disease. Conversely, an inadequate diet of cheap, less nutritious dog food can cause obesity, heart disease, joint pain, and a poorer quality of life. You have chosen to bring a Chessie into your life with the promise that you will take the best care of him. You owe it to him to feed him the best diet possible for a lifetime of health, energy, and fitness.

> **HELPFUL TIP**
> **Hunting Dog Nutrition**
>
> A 2001 study conducted by the dog food manufacturer Eukanuba sought to study the effects of nutrition on hunting dogs' performance. Two groups of dogs were studied throughout a season on a quail plantation. One group received a maintenance adult dog food, while the other received a "performance" dog food, which contained a substantially higher fat content than the maintenance food, as well as a higher content of high-quality protein. The dogs who received the "performance" food located more birds per hour and had more total finds per hunt than the control group.

The nutritional needs of your Chesapeake Bay Retriever will change as he moves through each season of his life. Chessie puppies need more protein and calories. A senior Chessie that leads a less active lifestyle will need fewer calories to maintain his ideal weight.

Always have a conversation with your veterinarian about the food you are feeding your Chessie, as well as the proportions. Discuss the many options that you have, as well as any concerns or special circumstances with the veterinarian. He or she will be able to answer your questions and guide your decision-making process. In fact, nutrition should be an ongoing topic of discussion at every vet visit. The veterinarian will be able to assess your Chessie's health and physical condition to determine if his current diet is satisfactory or if changes need to be made. Be sure to listen to the recommendations of your veterinarian, take notes, and ask plenty of questions.

Tips for Picking the Best Food for your Chessie

"Avoid foods with 'meat' by-products, corn or soy. Learn to read the ingredients on the sack or can and understand what they mean. Initially you should continue with whatever food the breeder has been feeding. I do not recommend puppy food as pups grow too fast, but rather I suggest a good adult food that is 24-26% protein and 14-16% fat with a specific meat and nutritious grains and veggies as the primary ingredients."

KATHY MILLER
Sandy Oak Chesapeakes

As a new Chesapeake Bay Retriever owner, there are a few starting places and tips to help you select the right food for your Chessie.

First, ask the breeder or rescue group that you got your Chesapeake Bay Retriever from what food they were feeding him. You should avoid abrupt diet changes with your Chessie. A sudden switch to unfamiliar food could upset his digestive system, leading to diarrhea, gas, and vomiting. Anytime you need to change his diet, do so gradually, by mixing in the new dog food with the old one. Alter the proportions each day so that you are gradually giving him more and more of the new food. This will help ease his digestive system into the new food.

Once you find out what food your Chessie is currently eating, you can discuss that brand of food with your veterinarian. He or she can offer an expert opinion about its quality. Your vet can help you decipher the wording on the label and examine the nutrition information on the label. If, after your conversation with your vet, you decide you need to make a switch, your veterinarian can offer some recommendations. This will give you a starting place when you go dog food shopping.

In the dog food aisle, take your time to read the labels on the packaging. Dog food manufacturers are required by law to list the ingredients and nutritional information on the packaging, as well as additional information. If you know how to decode the label, you will be armed with the information you need to make wise choices. Start with the list of ingredients. By law, the ingredients must be listed in the order of weight. The heaviest ingredient in the dog food is listed first. Regular meat contains about three-quarters of its weight from water. If meat is listed as the first ingredient, it is because it is predominantly water. If you see meat or chicken meal, however, the water has been removed. What is left is a concentrated protein. You will notice that cheaper dog foods will contain less meat and more grains and vegetables.

CHAPTER 14   Your Chessie's Nutrition

Watch for wording such as "beef dinner" or "chicken dinner" in place of phrases like "real beef." This usually means that there is considerably less protein in the product ... like 25 percent versus 95 percent. You may think that you should avoid products made with "animal byproducts," but not all animal byproducts are bad. Some, like blood, bone, brains, and stomachs, are nutrient rich and high in iron and vitamin A. These may sound disgusting to us, but your dog would probably love them. Other animal byproducts, like hair, horns, and teeth, cannot be included in dog food as per regulations established by the Association of American Feed Control Officials.

Let's take a moment to discuss what the Association of American Feed Control Officials does. AAFCO is the main governing body for the pet food industry. It sets the minimum nutritional standards for commercial dog food. Dog food products that meet or exceed the nutritional standards of the AAFCO are allowed to print a statement from the organization on their packaging. You should look for this statement when selecting food for your Chessie.

Lastly, you may want to look at recognizable brands when selecting your Chessie's food. There are a number of dog food manufacturers that have been in business for a considerable amount of time and have a reputation for producing quality pet food. There are some newer companies, as well, that have brought a fresh perspective to the pet food industry. Although they lack the longevity of older, more established companies, they have, nonetheless, built a solid reputation by focusing on quality. If you see a dog food brand that you have never heard of before, do some research on the company, in addition to reading the labels.

Wet or Dry, Which Food Is Best?

"Find a good quality of food. Do not keep changing brands of food since Chessies have a very sensitive stomach. If you find a brand that they do well with, then stay with that brand."

ANDREA HURT
Chessies R Us

The first major decision you will have to make while you are standing in the pet food aisle is whether to feed your Chessie wet (canned) dog food or dry dog food (kibble). Most commercial dog food manufacturers make both wet and dry dog food and there seems to be a 50-50 market split, therefore it is not an easy choice to make. If you are wondering, "Which dog food is best,

Karen HARRIS | The Complete Guide To Chesapeake Bay Retrievers

Photo Courtesy of
Andra Collins

CHAPTER 14 Your Chessie's Nutrition

wet or dry?" the answer is "Both!" There are pros and cons of each one. Your own lifestyle and personal preferences are the deciding factor.

Some Chessie owners prefer wet dog food because it has a higher water content and reduces stomach and intestinal bloating. They also like canned food because it is softer and easier to chew, making it ideal for older Chessies or dogs with dental issues. Wet food may be more appealing to senior Chessies because this type of food has a stronger smell and taste.

That stronger smell, however, can also be a drawback for people. The odor can be quite off-putting. Wet dog food comes in roughly 13-ounce cans. You will need to work with your veterinarian to determine how much canned dog food you should give your Chesapeake Bay Retriever at each meal. You will probably have a portion of one can left over. This will need to be immediately refrigerated to prevent it from spoiling. You and other family members will need to get in the habit of checking the fridge for unused cans before you open a new one. And you will have to make sure that the unused cans don't get shoved in the back of the fridge and forgotten. You run the risk of either feeding your Chessie old, spoiled food or having to throw away half-full cans. Since the price of canned dog food is higher than dry dog food, this could drive up your dog food budget.

Cost is one of the benefits of dry dog food. Just because it is lower in price does not mean it is lower in quality. Packaging accounts for much of the cost difference. The nice thing about dry dog food is that it doesn't spoil as fast. You can leave a bowl of dog food out during the day without worrying about it going bad. Kibble is more convenient to use because you can easily measure the correct amount you need. It is much easier to take kibble with you when you and your Chessie are on an adventure. A Ziploc® bag of dry dog food isn't as heavy as canned, so it won't weigh down your backpack. Also, you won't need to bring along a can opener or a container to store the unused portion.

The Raw Food Trend

One of the newest trends in dog food is the raw food diet. The theory supporting this trend sounds reasonable enough. Dogs in the wild, long before they were domesticated by humans, did not eat a diet of cooked meat and grains. They ate uncooked meat, gristle, raw eggs, fresh fruits and vegetables, bones, and skins. Fans of this type of dog food claim that raw food is better for dogs because it is the way they naturally ate. They add that dogs fed a raw diet have healthier bones and skin, more energy, and fuller fur. However, there is strong evidence to show that the digestive tract of modern dogs has evolved as a side effect of domestication.

Feeding your Chesapeake Bay Retriever a raw food diet takes a big commitment on your part. You will need to find a source of raw meat, bones, and gristle, like a local butcher, and arrange to buy the meat several times a week. Raw meat spoils quickly. You will also need to purchase raw vegetables, such as carrots, potatoes, peas, and green beans, from a reliable source, like a local farm store. The real work comes when you have to cut up the meat. The task is gruesome, messy, and bloody. It also smells bad. A Chessie owner has to be really committed to the raw food diet – and have the sources they need and the financial ability to pay for top quality meat – to make it work. Before you jump into the raw food diet trend, schedule a visit with your veterinarian and discuss this nutrition plan with them. They may give you some insight you had not thought about before that can help you determine if the raw food diet is the best choice for your Chessie.

Is a Vegetarian Diet a Good Choice for Your Chessie?

More and more people these days are opting to eat a meat-free diet, for both health and ethical reasons. Many of them want their dog to also follow these restrictions. That brings up a particularly good question. Is a vegetarian diet a safe and healthy option for dogs? The experts are divided on this subject. To understand why, we have to look back at the domestication of dogs thousands of years ago. Modern dogs descended from wolves, but the dog branch and the wolf branch diverged on the canine family tree. Both animals evolved independently. While wolves maintained their carnivorous diet, domesticated dogs evolved so that their systems can digest grain, vegetables, fruits, and dairy products. Because of this, it is possible for modern dogs to thrive on a vegetarian diet, whereas wolves can't.

If you are considering feeding your Chesapeake Bay Retriever a vegetarian diet, your first step should be to discuss your personal preferences regarding food with your veterinarian. Your veterinarian can give you guidance and tips for how you can satisfy your Chessie's nutritional needs with a plant-based diet. It is possible for your dog to eat a vegetarian diet, but your Chessie still retains some of the wild instincts of its wolf ancestor. He will crave meat.

CHAPTER 14   Your Chessie's Nutrition

The Pros and Cons of Homemade Dog Food for Your Chessie

For Chessie owners who want to know exactly what is in the food they feed their dog, one option is to make your own food. Before you do, discuss your plans with your veterinarian. Your vet may be able to offer some tips or provide you with some good dog food recipes that will fulfill your Chesapeake Bay Retriever's nutritional needs. He or she may even recommend that you schedule regular vet visits and weigh-ins so you both can tell if your Chessie is thriving on the homemade diet.

Offering your Chessie homemade dog food is a big time and financial commitment on your part. You will need to find a local source for high-quality meat that you can purchase from every day or every two days. Fresh meat begins to break down and spoil if it sits in the fridge for more than a few days. Never skimp on the quality of the ingredients. Doing so may mean that your Chessie's nutritional needs are not being met.

Once you have a homemade dog food recipe that both you and your vet approve of, you will have to block out time every day to prepare your Chessie's food. It can be a time-consuming process and, unfortunately, you cannot make the food in bulk and serve it throughout the week. It simply won't stay fresh that long.

The process of making homemade dog food is messy. Despite this, you need to be committed to cleanliness by sanitizing the work area, equipment, and utensils as often as possible. Bacteria can creep into your Chessie's food during the preparation process and make your dog sick. Despite the cost and the inconvenience, however, many Chesapeake Bay Retriever owners prefer the peace of mind and the feeling of control that they have by preparing their own food for their dogs.

Does your Chessie Need Vitamins and Supplements?

If your Chesapeake Bay Retriever is eating a well-balanced diet, you may be wondering if he needs to also take vitamins or supplements. A stroll through the pet store will show you that there are plenty of supplements on the market today that promise all sorts of things, like reduced joint pain, shinier coat, youthful energy, and more. It can be hard to know what supplements your Chessie needs, if any. To find your answers, you need to

Photo Courtesy of JD Odell

contact your veterinarian. He or she knows your Chessie and can assess his health history, lifestyle, and diet to determine if he is lacking in any areas. Any supplements that you give your Chessie should complement the diet he eats, instead of making up for a poor diet. Don't be surprised, however, if your veterinarian tells you that, as long as your Chesapeake Bay Retriever is eating a well-balanced diet, he doesn't need additional vitamins and supplements.

If you want to try supplements to alleviate a medical condition, such as arthritis, you definitely should talk to your vet about this. Some supplements can be harmful if taken in the wrong dosage or if taken with other medications. It is also important to continue with your Chessie's veterinarian prescribed treatment instead of foregoing traditional medicine in favor of supplements. The health of your Chesapeake Bay Retriever is too important for you to take it into your own hands unless you have the same educational background as a veterinarian.

Keep in mind that the supplement industry is not as regulated as the prescription drug industry. The supplement may not do what it claims on the label and the list of ingredients may not be complete. In the last two decades, the National Animal Supplement Council has worked to get more accuracy and transparency on pet nutrition supplement labels. Look for products that are manufactured by well-known brands, that have documentation on the label to verify that a clinical study of the supplement has been done and contact the customer service number listed on the packaging to ask questions. If the supplement promises something outlandish or sounds too good to be true, it is worth further investigation.

One final piece of advice about vitamins and supplements. Never assume that a product that is safe for human use is also safe for dogs. Many are not. Supplements that contain garlic, for example, can cause your Chessie to get sick. Additionally, dosing will be different for dogs than it is for humans. The best thing you can do to ensure that you don't give your dog anything that may harm him is to check with your veterinarian.

What Should You Know About Treats for Your Chessie?

Treats are ideal for positive reinforcement training. However, they should not be a replacement for dog food and should be given sparingly. The more you know about dog treats, the better equipped you will be to select the right treats for your Chessie.

When purchasing treats for your Chessie, be sure to read the labels. Some treats contain way too much fat and sugar. While your dog will find these delicious, they are not the healthiest option for him. Look for treats made with whole food ingredients that are low in fat and calories. Try to find products that use a natural sweetener, such as molasses, honey, or applesauce. If you are looking at meat-based treats, look for ones made with high-quality chicken, lamb, and fish.

Moderation is the key with treats. Veterinarians advise that dog treats should make up less than 10 percent of your Chessie's daily calorie intake. When you are doing a lot of training sessions, that may mean using an alternative reward in place of treats or breaking the treats into smaller pieces.

What Should You Know About Table Scraps for your Chessie?

Our Chessie, Hank, is a beggar. He doesn't sit next to us at the dinner table. He typically stands in the other room, staring at us and drooling. It's a terrible habit that he started because our kids would sneak him scraps of their food under the table when he was a puppy. It is easy to train dogs; it's much harder to train kids.

As tempting as it may be, you should avoid feeding your Chesapeake Bay Retriever table scraps. Most human foods are not good for dogs. They are too high in fat and calories and they don't contain the nutrients that dogs need. Your Chessie will fill up on tasty human foods that are low in vitamins and nutrients then won't want to eat his own dog food. As we discovered, you have to be diligent about table scraps. If you buckle to cute puppy dog eyes, even just once, your Chessie will never forget it.

Human Foods That Are Toxic to Chessies

Feeding your Chessie table scraps can lead to some unhealthy eating habits, but it can also be downright dangerous. It is up to you to make sure everything your Chesapeake Bay Retriever eats is safe.

Both onion and garlic are poisonous to Chessies, and they are often found in human foods, such as soups, stews, sauces, and burgers. There is a chemical compound in onions and garlic that can break down your dog's red blood cells, which makes the animal anemic.

Dogs should not eat any kind of nut as they are high in fat and salt and can also be a choking hazard. Some nuts, including macadamia nuts, are

CHAPTER 14 Your Chessie's Nutrition

extremely toxic to dogs and can cause kidney problems. Unfortunately, macadamia nuts are a favorite around Christmas time and many people leave them sitting out in dishes, which is tempting to a Chessie.

Grapes and raisins are toxic to dogs' kidney function and should be avoided. Some baked goods, like cookies and quick breads, contain raisins so you must be especially mindful to not give these to your Chessie.

The skins of potatoes, tomatoes, and avocados should also be avoided as they can make your Chessie sick. Recently, Hank acted sick for a few days. He had gas and his stomach made weird gurgling noises. He just seemed down. Early one morning, I heard him vomiting so I bolted out of bed in an effort to save my carpeting. I found a small pile of vomit and, in the center, was a fully intact avocado pit! I thought back and determined that three days prior, I had avocado toast for breakfast. I put the skin and pit in the trash and left the house. When I returned, I remember, Hank had knocked over the trash. Apparently, he ate the avocado pit, which sat in his stomach for three days, making him ill until he managed to throw it up.

Dark chocolate can be toxic to dogs and can damage their central nervous system. Drinks containing caffeine can do the same thing, including coffee, hot chocolate, tea, and soft drinks.

Lastly, dogs should never be given alcoholic beverages. Ignore those frat boy movies that make it seem hilarious to get a dog drunk. It is not funny; it is dangerous. Dogs cannot metabolize alcohol like people can. Small amounts can be deadly.

The health and longevity of your Chesapeake Bay Retriever is closely tied to the diet he eats. When you make the commitment to bring a Chessie into your family, you are committing to providing this family member with the best quality of life. This starts with a well-balanced, healthy diet, nutritious treats, and abstaining from potentially harmful human food.

CHAPTER 15:
The Overweight Chessie

Hank is overweight. Every time we visit the vet, Hank is fat shamed. We are working hard to help him shed those extra pounds, but it has been slow going. At eight years old, Hank is beginning to slow down. He appreciates couch time more and more, especially during the cold and snowy winter months (don't we all?). The other problem is that he likes food. While everyone loves a chubby, roly-poly puppy, a chunky adult dog is at risk for health problems, a diminished quality of life, and a shorter life span.

How Can I Tell if my Chessie is Overweight?

"Don't overfeed. Dog food bags have suggested amounts...but remember; their goal is to sell dog food, so overfeeding is likely. A Chessie should have a waistline, and you should easily be able to feel ribs when you push in on their side."

SHARON POTTER
Red Branch Kennels

Those extra pounds can sneak up on you and your Chesapeake Bay Retriever then, one day, you have a tubby puppy on your hands. Your veterinarian can help you determine if your Chessie is overweight, but there are ways you can tell yourself.

First, look at the breed standards for your dog. According to the American Kennel Club, an adult male Chesapeake Bay Retriever should weigh between 65 and 80 pounds, while a female should be between 55 and 70 pounds. Of course, there are some variables that factor into this, such as age and height, but if your Chessie exceeds these averages, it may be time for a diet.

Look down on your Chessie as he stands. Do you see a curve in at his waist, giving him an hourglass shape? A Chessie that is at his ideal weight will have a defined waist that you can see from above.

CHAPTER 15 The Overweight Chessie

Another way to see if your Chessie is overweight is to feel his rib cage just past his shoulder blades. If you put your hand flat on a table with the palm down, then take your other hand and run your fingers across the backs of each fingers, you would feel the bony knuckles and the dips between your fingers. That's how your Chessie's ribs should feel. Ideally, you will be able to feel the ribs and the spaces between them.

Health Problems Associated with Excess Weight

Being overweight is not healthy, in humans or in dogs. If your Chessie is tipping the scales beyond his ideal weight, he could be at risk for developing life-threatening diseases. Insulin-resistance diabetes occurs when a dog's body is not responding to the insulin being produced by the pancreas. Glucose remains in the dog's bloodstream instead of being effectively use by the body's cells. The result is that the bloodstream of the Chessie is so high in sugar levels that it could damage the kidneys, heart, eyes, and vascular system.

An obese Chessie can also develop osteoarthritis and joint pain. As a large-breed dog, Chesapeake Bay Retrievers are prone to hip dysplasia. Excess weight can speed up the degenerative effects on your dog's joints. You may notice your Chessie appears to have trouble getting up or seems reluctant to jump into your car or up on the bed. Maybe he is walking stiffer or limping. He may wince or jump if you pet him in certain places, such as his hips. All of these are indicators that your Chessie is experiencing chronic joint pain that could be osteoarthritis exacerbated by extra weight.

One of the leading causes of high blood pressure is obesity. Hypertension, or high blood pressure can damage the heart, as well as the kidneys, eyes, lungs, and bladder.

> **HELPFUL TIP**
> **Swimming for Overweight Chessies**
>
> Chesapeake Bay Retrievers love to swim. Bred as waterfowl hunting dogs, it's almost in their genes to crave water exercise. Swimming is also an excellent low-impact exercise for overweight dogs since the water creates a supportive environment that takes the pressure off of your dog's joints, which could be stressed if they're supporting extra pounds. Be sure to observe swimming safety with your dog, and consider using a safety vest in natural bodies of water if your dog is not a strong swimmer. Some communities even have aquatic centers specifically for dogs.

Signs of high blood pressure in dogs include disorientation, blindness, bloody urine, seizures, and circling.

Obesity can greatly reduce the life span of dogs, especially larger dog breeds like the Chesapeake Bay Retriever, by as much as two years. Even being moderately overweight reduces longevity.

Preventing Obesity in your Chessie

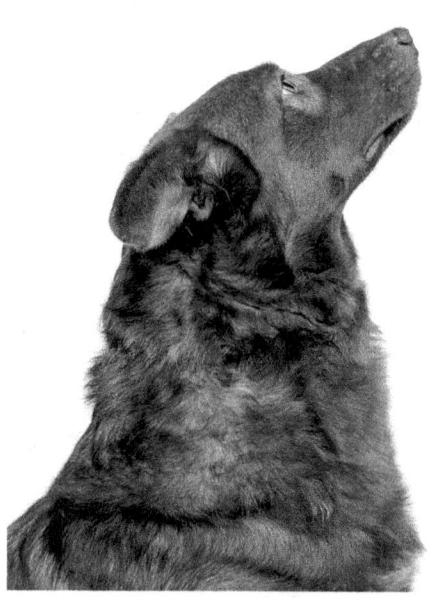

It is much easier to prevent obesity than it is to lose weight. Starting your Chessie on a top-quality dog food from puppyhood is a good start. It is important to make good nutrition a habit from the moment you bring your Chessie home. That means not overfeeding him and keeping treats to a minimum. Avoid all table scraps, too. Regular checkups with the veterinarian will ensure that your Chesapeake Bay Retriever stays in great shape.

Food is just half the battle. Chessies are powerhouses. They need to have physical activity on a daily basis for optimal health and to keep their physique trim. Part of owning a dog means you must commit to daily walks or play time in the yard, even on the days when you are exhausted or it is raining.

Putting your Chessie on a Diet

Hank's vet has put him on a strict diet, and Hank is not happy about it. As per the veterinarian's instructions, he eats a small portion of his healthy-weight dog food twice a day. In addition, he eats some cooked green beans and a raw apple each day. He has responded to this diet by eating out of the trash and stalking my daughters for table scraps. Bad habits aside, the diet is working. Hank has shed some pounds and is getting closer to his ideal weight.

CHAPTER 15 The Overweight Chessie

If you need to put your Chessie on a diet, the best thing you can do is to get some guidelines from your veterinarian. Even if you decide to switch your dog to a healthy-weight dog food formula, you should discuss this first with your vet.

You can also help your Chesapeake Bay Retriever drop some pounds by taking him for more walks, longer walks, or increasing play time. The more active your Chessie is, the easier it will be for him to lose weight. If your Chessie is not regularly active, be sure to start slowly with the new exercise routine. Go for shorter walks and build up to longer ones. Be sure to check with your veterinarian if you have any concerns about your Chessie increasing his activity level.

CHAPTER 16:
Chessies and the Holidays

Holidays are an important part of our lives and, naturally, we want to include our Chesapeake Bay Retriever in our celebrations. However, the holidays also bring added dangers for our pets. Even if you diligently puppy proof your home and are careful about leaving human food within reach of your Chessie, there are still some holiday-specific special circumstances to consider. Let's address these so that your holidays are not ruined by an unforeseen incident with your Chessie.

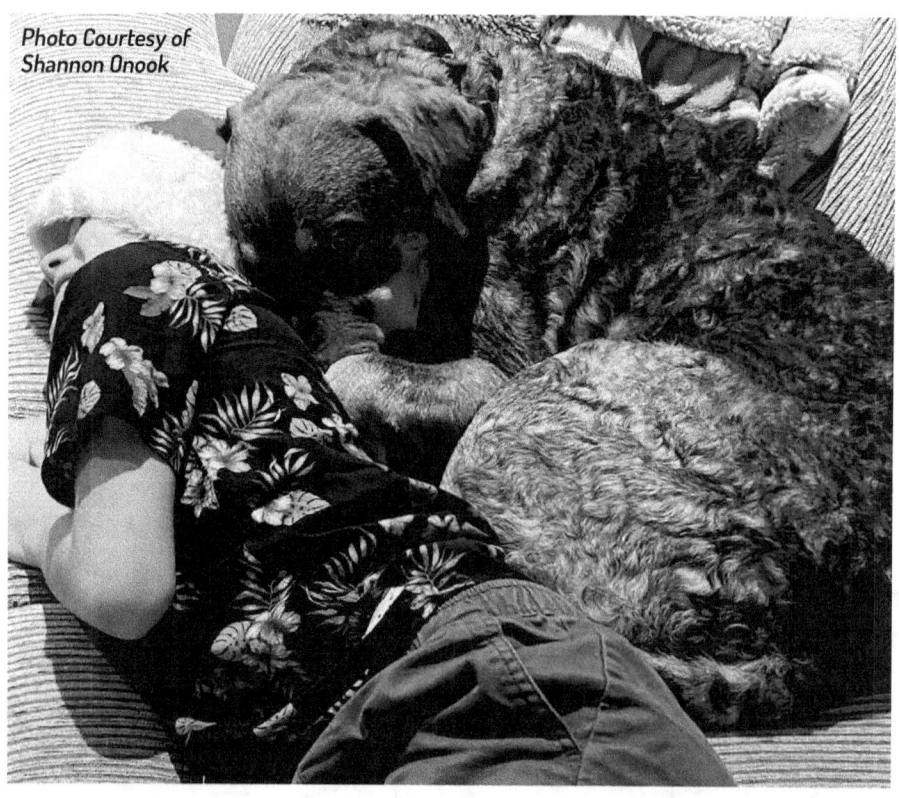

Photo Courtesy of Shannon Onook

CHAPTER 16   Chessies and the Holidays

Christmas Dangers

It is supposed to be the most wonderful time of the year, but for your Chessie, Christmas is a time of new smells, new routines, new distractions, and new hazards. From holiday decorations to your Christmas cookies, there are plenty of Christmas related things that can make your Chessie sick, or worse.

HOLIDAY DÉCOR

Consider using an artificial Christmas tree. Your Chessie may want to chew on a real Christmas tree because it is attracted to the smell. Real trees also drop their needles, which can pose a health hazard. For curious puppies, you may want to consider putting your tree up for a few days before you decorate it. This way, your dog will get used to the strange, new object in the house before you add the temptation of ornaments and lights. Your Chessie may jump up on the tree or bite and pull the branches, knocking it over. You can keep the tree upright by tethering it to the wall or ceiling. You can protect it even more by putting a baby gate around it.

When you add ornaments to your tree, be sure to keep potentially dangerous ornaments off the lower branches. Chessies have been known to chomp down on dangerous glass ornaments and eat homemade salt dough ornaments. I have one last bit of advice to keep your Chessie safe around your Christmas tree. Once you put the lights on your tree, tape the cords down or run them through a piece of PVC pipe to prevent your dog from chewing on the cords.

In addition to Christmas trees, we also bring other plants into our homes during the holidays, such as holly, poinsettias, ivy, and mistletoe. Holly has spiky leaves so dogs tend to avoid them. It is a good thing, too, because there are toxins in all parts of the holly plant: the stalk, leaves, and berries. The reaction to the toxin is generally mild, ranging from mouth irritation to diarrhea and vomiting.

We often hear stories about how poisonous poinsettias are,

> **FUN FACT**
> **Chessies in the White House**
>
> President Theodore Roosevelt, the 26th president of the United States, welcomed a Chesapeake Bay Retriever named Sailor Boy into the White House on May 26, 1902. In his autobiography, Roosevelt described Sailor Boy as "not only exceedingly fond of the water, as was to be expected, but passionately devoted to gunpowder in every form, for he loved firearms and fairly reveled in the 4th of July celebrations..."

but the truth is, this holiday favorite is the victim of some bad press. The white sap found inside the poinsettia can irritate your Chessie's digestive system, but it generally only causes excess drooling and maybe some diarrhea.

Photo Courtesy of Brad and Meghan Phillips

CHAPTER 16   Chessies and the Holidays

Ivy is not particularly dangerous, but your Chessie can get an upset stomach if he eats it. The bigger concern with ivy is that some dogs develop allergic dermatitis from it.

In general, mistletoe is low in toxicity, but if your Chessie eats enough of it, he could experience a tummy ache or have diarrhea.

The best thing for your Chesapeake Bay Retriever is to make sure that all holiday plants you bring into your home for seasonal decorations are kept well out of reach of your dog.

During the holiday season, we may also decorate with scented candles, potpourri, and knickknacks. The smell of the candles and potpourri may entice your Chessie to take a nibble. After all, it smells like apple pie! Just make sure you keep these items away from your dog. That probably means you can't decorate your coffee table like you did pre-Chessie.

Our friends have a two-year-old Chesapeake Bay Retriever named Bodi. Last Christmas, her eight-year-old daughter came running into the kitchen in tears, exclaiming, "Bodi ate Baby Jesus!" Sure enough, Bodi had snatched the figurine of Baby Jesus from the nativity set and swallowed him whole, which made for an interesting story to tell the veterinarian.

HOLIDAY FOOD DANGERS

Many people like to leave food items sitting out during the holidays. It is not uncommon to see a bowl of hard candies on an end table or a dish of mixed nuts on a coffee table, but you may have to find a different spot to put these so your Chessie won't help himself. The same thing goes for cheese and cracker trays and cookie platters. Your Chessie would love to sample the cheese and sausages on the tray and small portions of these won't cause any health issues, but too much of a good thing can be bad news for your Chessie. Cheese is high in fat and calories and sausage is high in fat and sodium. As for the Christmas cookies, they contain way too much sugar for your dog and may contain nutmeg. Nutmeg can be toxic to dogs, especially when eaten in large quantities.

During holiday celebrations, remind your family members and guests not to give your Chessie human food. At the minimum, it will upset his digestive system to eat unfamiliar foods. Turkey bones can splinter when your Chessie chews on them, creating a choking hazard. Make sure your guests don't give your Chessie a bone and make sure to take the trash out to the dumpster immediately after you enjoy your dinner.

Every holiday season, there are people who think their dogs should celebrate with them, so they give them beer or alcoholic beverages. This is never a good idea. Dogs cannot metabolize alcohol like humans can. Your Chessie could become sick, vomit, and even have alcohol poisoning.

CHAPTER 16   Chessies and the Holidays

CHRISTMAS PRESENTS

If your Chesapeake Bay Retriever is especially curious about your Christmas tree, it may be best to avoid putting the presents under the tree too early. Dogs have been known to unwrap gifts when no one is looking. And even when people are looking! In addition to that box of Skittles that Hank unwrapped and ate, he has also tried to unwrap a cashew gift set and some random pair of socks. We have gotten into the habit of only putting a few, benign Christmas gifts under the tree and stashing the rest in a closet until Christmas Eve.

During the Christmas morning gift opening frenzy, there are several things to watch out for. Plastic and metallic ribbons can cause trouble if your Chessie eats them. Some toys have tiny parts that your Chessie may want to chew on and even swallow. I am embarrassed to say how many Barbie Doll shoes Hank has destroyed. Those little, round batteries that are found in some toys and games can be lethal to your dog. If your dog bites into a battery and breaks it open, the chemicals inside can cause burns and heavy metal poisoning. Also watch out for the silica gel packets that are placed in shoe boxes, backpacks, and purses. While they are non-toxic, they can cause blockages if your Chessie eats them.

Easter Dangers

Like Christmas, Easter is a holiday that involves a lot of decorations and food. Both of these can pose dangers to your Chesapeake Bay Retriever.

EASTER DECORATIONS

Perhaps the biggest threat from Easter decorations is the plastic Easter grass. Your Chessie may accidentally eat the plastic grass if he samples some of the jellybeans or other goodies in an Easter basket. The problem is that dogs cannot digest the plastic. As it passes through your Chessie's gastrointestinal tract, it can get stuck. If your Chesapeake Bay Retriever is vomiting, has decreased appetite, stomach pain, and acts lethargic, it could be a blockage from Easter grass.

CHESSIES AND CHOCOLATE

One Easter, the kids opened their Easter baskets in the morning before we headed out to my parents' home for brunch. When we returned home, Maizie had taken a chocolate Easter bunny, still in the packaging, from one of the kid's baskets. She ripped open the package and ate the entire thing. Thankfully, she had no ill effects from this incident, but dogs should not eat chocolate. Milk chocolate isn't quite as bad as dark chocolate, but none of it is safe for dogs. Ingesting chocolate could cause tremors, seizures, vomiting, diarrhea, elevated heart rate, and pancreatitis in dogs. We learned our lesson after the incident with Maizie. Now, we double check that all the Easter baskets are put on top of the refrigerator.

Fourth of July Dangers

We celebrate Independence Day with backyard barbecues and fireworks. While your Chesapeake Bay Retriever will probably love the backyard barbecue, the fireworks part may not be his favorite. There are some ways to make sure your Chessie stays safe on the Fourth of July.

BACKYARD BARBECUE HAZARDS

Cookouts and bonfires are a big part of summer fun, particularly around Fourth of July weekend. With friends and family gathering for hot dogs and burgers, there are plenty of temptations for your Chessie. Be sure to keep all the food out of reach of your Chessie. That includes the table with the potluck food, the grill, and the tray of s'more supplies by the bonfire. Hopefully, you have trained your Chessie well enough that he won't surf the food table or stalk your guests for handouts, but your guests may try to make friends with your Chesapeake Bay Retriever by sneaking him a few bites of their brats or baked beans. Even though you will be busy socializing and flipping the burgers, you still need to monitor your Chessie to make sure that he isn't indulging in human food that will make him sick.

When you grill fatty meat on a charcoal or gas grill, fat drips down into the coals. Dogs typically leave the grill alone while it is still hot, but I know of some dogs – not Hank, thankfully – that have gotten into the grill after it has cooled down and licked the fat off the charcoal. You can stop your Chessie from doing this by remembering to close the lid on the grill once the coals have cooled.

FIREWORKS ANXIETY

The Fourth of July is a day filled with scary noises that can cause your Chesapeake Bay Retriever to experience anxiety. Forty percent of all dogs have anxiety and stress from fireworks. In fact, the Fourth of July is the number one day of the year that dogs run away. The sudden, loud noises and flashes of light are so frightening to some dogs that they run in fear for their lives. In the days or weeks leading up to Fourth of July, make sure that your Chessie's microchip information is up to date and that he is wearing

CHAPTER 16   Chessies and the Holidays

an identification tag on his collar with your contact information on it. Once the fireworks start, keep your Chessie safely indoors. If you have to take him outside to relieve himself, keep him on a leash and hold it securely. An unpredictable bang may cause him to bolt.

If you know when the fireworks will start, take your Chessie for a quick walk an hour or so before so you can be safely home when the noise starts. Make sure that the gates in your yard are securely latched, your doors are closed, and the doggie door is blocked.

Play some calming music at a moderate level when the fireworks start. The goal is not to have the music drown out the sound of the fireworks, but to distract your Chessie from the noise. You and your family members should remain calm as well. Dogs pick up their cues from us. If your family is excitedly watching fireworks from the window and exclaiming over the light display, your Chessie will sense that things are not normal and this will increase his anxiety.

Give your Chessie plenty of attention with calm petting and a soothing voice, but if he wants to cower under your bed, let him. He will go to a place where he feels safe and if you force him to come out, he will experience more stress.

A snug-fitting jacket like a Thundershirt is comforting to dogs and helps to calm them in anxiety producing situations, such as fireworks.

Halloween Dangers

Like Christmas, Easter, and Valentine's Day, candy is the focus of Halloween. When you kids return home from trick or treating, you will need to make sure that their Halloween haul is safely out of reach. The top of the refrigerator is an ideal spot. Personally, I don't trust my kids when they say they are taking their candy-filled plastic pumpkins up to their bedrooms and promise they will keep it out of Hank's reach. There have been too many times when they have "forgotten" to secure the candy and Hank tried to raid it. So, the rule now is that no candy goes upstairs. It all has to stay on top of the fridge where we know it will stay out of Hank's mouth.

As a good Chesapeake Bay Retriever owner, you have taken all the precautions you can to make sure your dog is safe. Don't let your guard down during holidays. In fact, this is a time to double your efforts. There are holiday-specific dangers that can harm your Chessie. Fortunately, all of these dangers can be prevented if you are aware of the potential hazard and take the necessary steps to remove the temptation from your holiday celebrations.

CHAPTER 17:
Grooming your Chessie

"Never, ever clip a Chessie or use any kind of straight edged metal tool, like a furminator. It breaks the hair and ruins the coat. That heavy Chessie coat insulates against heat in summer and repels water when swimming or hunting. Bathe rarely if at all, as too much bathing strips the oil from their coat. A simple once-over with a grooming glove works best to remove any loose hair."

SHARON POTTER
Red Branch Kennels

Photo Courtesy of Emma Totten – @daisy.the.chessie on IG

CHAPTER 17   Grooming your Chessie

In general, Chesapeake Bay Retrievers are no-fuss dogs. They require only minimal maintenance to keep them well-groomed and looking good. The Chessie has a unique coat that repels water and protects the dog's skin. Because of this, Chessies require less bathing than other dog breeds. In this chapter, we will discuss grooming the Chessie's coat, as well as proper eye, ear, and dental care, as well as nail care.

The Chessie's Unique Coat

The coat of the Chesapeake Bay Retriever was developed to be ideal for duck hunting. The thick, woolly undercoat keeps the dog warm in cold temperatures and frigid water. The outer coat is dense, rough, and oily. The oil helps water run off the Chessie's coat, which keeps the dog warmer and drier. When the Chessie emerges from the water and does that iconic dog shake, most of the water flies off, leaving the fur barely damp.

Bathing

If you bathe your Chesapeake Bay Retriever too much, you run the risk of stripping away too much of the fur's natural oil. Doing so will decrease the water repelling quality of the coat and dry out the dog's skin. Even if your Chessie isn't able to swim regularly, he still only needs a bath a few times a month. Hank gets a bath about every two or three weeks unless he rolls in something stinky, which is one of his favorite hobbies.

HOW TO BATHE YOUR CHESSIE

Chessies are big and energetic so you may think that you need a small army to help you bathe your dog, but in my experience, that's not the case. Chessies love being in water so they generally don't protest too much when it is bath time. In fact, sometimes, Hank goes and stands in the tub as if to tell us he wants a bath.

Bathing a dog as large as a Chesapeake Bay Retriever may seem like a daunting task, but with proper planning, and maybe some extra manpower, it can be done quickly and stress free.

First, determine where you will bathe your Chessie. For Hank's first bath when he was an energetic puppy, we chose to do it outside in a large, metal feed trough. It worked, but it took a long time to fill the feed trough. After that, we moved to the bathtub. I'd love to one day have a house with a dedicated dog bath area, but until then, Hank shares the tub with the rest of the family.

Next, gather all the supplies you will need. This includes doggie shampoo, a large plastic tumbler cup, a non-slip bathmat, and several large towels. Keep everything you need close at hand, so you don't have to leave your Chessie unattended in the bathtub while you run to get something. It has been my experience that Chessies like to splash around in the water

Photo Courtesy of Paxton Gray

and make a big mess. They also like to jump out of the tub, run around the house, and shake water everywhere. It is better for your walls, furniture, and carpeting if you stay close while your Chessie is in the bath water.

Not all dog shampoos are created equal. Look for a shampoo that is strong enough to remove the dirt, yet mild enough that it doesn't strip the protective oils from your Chessie's fur. There are some excellent dog shampoos on the market that are made with all-natural ingredients, such as oatmeal, lavender oil, and aloe vera. Never use your own shampoo on your Chessie. Shampoos for humans have a different pH balance and may contain ingredients that are too harsh or potentially harmful for dogs, especially if the product gets in his eyes. If you are at a loss about which dog shampoo to use, talk to your groomer or your veterinarian and get their advice.

Once our supplies are gathered for Hank's baths, we start filling the bathtub. Lukewarm to warm water is best and makes the bathing process more comfortable for you, but your Chessie probably won't mind cold water. By now, Hank understands that when we fill up the bathtub with the bathroom door open, it means he's getting a bath. He happily runs into the bathroom and jumps in the tub, often before we are ready for him. But you may have a Chessie that is less excited about bath time or a Chessie puppy that fears the loud running water. You might need to coax him into the bathroom with a treat. If he's not too big, you may need to scoop him up and gently set him in the water. Shutting the water off at this point helps ease his anxiety.

Next, get your Chessie's fur wet. Since we can never get Hank to sit down in the bathtub, and we don't have a spray attachment on the faucet, we use a large plastic tumbler cup to gently pour water over his back, hindquarters, and chest. Shield your dog's eyes before you pour water on his head and even then, use small amounts and pour slowly so you don't get water in your Chessie's eyes. Get his coat thoroughly wet.

Pour some shampoo onto your Chessie's back and near his neck. Rub it in to suds it up. Work the suds carefully onto his head, ears, and face, taking care to avoid his eyes. You can even use a washcloth for this task. Slowly and gently rinse the shampoo away, working through the fur with your fingers to make sure the water reaches the skin. Once your Chessie's head and face are washed, do a quick towel dry of this area, just so he doesn't have water dripping into his eyes as you wash the rest of him.

There should still be plenty of shampoo on your Chessie's back, but if there isn't, add some more. You may also need to add more water so you can get the shampoo lathered up. Work along your dog's back and rump, including his tail. Put some shampoo in the palm of your hand and wash his chest and front legs. Carefully lift one leg at a time and wash his underside.

Photo Courtesy of Lori Stine

Do the same with his back legs. When your dog is completely washed, repeat the whole process and wash him again. This time, you can skip his face and head unless he is really dirty.

Thoroughly rinse all the shampoo out of his fur. If you have a spray attachment in your shower, you can do this much quicker than using a plastic cup. Rinsing takes the most time. Be sure to rinse out all of the shampoo. If you don't, the shampoo could irritate your dog's skin. It also gives the fur a greasy feel that actually attracts dirt. Without proper rinsing, your dog could look like he never got a bath at all.

Once your Chesapeake Bay Retriever is completely washed and rinsed, drain the water from the tub, but keep him in place. Towel dry him using as many towels as it takes to remove all the moisture you can. We always plan on three with Hank. At this point, Hank often gets anxious to jump out of the tub, but it is slippery. We lift him out (no easy task!) or put a non-slip bathmat in the tub so he can get his footing enough to jump out and onto another non-skid bathmat. Then stand back! Your Chessie will shake the excess water off his fur by shaking his whole body. For some reason, Hank always gets the zoomies after a bath. Weather permitting, we let him outside after his bath and he runs full speed around the yard. Maybe this is his way of drying himself off. He also likes to roll around on the ground, so we have to watch him to make sure he doesn't roll in dirt and negate all the work we just did to bathe him.

Do not use a blow dryer on your Chessie's fur. The forced air is quite hot and can cause injury.

Brushing

Chessies, like all members of the retriever family, are heavy shedders. Routine brushing will help remove all the loose fur from their coats. The shedding is particularly heavy in the spring and fall. In the spring, the dogs shed their thick, coarse winter coat. In the fall, Chessies shed their undercoat in preparation for the new season's growth. Routine brushing is even more important during these times as it helps remove the old hair and make room for new fur.

Firm brushing on a regular basis also helps to keep your Chessie's coat healthy by distributing the natural oils evenly throughout his fur. A soft rubber curry brush is preferred over wire or metal ones. The wire brushes are too harsh on the Chessie's unique coat as they can break the Chessie's wavy fur.

HOW TO BRUSH YOUR CHESSIE

Because Chesapeake Bay Retrievers are short-coated dogs, they don't require brushing as frequently as dog breeds with long coats. Their fur doesn't get tangled, but it is still important to brush your Chessie once every one or two weeks, just to remove loose hair and dirt.

When brushing your dog, start with the ears. From there, move to his back and sides. Always brush in the direction that the fur grows, but do so with an outward, lifting move so you bring the dirt and loose

> **HELPFUL TIP**
> **Choosing a Brush**
>
> Chesapeake Bay Retrievers shed, so it's important to have a consistent grooming routine in place for your dog. Consider using a rubber brush or rubber brush gloves throughout the week to remove dead fur from your dog's coat before it ends up on your furniture and clothes. Frequent brushing will also help redistribute natural oils through your Chessie's coat, keeping his skin and fur healthy. Chessies have a naturally oily and water-resistant coat, which is an excellent asset for a duck-retrieving dog.

hair out of the coat. Brushing your dog's coat against the natural direction is off-putting and anxiety producing. You want the experience to be a pleasant one for your Chessie.

If you encounter tangles, be gentle. Don't pull them or brush vigorously. This will just upset your dog. Because Chesapeake Bay Retrievers' hair is so short, you generally won't find large, matted tangles of fur, but if you do encounter a rough patch, be as gentle as possible. You can spray a doggie detangler on the spot or try a wide-tooth comb to unsnag it.

Finish brushing you Chessie by carefully brushing down his legs to his paws. There isn't much hair on your Chessie's belly, but you can brush that area too. Hank finds it so relaxing that he rolls onto his back to let us brush his belly and chest.

After I'm done brushing Hank, I wipe down his coat with a damp washcloth. It helps to catch all the stray hairs that the brush loosened but didn't remove.

Ears, Teeth, and Eyes

Your Chessie's Ears

The ears of the Chesapeake Bay Retrievers are delicate and sensitive. If you have ever flipped up your Chessie's floppy ear and peered inside, you will have noticed a labyrinth of nooks and crannies. The environment is moist and has plenty of hiding places for yeast, bacteria, and parasites, such as ear mites. Proper care can reduce the chances of infection, so routine ear care should be part of your dog grooming regimen. For Chessies, monthly ear cleaning should be sufficient.

From puppyhood, get your Chesapeake Bay Retriever used to having his ears touched. Stroke his ears frequently and get your puppy used to the sensation of having his ear flaps flipped up and the inside inspected. He will learn to sit quietly as you clean his ears. Always inspect your Chessie's ears before you clean them. Visit the veterinarian if you see redness, swelling, or oozing, and notice a foul smell. If you see black or brown clumps that resemble coffee grounds, these could be ear mites and also require a vet appointment.

If you don't see any red flags when you inspect his ears, you should be able to clean your Chessie's ears yourself. When cleaning your Chessie's ears, most veterinarians advise against using cotton swabs or similar hygiene tools. Anything inserted too deeply in your Chessie's ear canal can potentially cause damage. Even if you intend to use the cotton swab just on the inner ear flap, your dog may wiggle and squirm, causing the swab to accidentally enter his ear canal.

HOW TO CLEAN YOUR CHESSIE'S EARS

To start, moisten a cotton ball or a cotton cleansing pad with warm water, mineral oil, or a gentle over-the-counter dog ear cleanser.

Next, lift the ear flap up and gently wipe the inner ear, starting just outside the ear canal and working your way out. If needed, you can squirt a small bit of the ear-cleaning solution in the ear and gently massage it in by rubbing the outer ear flap for about 30 seconds to loosen the debris in the ear. This should make it easier to wipe the dirt away.

Be sure that you do not clean your Chesapeake Bay Retriever's ears too aggressively or too frequently. You could accidentally cause irritation or damage that could lead to infection.

Your Chessie's Teeth

If you had dogs when you were a kid, chances are you and your parents never brushed the dog's teeth. In fact, you probably didn't concern yourself with your dog's dental health at all. That doesn't mean your parents slacked on their dog care; it is because doggie dental care was not a thing a generation or so ago. In the last few decades, we have learned quite a bit about the importance of dental hygiene for dogs. Gum disease and tooth decay are two of the most common medical conditions in dogs, yet they are both preventable with proper hygiene.

Most Chesapeake Bay Retrievers have all their adult teeth by the time they are about seven or eight months old. Prior to this time, however, your dog will have baby teeth. This is when you should hone your dog teeth-brushing skills as you get your Chessie acclimated to the process. Then he will know what you are doing and how he should behave when you brush his teeth.

Dogs have strong teeth with thick enamel, so tooth decay doesn't happen as frequently in dogs as it does in humans. You only need to brush your Chessie's teeth two to three times per week to reduce tartar buildup, remove plaque, and prevent gum disease. In between brushings, you can give your Chessie a chew treat that is designed to reduce plaque. These can be found in the canine dental care aisle of the pet supply store or from an online pet retailer.

Visit your local pet supply store and purchase a toothbrush and toothpaste that is especially formulated for dogs. Never use human toothpaste on your dog. Many human toothpastes contain an artificial sweetener called Xylitol. This substance is toxic to dogs. It causes an unsafe drop in blood sugar and can even damage your dog's liver. There are plenty of quality dog toothpastes on the market that are much safer for your Chessie.

Likewise, avoid using a human toothbrush to clean your Chessie's teeth. Human toothbrushes are designed for human mouths and will be

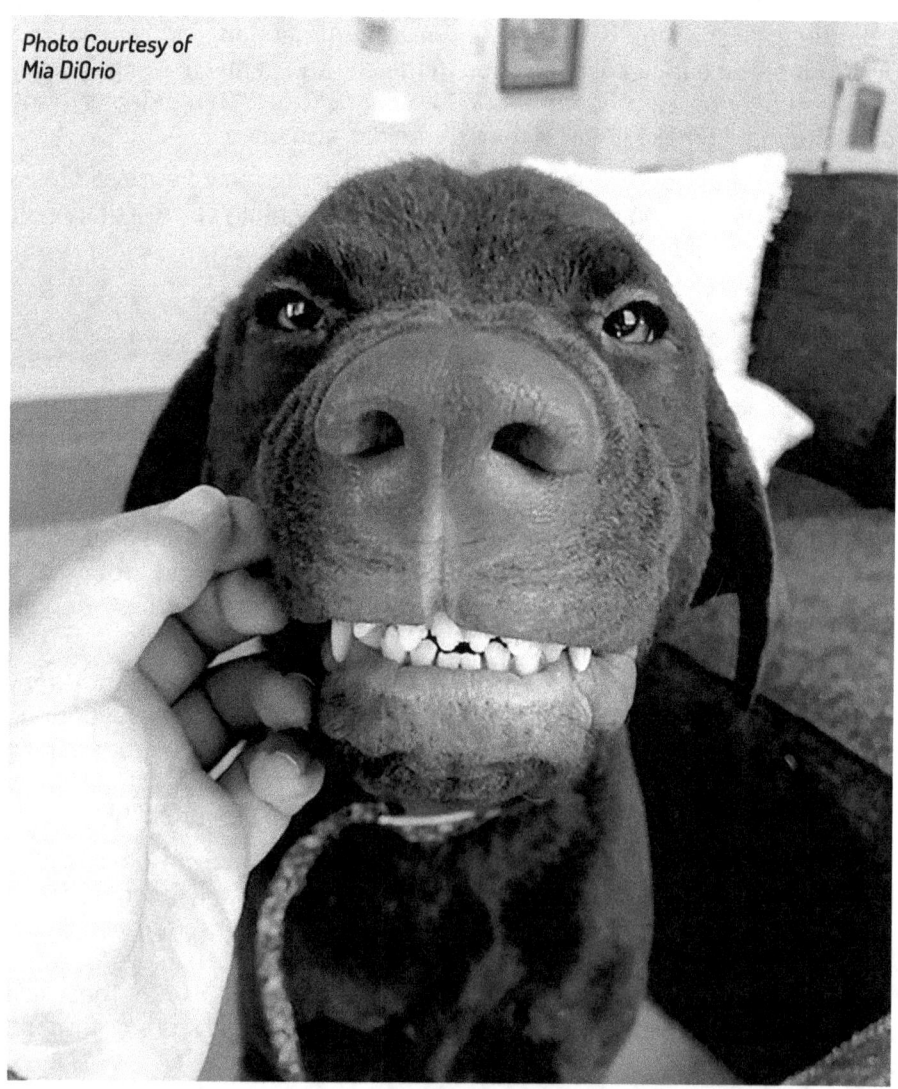

Photo Courtesy of
Mia DiOrio

CHAPTER 17   Grooming your Chessie

less effective on a dog's mouth. Toothbrushes for humans are not as tough either. You Chessie might be able to break them with his powerful bite. Instead, purchase one of the large-breed dog toothbrushes you find at your local pet store. It is a much better tool for the job.

HOW TO BRUSH YOUR CHESSIE'S TEETH

First, gather the supplies that you need. A good-quality dog toothbrush, available from your local pet supply store or an online pet retailer, should be tops on your list, as well as dog toothpaste, a bowl of water, and a towel.

Next, select a proper time and place to brush your Chessie's teeth. Ideally, you should do this task when your dog is calm and the activity level in your home is low. This will make it less stressful on your dog. You also need to find a place in your home where your Chessie feels comfortable. The spot should also have good lighting so you can see well in your dog's mouth.

The next step is to gently lift the top lip of the dog to expose his teeth. You can get your Chessie used to the teeth brushing process by carefully brushing using just water at first. Go slowly, starting in the front top, moving to the back top teeth, then repeating the process with the bottom teeth.

Now, your Chessie should be used to the feeling and is ready for a good brushing using dog toothpaste. Apply a small amount of the toothpaste to the dog toothbrush and start again in the top front of your Chessie's teeth and work your way to the back on each side. Be sure to praise your Chessie as you brush, speaking in a calming and soothing voice. Gently, peel back your Chessie's bottom lips to brush his lower teeth.

Grasp your Chessie's snout to open his mouth, if your dog will let you without it causing too much distress. This will allow you to brush the insides of his teeth. Most dogs don't like it when their snout is held, so work quickly to finish brushing.

You don't need to rinse the toothpaste from your Chessie's mouth. Dog toothpaste is edible, so it won't hurt your dog to leave it in his mouth. But you may want to offer him a drink of water when you are done brushing his teeth and wipe off his face.

Your Chessie's Eyes

Most of the time, you won't need to do any maintenance or hygiene care on your Chessie's eyes. Occasionally, however, your Chesapeake Bay Retriever's eyes may be impacted by pollen or other irritants. They can get weepy, itchy, and red. You may notice your Chessie pawing at his eyes or see tear stains in the corners of his eyes. Although Chesapeake Bay Retrievers are not prone to chronic eye drainage like some other breeds, they are not immune to occasional eye goobers and gunk.

If you notice discharge and eye boogers around your Chessie's eyes, you can remove them yourself. Using a clean washcloth or a cotton cleansing pad dampened with warm water, gently wipe the area around your Chessie's eyes. You can also purchase an eye-wash product for dogs at your local pet supply store. Always use solutions that have been especially formulated for dogs. These have been designed and tested to be safe for your dog's eyes.

In addition, there are products that you can use to flush your Chesapeake Bay Retriever's eyes if you believe there are irritants that need to be removed. Some veterinarians, in fact, recommend routine eye flushing for Chessies that do a lot of swimming and romping through tall grassy areas. Regular eye flushing, they say, reduces opportunities for infections by removing dust, dirt, and debris. Other experts take a more hands-off approach, relying on the Chessie's natural tearing mechanisms to rid the eye of irritants.

You should discuss your Chessie's eye care with your veterinarian. Explain your dog's lifestyle and have a frank conversation about the possible irritants that your Chessie may come into contact with. Your veterinarian will be able to help you establish an eye-care routine that is best for your dog and your situation.

Trimming your Chessie's Nails

Hank gets regular pedicures. His toenails grow so fast that he can't keep them worn down naturally. We tried to clip them ourselves, but his nails are so thick and tough – and he is so big and strong – that it turned into a traumatic experience for Hank and for us. When we tried to clip his nails, we occasionally caused the nail to crack and split. A few times, we clipped too low and caused bleeding. The dog groomer charges us $10 to trim Hank's nails and, to me, it is worth every penny. The groomer is better equipped to do the task than we are. First, she has years of experience. Second, she has a harness contraption that holds Hank in place. Third, she uses a Dremel tool that quickly files down the nails. The groomer can get all four paws done in less than 10 minutes and Hank usually stays still for her. I think he likes the feeling of the vibrations on his paws from the Dremel. He also knows that he will get a tasty dog biscuit if he is a good boy.

I don't mean to discourage you from trimming your own Chessie's nails. I know plenty of Chessie owners who do. My advice would be to get your Chesapeake Bay Retriever used to you handling his paws from an early age.

CHAPTER 17   Grooming your Chessie

That way, he won't struggle and resist when you try to trim his nails. My second suggestion would be to invest in a high-quality pair of dog toenail clippers or even get the correct Dremel tool to file down the nails. Having the best tools to use will make the job go smoother for both you and your Chessie. Alternatively, you can also reduce the need for regular nail trimming by walking your dog on rough surfaces, such as cement sidewalks and stone paths. After all, your Chessie's wild cousins, wolves and coyotes, don't schedule routine pedicures like Hank gets. They rely on the rough surfaces of their surroundings to get the job done.

HOW TO CUT YOUR CHESSIE'S NAILS

Many dog owners trim their own dogs' nails with great success. They make it part of their regular grooming and hygiene for their Chesapeake Bay Retriever. Following these steps, you can keep your Chessie's nails an appropriate length.

First, you need to determine if your Chessie's nails are ready to be trimmed. When your dog's paw is resting on the ground, the nail should hover above the floor. If it curves down to reach the floor, it is probably time for a trim.

Begin by gathering the tools you will need. They include a good, quality nail clipper that is appropriately sharp, a pair of trimming scissors, a Dremel tool with the nail grinding attachment, a towel, a flashlight, a styptic pencil, and some paw balsam.

Pick a time and place when your Chessie feels comfortable and calm. You could even offer him a treat and some cuddles to make him feel secure. You could sit on the floor with your Chessie so you can hold his paw in your hand or position yourself in a chair with his paw in your lap.

Next, you need to determine the cutting range of the nail. There is a blood vessel that extends into each of the dog's nails. If you cut the nail too short, you will hit the blood vessel – or cut to the quick, as it is called. Using your flashlight, you can shine the light through the nail to see when the blood supply ends. In general, the nails on the dog's front paws will be longer than his back paws, you can clip off more of the nail.

Hold the clippers securely in your hand while you hold your Chessie's paw in your other hand. Clip small sections of the nail, keeping the cut parallel to the floor. Stop trimming before you get to the blood vessel. Praise your Chessie and give him a snuggle before your move on to the next nail.

If you are using a Dremel tool to file down your Chessie's nails, the same concept applies. Firmly hold your dog's paw and separate out one of the nails with your fingers. Run the Dremel head back and forth across the nail in a smooth, gliding motion. Take care not to file too much off or you will hit the blood supply.

As careful as you are, there will still be times when you accidently go too far and cause your Chessie's nail to bleed. Don't panic. Just apply your styptic pen or styptic powder to the area to stop the bleeding. You can also try holding an ice cube to the nail. Bleeding is usually minimal, but if you cannot get it to stop after a half hour, call your veterinarian.

While you are clipping or filing your Chessie's nails, you should also trim any long fur between his toes. Using the small trimming scissors, quickly snip off any fur that is growing up between the pads. No need to go too short; just remove any hair that could be impeding your Chessie's traction.

When you are done trimming your Chesapeake Bay Retriever's nails, wipe down his paws with a towel to remove any shavings or clippings that may be stuck in his fur. Then give him a treat and praise him for being such a good boy during the ordeal.

Using a Groomer Versus Grooming Your Chessie Yourself

"The most important thing to always remember about grooming your Chessie is do not under any circumstances, remove their undercoat. Their undercoat is like feathers to a duck or feathers to a goose, it is a necessary element of their coats. Removing this undercoat can permanently damage your Chessie's coat. Chessie's love being groomed, whether by you or a professional. Make sure anyone who is grooming your Chessie knows what tools to not use and knows to not remove their undercoat. Do not assume that a professional will know this about the breed. They are not a common breed, and not all of them need professionally groomed, so your groomer may not be aware of their needs."

LEAH SPRADLIN
Hickory Creek Chesapeakes

From bathing to nail trimming to toothbrushing, the basic grooming needs of your Chesapeake Bay Retriever are not too overwhelming or laborious. You should be able to do them all yourself with a little practice and a lot of patience. Grooming your Chessie yourself saves money and is less stressful for your dog. When you take your Chessie to a groomer, your dog

CHAPTER 17   Grooming your Chessie

will experience some anxiety about being in a new place with a stranger manhandling him. At home, your dog will be more comfortable.

There are benefits to using a groomer, though. Typically, a good dog groomer will be able to groom your dog much faster than you can and will most likely do a better job than you could do on your own. Groomers have the experience, tools, and equipment to get your Chessie looking his best. The downside to using a groomer is, of course, the cost. You can expect to spend between $50 and $75 per grooming visit. However, Chessies are low-maintenance dogs. You can schedule your Chessie's grooming appointments for every six weeks or so.

Whether you choose to use a groomer or take care of your Chesapeake Bay Retriever's grooming needs yourself, you need to assess your ability, situation, time, and budget. In the end, you want grooming to be a quick, low-stress process for your Chessie.

CHAPTER 18:
Your Chessie's Health

Your Chesapeake Bay Retriever's health and happiness are your top priority. Just like the human body, the canine body needs routine medical care and maintenance to stay in peak condition. The more you are aware of potential medical problems that could arise, the better prepared you can be to keep small health issues from becoming big ones. Being diligent about preventative health measures can ensure that your Chessie lives a long and healthy life. In this chapter, we will look at routine health care and preventative medicine, as well as some of the common ailments that Chessies are prone to developing.

Photo Courtesy of Angela Nester

CHAPTER 18   Your Chessie's Health

The Benefits of Building a Good Rapport with Your Veterinarian

Your veterinarian is your trusted partner and ally on your Chessie's medical team. It is important to have a partner who is on the same page as you when it comes to dog care, so choose your vet wisely. Although it may be convenient to go to the vet clinic closest to your house, if the veterinarian and staff at this clinic don't mesh with your personal beliefs, you may find yourself conflicted about the medical information you are receiving. As we discussed in Chapter 5, you should take your time and personally meet several veterinarians before you select the one who will help you care for your Chesapeake Bay Retriever.

Ideally, the vet you pick will be your Chessie's doctor for life. But remember that you will be interacting with this person just as much as your dog will. You want to find a veterinarian that makes you feel comfortable enough to ask questions. You want a person who listens to your concerns and answers you truthfully and honestly. A person who is dismissive of your questions, who is too rushed to listen to you, or who answers your questions in a condescending manner is not the person you want as your Chessie's healthcare partner. Instead, you want a person who will put your mind at ease, offer sound advice based on experience, and who genuinely loves your Chessie. Building a good rapport with your veterinarian is an important step to productive checkups and a healthy Chessie.

The Importance of Routine Checkups

Your veterinarian will want to schedule yearly checkups with your Chesapeake Bay Retriever but may suggest more frequent visits when your Chessie is a puppy, entering his golden years, or has a chronic health condition. The goal of annual vet visits is to give your veterinarian an opportunity to assess your Chessie's overall health and fitness, to look for signs of potential medical problems, and to proactively address any concerns before they become serious issues. It is also a time to update your Chessie on his vaccinations, if needed.

Routine vet checkups differ from the vet visits you have if your Chessie is sick or injured. During those visits, your vet will focus exclusively on the illness or injury. At a routine checkup, however, the veterinarian will assess the whole dog and evaluate his health and fitness level. The vet will compare your Chessie's health against the notes and information from his last checkup to determine if there have been any significant changes. In addition to listening to your Chessie's heart and lungs, examining his eyes, ears, and teeth, and feeling his abdomen for any abnormalities, the veterinarian will ask you general questions about your Chessie's appetite, activity level, and disposition. If anything seems amiss, your veterinarian may run additional tests or ask you more questions to get to the root of the problem.

At your yearly vet visit, you can also expect your veterinarian to check for heartworms and other internal parasites. You and your vet can discuss preventative options for fleas and ticks, two common parasites that can carry diseases. These parasites are discussed in a later section of this chapter. Depending on the region you live in, most vets will recommend putting your dog on a flea and tick medication. Lastly, your vet will make sure that your Chessie's microchip is still working.

Photo Courtesy of Jessica Richmond

CHAPTER 18   Your Chessie's Health

Different Kinds of Vaccinations

Vaccinations are an important way to prevent potentially deadly diseases. Keeping up to date on your Chessie's vaccinations is also required by law in some areas. It can be inconvenient and costly to schedule vaccination appointments for your dog, but it is in the best interest of your Chesapeake Bay Retriever to follow the recommended vaccination schedule. It may save you some heartache in the future.

There are many vaccinations available for dogs. Depending on where you live, some vaccines may be required and some may be optional. Below is a brief overview of the different vaccines and what they are used for.

CANINE DISTEMPER

Canine distemper is caused by a virus that gets into the respiratory, nervous, and gastrointestinal systems of dogs, as well as other mammals. It is highly contagious and spreads through exposure to airborne droplets when an infected dog coughs or sneezes. It can also be spread through shared water bowls, feed dishes, or chew toys. The symptoms of distemper are coughing, sneezing, watery eyes, nasal discharge, diarrhea, vomiting, convulsions, seizures, and in many cases, death. Currently, there is no cure for distemper. The best veterinarians can do is to try to stop secondary infections from taking an unnecessary toll on the dog's immune system while he is still trying to fight off the distemper.

RABIES

Also caused by a virus, rabies is so deadly and so contagious that nearly every state has laws requiring owners to vaccinate their dogs against it. Your veterinarian will know if your state requires it. When the rabies virus infects a dog or other mammal, it attacks the central nervous system. Dogs may also have excessive drooling and show signs of headache, hallucinations, and anxiety. In the final stages of the disease, dogs will become paralyzed and die.

PARVOVIRUS

Parvo is caused by the parvovirus. A highly contagious disease, parvo impacts the gastrointestinal system. It causes vomiting, diarrhea, loss of appetite, and fever. The disease typically strikes quickly and the dog will suffer from such severe dehydration that it will die in two or three days.

Puppies are vaccinated for parvo at two months old. Until then, they are at risk for contracting the disease; therefore, they should avoid places where there are many dogs, such as doggie day cares or dog parks. Since puppies can succumb to parvo and the effects of dehydration within a few days of contracting the illness, it is important to seek prompt medical care as soon as you suspect your unvaccinated puppy has parvo. It has no cure, but your veterinarian will help reduce the risk of secondary infections and help your dog's immune system fight off the parvovirus.

BORDETELLA

Kennel cough is a catch-all phrase to refer to an upper respiratory illness in puppies and dogs that can be caused by bacteria, viruses, or a combination of them. The Bordetella vaccine is given to dogs, along with the canine parainfluenza vaccine, as part of routine vaccinations to prevent highly contagious kennel cough. Kennel cough is usually mild, with dogs exhibiting a dry, hacking cough that can sometimes lead to vomiting.

LYME DISEASE

Lyme disease is caused by bacteria called spirochete that is transmitted through tick bites. If you live in an area where ticks are prevalent, your veterinarian may recommend that your Chessie get the vaccine for Lyme disease. A dog infected with Lyme disease will spike a fever and limp. He may experience a loss of appetite and swollen lymph nodes. Lyme disease will progress to the dog's joints, kidneys, heart, and brain. If Lyme disease is caught in time, it can be treated with antibiotics.

HEPATITIS

Canine hepatitis is not the same virus that causes human hepatitis. But like human hepatitis, this viral infection is highly contagious and impacts the liver, kidneys, and spleen of the dog. A hepatitis infection in dogs can range from mild to severe. It can even be deadly, especially if untreated. While there is no cure for canine hepatitis, prevention is the best treatment, which is why hepatitis vaccines are recommended. Your veterinarian can take steps to lessen the severity of the symptoms.

LEPTOSPIROSIS

Leptospirosis is not a viral disease like most of the others on this list. It comes from bacteria that is found naturally in soil and water. In many cases, an infected dog may not show any symptoms. If a dog does exhibit signs of the disease, it may have a fever, diarrhea, vomiting, muscle weakness, stiffness, lethargy, and kidney failure. While antibiotics are helpful in treating the disease, preventative vaccines are recommended to avoid the problem altogether.

Your Chessie's Vaccination Schedule

Generally, all veterinarians follow the same vaccination schedule for puppies.

- 6 to 8 Weeks – Distemper, parainfluenza (optional: Bordetella)
- 10 to 12 Weeks – DHPP (a combination vaccine for distemper, hepatitis, parainfluenza, and parvovirus (optional: Lyme disease, Bordetella, Leptospirosis, Coronavirus)
- 12 to 24 Weeks – Rabies
- 14 to 16 Weeks – DHPP (optional: Lyme disease, Leptospirosis, Coronavirus)
- 12 to 16 Months – Rabies, DHPP (optional: Lyme disease, Leptospirosis, Coronavirus)
- Every 1 to 2 Years – DHPP (optional: Lyme disease, Leptospirosis, Bordetella, Coronavirus)
- Every 1 to 3 Years – Rabies

Tips For Preventing and Treating External Parasites

External parasites live on the outside of your Chessie's body, typically in his fur. They include fleas and ticks, as well as mites, ringworm, and lice. Parasites are not just annoying and bothersome for your dog; they can be a vector for disease as well. Untreated external parasites can make your Chesapeake Bay Retriever quite miserable and may even cause death. Preventing and treating external parasites in your Chessie is one of your tasks as a responsible dog owner. Fortunately, there are steps you can take, with the help of your veterinarian, to keep external parasites away.

Fleas

Fleas have been the scourge of dogs since the dawn of time. Dogs can pick up fleas anywhere, from other dogs, from cats, or from the grass and sand in their own yards. They feast on your dog's blood and multiply quickly. My granddad used to say, "If you kill one flea, one hundred more will come to its funeral." The tiny fleas live on your dog's skin and hide in his fur. And they bite. Flea bites can cause an allergic reaction in some dogs, a condition known as flea allergic dermatitis. It is itchy, so your dog will scratch and bite at his skin, seeking some relief. Many times, dogs will break open their skin, leaving them vulnerable to infection.

Fleas are tenacious. They invade not only your dog, but your dog's bedding, your carpeting, and other organic surfaces. For this reason, you must treat both your Chessie and his living environment when you suspect fleas. This includes frequently washing your dog's bedding, spraying veterinarian-approved pesticides, and treating all the other pets in your household.

Both pills and topical treatments for fleas are available. You can purchase them from your veterinarian, online, or at your local pet supply store. Be sure to discuss the different options with your veterinarian. Based on where you live and your lifestyle, your vet will be able to recommend the flea prevention product that is best for your situation. Note that some flea prevention products are toxic to cats and possibly to children.

Ticks

We live in an area where ticks are common. Every spring, we have to do nightly tick checks on Hank. With his brown fur, it can be a challenge, but we have learned that ticks seem to like his ears and his underside the best. Unlike fleas that administer a series of quick bits, ticks will latch onto your dog's skin and burrow into his flesh. A tick can stay attached for days, drinking your dog's blood until it becomes engorged. Ticks, like fleas, can transmit diseases, like Lyme disease and Rocky Mountain spotted fever, so it is important to be diligent in checking for ticks and promptly removing them.

TIPS FOR REMOVING A TICK

Removing a tick from your Chessie is not difficult, but there are a few things to keep in mind so that you do not increase the potential for infection. The best tool for the job is a pair of fine-tipped tweezers. Your average tweezers have a larger, squarer tip that will get the job done, but is less effective than fine-tipped tweezers. Tweezers are fairly inexpensive. It is worth purchasing a pair of fine-tipped tweezers to have on hand during tick season.

When you locate a tick on your Chessie's body, spread the fur away so you can get a good view of the tick. With the tweezers, grasp the tick's body as close to the dog's skin as you can. Holding tight to the tweezers, pull the tick straight up. Don't yank it too quickly. A slow and steady movement is best. Your goal is to keep the tick intact and remove the entire insect.

Contrary to popular belief, ticks don't have separate heads that they burrow into the dog's skin. Ticks are not segmented like some other insects. Their heads are a continuation of their bodies. They do, however, have pincer-like mouths that embed in the animal. If the tick breaks apart when you try to remove it, it is the mouth of the tick that stays attached. Fine-pointed tweezers will help you to grasp these tiny parts and remove them.

Do not try to remove a tick with your fingers or fingernails. By doing so, you squeeze the ticks body which could force more infectious substances into the dog's body.

After the tick is removed and discarded, use a cotton ball with rubbing alcohol to clean the bite area. Thoroughly wash the tweezers with a disinfectant soap and, of course, wash your hands. Make a mental note of where the tick bite was so you can keep an eye on the spot. Contact your veterinarian if the site becomes infected.

Nightly tick checks are one way to rid your dog on ticks. Another way is to use a tick preventative medication. Most manufacturers make one pill for both fleas and ticks, which is easy and convenient. Dosage is determined by your dog's weight, so, yes, Hank has the highest dosage. We have found that his flea and tick medicine works extremely well, but we continue to do tick checks, especially in the spring when the ticks are prevalent.

Mites

We can check Hank over for ticks, but not mites. That's because mites are so small, they cannot be seen with the naked eye. There are several different types of mites, such as ear mites and mange mites. These microscopic organisms live on the dog's skin or fur, but they burrow into the skin to lay their eggs. Mites spread easily, hopping from one animal to the next.

When mange mites burrow into your Chessie's skin, it causes itching and irritation. To find some relief, he will dig at his skin with his nails or bite his skin. Your Chessie could experience infections, loss of fur, and scarring of the skin.

You can tell if your Chessie has ear mites because you will see your dog vigorously shake his head back and forth and paw at his ears. Inspect the inside of your Chessie's ears. Telltale signs of ear mites are specks of dried blood, chunky stuff that looks like coffee grounds, and dark earwax. Your dog could get an ear infection as a result. Your veterinarian can give you ear drops to treat ear mites. As for preventative measures, the same flea and tick medication that you give your Chessie is also effective at keeping mites at bay. You could also use preventative ear drops if your dog is prone to ear mites.

Lice

Canine pediculosis, a form of lice, can invade dogs and infest the fur and skin of the animal. To reproduce, individual lice must suck on the dog's blood. If the lice infestation is severe enough, your dog could become anemic. Like fleas and mites, lice bites are very irritating to dogs. They itch terribly, leading to open wounds and possible infections. There are lice treatment medications available from your veterinarian, as well as online and at pet supply stores. The flea and tick medication that you use could also be effective at preventing lice infestations. If your Chessie has bites on his skin and is itching, schedule a visit with your veterinarian to determine the cause and the best course of action.

Ringworm

Despite its name, ringworm is not caused by worms. It is actually a fungal infection that manifests in the shape of a ring on your Chessie's skin. It will cause the fur in that area to fall out. Ringworm can be easily passed from animal to animal. Ringworm can be prevented by frequent baths and by treating the dog's skin with an antifungal cream.

Tips For Preventing and Treating Internal Parasites

Some parasites live within dogs' bodies, in various organs, and cause illness and even death. Heartworms are probably the most commonly known internal parasites, but they certainly aren't the only ones. Dogs are also susceptible to hookworms, tapeworms, roundworms, and whipworms. All of these can be dangerous and cause severe health issues for your Chesapeake Bay Retriever. During your routine veterinary visits, your vet will test for internal parasites. If a test comes back positive, your veterinarian will want to take prompt action and will talk to you about treatment plans to start, depending on the type of internal parasite. Below, we discuss various kinds of internal parasites that may affect your Chessie.

Heartworms

Heartworms are the most serious kind of internal parasite and can be fatal if not treated promptly and aggressively. Dogs contract heartworms from bites from infected mosquitoes. The parasite migrates to the dog's heart and lungs, where it multiplies and causes major tissue damage. Heartworms clog the arteries, making your Chessie tire easily. The dog's exercise routine must be restricted so his heart isn't strained too much. Because heartworms are such a threat to the health of dogs, your veterinarian will put your Chessie on a preventative heartworm medication that he will take once a month. You can expect your veterinarian to also check your dog for heartworms on an annual basis. A simple blood test can detect antigens from heartworm proteins that the parasite releases into the dog's blood stream.

When a dog is diagnosed with heartworms, your veterinarian will most likely treat the condition with a series of injections of melarsomine, a medication that kills adult heartworms. The number of injections and the frequency of the treatments will be set by your veterinarian after the severity of your dog's condition has been determined. It is an unpleasant and painful process for dogs, but it has been proven effective at ridding stricken dogs of heartworms.

Hookworms

If a dog is suffering from severe or chronic anemia, it could be that the dog has a case of hookworms. One of the most common internal parasites, hookworm larvae penetrate a dog's body, usually through the feet, but occasionally through the mouth. Once inside, the larvae invade the dog's small intestine and attach themselves to the lining. Adult hookworms are between a half inch and one inch long. They feast on blood through the intestinal lining, causing anemia, diarrhea, weight loss, and bloody stool.

To prevent hookworm, be sure to promptly remove dog droppings from your yard and to avoid communal dog runs where your Chessie may come into contact with the droppings from other dogs. Also, put your dog on a preventative heartworm medication. These medications are effective at preventing hookworms, too.

Your veterinarian will be able to easily detect hookworms in your Chessie. The hookworm eggs can be seen when examining a stool sample under a microscope. There are medications available that will kill the adult hookworms and flush them from your dog's intestines. Your vet may suggest that you repeat the course of medication two weeks after the initial treatment, to be sure to remove any lingering hookworms or new hookworm larvae.

Tapeworms

Unlike hookworms, your dog cannot get tapeworms from his environment. Tapeworms immediately die if they are not in a host, like a rodent or bird. In fact, tapeworms are species- specific, meaning they require certain animals to host them, or they cannot complete their life cycle. For this reason, your Chessie cannot get tapeworms from cats or other dogs. In order to become infected with tapeworms, a flea must bite an infected rodent then bite your dog, transferring the parasite from one animal to the next. One kind of tapeworm, however, is transmitted when dogs eat an infected flea, which is common when your dog nibbles at flea bites.

Tapeworms make their home in your dog's digestive system. Your dog may experience diarrhea or weight loss. In severe cases, tapeworms can cause intestinal blockage, a life-threatening condition.

Your dog may have tapeworms if you see him nibbling or licking his anus or he scoots his rear end on the carpet. This is your dog's way of relieving the itching he is experiencing. If you inspect your dog's anus, you may even see small, rice-like worms wiggling around. Likewise, you may observe these small worms in your dog's fresh droppings. Schedule an appointment with your veterinarian as soon as possible and bring along a stool sample so your vet can confirm a tapeworm diagnosis.

Fortunately, there are effective ways to prevent and treat tapeworms. Since tapeworms are passed to dogs via fleas, having your Chessie on a good flea and tick medicine is the best way to prevent the parasite from getting into your dog's system. If your Chessie has been diagnosed with tapeworms, your veterinarian will prescribe praziquantel, a parasiticide medication that will cause the adult tapeworms to detach from your dog's intestinal wall and pass through his system. Praziquantel is manufactured as both an oral pill and an injection. Your veterinarian will take into consideration your dog's weight, the severity of the parasitic infestation, and the type of tapeworm when determining which variety of the medication would be best, the dosage, and the frequency of treatment.

Round worms

Roundworms differ from tapeworms and hookworms in that they do not attach themselves to the dog's internal organs. They free-float in the intestines. Additionally, roundworms don't need a vector to infect dogs. Roundworm eggs in the feces of infected dogs can live for a long time in your yard or at the dog park. When a dog eats the feces, which some dogs seem to enjoy doing, the roundworm eggs move to the intestines when they mature and multiply.

Roundworms can spell trouble for young puppies. The internal parasite can interrupt the puppy's growth. It can also create digestive issues such as diarrhea and vomiting that can, in turn, cause a build-up of excess gas. This will give the pup a bloated or pot belly appearance.

You may see the roundworms in your dog's stool. If that is the case, get a stool sample and call your veterinarian right away. Your vet may routinely do a fecal exam during your puppy visits just to make sure there are no signs of this parasite. A roundworm infestation can easily be treated with a course of de-wormer, administered every few weeks. The monthly heartworm medication that your dog takes once he is old enough is also effective at preventing roundworms.

Whipworms

Whipworms are the internal parasite responsible for causing the most disease in dogs. The tiny, quarter-inch-long parasite sets up shop in a dog's large intestines, where it wreaks havoc with the intestinal lining. The result is watery and bloody stool, weight loss, fatigue, and debilitation. Dogs get whipworms by ingesting the eggs, which are extremely hardy. They can remain alive, albeit in a dormant state, for as long as five years. Even high temperatures and drying won't kill them. Only after they are eaten by a dog can the eggs hatch and complete their life cycle in the animal's large intestines.

Whipworm eggs are easy to detect by examining a stool sample under a microscope, however, you often need to bring in several different stool samples. This is because whipworms pass their eggs sporadically; therefore, the veterinarian may miss seeing the eggs if only one sample is examined. If your Chessie is suffering from chronic diarrhea, your vet may run tests on multiple stool samples and may even prescribe a de-wormer, just in case.

A de-worming medication is used to treat dogs with whipworms. The reinfection rate with whipworms, however, is high. When dogs are diagnosed with whipworms, most veterinarians suggestion the dog be retreated for whipworms every few months. Luckily, the number of cases of whipworm in dogs is on the decline because more and more dogs are taking preventative heartworm and flea and tick medications.

The Importance of Spaying and Neutering Your Chesapeake Bay Retriever

One of the biggest decisions you need to make when your Chesapeake Bay Retriever is a puppy is whether to spay or neuter your dog. The only reason you would want to keep your Chessie unaltered is if you plan to breed your dog. Unless you are an experienced, responsible dog breeder with your own kennel and the goal to improve the Chesapeake Bay Retriever breed by producing top-quality dogs, I would advise against trying to breed your Chessie. You would only be contributing to the problem of poor quality and irresponsible breeding practices that run rampant through the puppy mill and backyard breeder industry. That being said, most people opt to spay or neuter their dogs. Not only is it the responsible thing to do as a pet owner, but it is actually beneficial for your dog.

Statistically, spayed and neutered dogs live longer lives and enjoy better overall health. Unaltered dogs may be more aggressive or try to display dominance. They are more apt to escape from your backyard and run off, looking for love in all the wrong places. This puts them at a greater risk of becoming lost or getting hit by a car.

For female dogs, spaying ends their heat cycle and all the unpleasant side effects of it, such as bleeding, whining, anxiety, crying, and nervous nipping. For male dogs, that embarrassing tendency to hump someone's leg will be reduced.

Chessies that have been spayed and neutered are much calmer, less aggressive, and friendlier. Hyper puppies tend to be less crazy after they have been spayed or neutered. In general, spayed and neutered Chessies are more affectionate and are better adapted to family life. They will be less distracted and can focus more on their training and obedience lessons.

Spaying and neutering has some health benefits as well. Spaying your female Chessie before her first heat cycle drastically reduces her chances of developing various cancers of the reproductive system as she ages. Similarly, neutered dogs, especially those that were neutered before the age of six months, have a much lower occurrence of testicular cancer.

Lastly, spaying and neutering your pets is the ethical thing to do. It helps to control the overpopulation of dogs, particularly mixed breed dogs. It reduces the number of dogs that end up in animal shelters. It also lowers the chance of your dog busting out of your yard, impregnating unsuspecting dogs, and killing local wildlife. Save the dog breeding to the experts and have your Chesapeake Bay Retriever spayed or neutered.

CHAPTER 18 Your Chessie's Health

Photo Courtesy of Shelby Ethier

Common Diseases and Medical Conditions in Chessies

In general, Chesapeake Bay Retrievers enjoy good health, but there are some genetic illnesses and medical conditions that occur more frequently in some dog breeds over others. Of course, that does not mean that every dog within that breed will develop the same disease; it just means that they are at an increased risk for contracting it. Knowing the specific diseases and disorders that are common in Chessies will help you to take preventative measures and to be on the lookout for early warning signs that may indicate the onset of disease. It also allows your veterinarian to be proactive about your Chessie's health care needs. Below are some of the most common genetic disorders in Chessies and a brief explanation of each. If you suspect your Chesapeake Bay Retriever may have a genetic disorder, discuss your concerns with your veterinarian.

CONGESTIVE HEART FAILURE

Congestive heart failure is what killed our first Chessie, Maizie. While there are medications that can help relieve some of the symptoms and prolong the dog's life, there is no cure for congestive heart failure.

With congestive heart failure, the dog's heart can no longer adequately pump blood throughout the body. Congestive heart failure can be caused by either a leaky mitral valve or by dilated cardiomyopathy. The heart becomes enlarged, resulting in the buildup of fluid in the lungs.

The first sign of congestive heart failure in your Chesapeake Bay Retriever is a constant cough. With Maizie, we first noticed the coughing when she went on walks or when we played ball in the yard. We assumed she was coughing because she was getting older and had put on a few pounds. We thought we were exercising her too hard. When the coughing persisted, we took her to see the veterinarian who ran some tests. The vet also asked us questions about Maizie's appetite and activity level. We admitted that Maizie didn't run and play like she used to, but we had chalked it up to age. We were devastated when the test results indicated that Maizie had congestive heart failure. We immediately started her on medication and devoted ourselves to making her as comfortable as possible.

As the disease progressed, Maizie's stamina became depleted. We noticed her panting a lot and she even coughed in her sleep. She lost weight, probably because she didn't have much of an appetite. Her condition seemed to plateau for a while, but then took a sudden and sharp turn for the worse. When she became too tired to stand and we had to carry her outside to relieve herself (did I mention that she was a big girl?), we knew it was time to make some difficult and heartbreaking decisions. We take comfort in knowing that she lived a wonderful life surrounded by people who loved her.

HIP DYSPLASIA

A skeletal deformity common in large-breed dogs like the Chesapeake Bay Retriever, hip dysplasia impacts your dog's mobility and quality of life. It is caused when the ball and socket of your dog's hip joints do not fit together properly. Instead of moving in a smooth, gliding motion, the ball grinds and rubs as it moves in the socket. The bones deteriorate from this wear and tear and, eventually, the function of the joint greatly diminishes.

Hip dysplasia is a genetic disorder that tends to impact large breed dogs the most. There are, however, some other factors that can determine the severity of the condition. For example, if a puppy does not get adequate nutrition and his growth is impacted, the rate of growth and development of his joints can be affected. As an adult Chessie, weight management is an important factor in hip dysplasia. Excess weight can put a strain on a Chessie's hip joints and exacerbate the preexisting condition. Following your veterinarian's guidelines on food and nutrition can help stave off some of the symptoms of hip dysplasia.

Chesapeake Bay Retrievers can show symptoms of hip dysplasia as young puppies, around four months old, or as aging dogs entering their golden years. No matter the age, many of the symptoms of hip dysplasia remain the same. They all have to do with mobility.

You may notice that your Chessie no longer wants to jump or climb, or wants to, but seems hesitant. This can include jumping into the back seat of the car, climbing the stairs to sleep with the dog's favorite human, or stepping up onto the couch for

> **HELPFUL TIP**
> **Recognizing Hip Dysplasia**
>
> Hip dysplasia is a somewhat common ailment for larger-breed dogs, including Chessies. Some dogs begin to display symptoms early in life, while others develop this condition as they age. Signs that your dog could be suffering from hip dysplasia include:
> - Decreased activity or range of motion
> - Reluctance to jump, climb stairs, or run
> - Rear-leg lameness
> - Stiffness or pain
> - Swaying gait
> - Loss of thigh muscle mass
>
> There are many treatments available for canine hip dysplasia, so it's important to bring up any concerns you may have with your vet to get the best treatment plan for your dog.

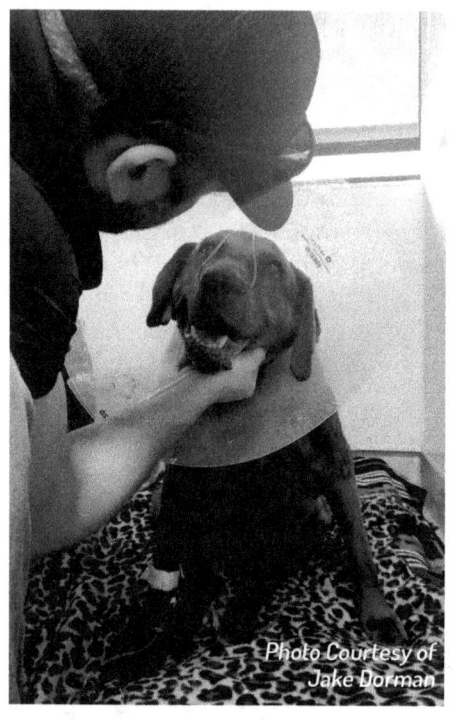

Photo Courtesy of Jake Dorman

a snuggle. You may also notice that your Chessie is slow to get up from a lying position or seems reluctant to come to you. He may no longer want to chase the ball, go on long walks, or catch the Frisbee, even though he always loved these activities. Your Chesapeake Bay Retriever may limp when he walks. He may show signs of stiffness, especially when he first gets up.

To test for hip dysplasia, your veterinarian will physically manipulate your dog's rear legs to gauge how stiff or loose the joint is. The vet will also feel for grinding within the joint. You should also expect your vet to do a blood test—the blood count can differ depending on the amount of inflammation—and an X-ray to see the structure of the joint. Based on all this information, your veterinarian will be able to make the diagnosis of hip dysplasia.

Treatment for hip dysplasia ranges from surgical to non-surgical options. If your veterinarian suggests a non-surgical approach, it probably means that your Chessie does not have a severe case of hip dysplasia. Non-surgical treatment options could include restrictions on exercise, weight loss to reduce stress on his joints, anti-inflammatory medications and joint support supplements, and even physical therapy. Your veterinarian, however, may feel that your Chessie is a good candidate for surgery to help relieve the pain and immobility of hip dysplasia. Surgical options could include procedures to remove bone from either the pelvic socket or the ball head of the leg bone. Another option is a total hip replacement. Your veterinarian will weigh all the factors and determine the best course of treatment for your Chesapeake Bay Retriever.

GASTRIC DILATATION AND VOLVULUS (GDV)

Commonly known as bloat, gastric dilatation and volvulus, or GDV, is more prevalent in dogs with deep chests like the Chesapeake Bay Retriever. The shape of the Chessie's chest makes it easier for bloat to occur. This happens when the stomach fills with gas and twists around, pinching off the blood flow to the stomach and spleen. When this occurs, the dog's life is in imminent danger. Without immediate emergency medical treatment, the dog could die in as little as a half hour. Prompt attention is needed if you suspect your Chessie has bloat from GDV.

Often, bloat occurs after the Chessie has consumed a large meal. In fact, it is more common in dogs that are fed one large meal per day, which is why veterinarians suggest feeding your Chesapeake Bay Retriever smaller portions, two or three times per day.

Your Chessie may be suffering from GDV bloat if he is retching and dry heaving with nothing coming out and appears to have an enlarged abdomen. You may also notice your Chessie sitting in a strange position, with his front legs and chest on the floor with his back legs standing up and his rump in the air. He may also be drooling excessively, acting in an anxious or panicked manner, or having difficulty breathing. Take your Chessie to your veterinarian or emergency animal hospital at once.

The veterinarian will stabilize your Chessie; the dog will most likely be in shock at this point. Emergency surgery will be required to untwist the stomach and return it to its original position. At this time, the vet will also assess the condition of the stomach, spleen, and other organs to see if any permanent damage has been done.

To reduce the chances of your Chessie getting bloat related to GDV, feed him smaller meals throughout the day and try to keep him from gorging himself on a lot of food in a short amount of time. The best way to ensure that your Chesapeake Bay Retriever doesn't get bloat is to have a preventative surgery done to tack his stomach into place. This way, the organ cannot twist and turn.

PROGRESSIVE RETINAL ATROPHY

Chessies have a higher-than-average risk of developing progressive retinal atrophy, or PRA. A genetic eye disorder, progressive retinal atrophy is passed to puppies from their parents and leads to eventual blindness. The only way to know if a Chesapeake Bay Retriever puppy is hardwired to lose his sight is to have him genetically tested. Unfortunately, there is no cure for PRA and, as the name suggests, it gets progressively worse as the dog ages.

Typically, symptoms of PRA begin to manifest when the Chessie is between three and five years old. You may notice that your Chesapeake Bay Retriever has trouble seeing at night. He may bump into furniture or walls or become easily confused in unfamiliar surroundings. He may be timid about going down steps or jumping down from a tall object. When you look into your Chessie's eyes, you may observe a cloudy or gray sheen over the eyeballs. The pupils might appear dilated. The symptoms will get progressively worse over time. The good news is that PRA is not painful for your Chessie. The bad news is there is no cure.

Genetic testing is available so you can find out if your Chesapeake Bay Retriever will lose his eyesight. While there is nothing you can do to prevent the inevitable, there are things that you can do to help him transition to a sightless life. For example, when you go for walks, always follow the same route. Your Chessie will get to know the route while he can still see and will feel comforted in future walks. Even though he won't be able to see, the sounds and smells will be familiar to him.

Keep the furniture in the same place in your home. Rearranging the furniture is downright cruel when you have a blind dog in the house. You should try to keep his surroundings as unchanged as possible. It is surprising how adaptable dogs can be. Even without vision, your Chessie can live a happy and fulfilling life.

DEGENERATIVE MYELOPATHY

A debilitating genetic disease, degenerative myelopathy targets the spinal cord of dogs, resulting in muscle weakness and loss of mobility in the back legs of the dog. In fact, it is related to Lou Gehrig's Disease in humans. Scientists have identified a genetic mutation as a risk factor for degenerative myelopathy in certain breeds of dogs. That list, unfortunately, includes the Chesapeake Bay Retriever.

The early signs of degenerative myelopathy can mimic hip dysplasia or arthritis, so an accurate diagnosis can be delayed. Other early symptoms of degenerative myelopathy can include difficulty standing up from a sitting or lying position, rear paws turn under leaving the dog to walk on his knuckles, and the hind end of the dog appears unstable when standing. Symptoms get worse as the disease progresses. In time, the Chessie's hindquarters will be completely paralyzed. The majority of the dogs stricken with degenerative myelopathy don't seem to be in pain. They are weak and may suffer from urinary and fecal incontinence, though.

When diagnosing degenerative myelopathy, your veterinarian will first run a series of tests to rule out other conditions, such as osteoarthritis, spinal tumor, or hip dysplasia. Based on the symptoms that the Chessie presents—and knowing that the Chesapeake Bay Retriever is one of the breeds more susceptible to the disease—your veterinarian may do a DNA test to look for the genetic mutation that is responsible for the disease.

There is no cure or effective treatment option for degenerative myelopathy. Good nutrition can help prolong mobility, as can physiotherapy. Swimming is a great exercise because it puts less strain on the dog's joints

CHAPTER 18 Your Chessie's Health

and because Chesapeake Bay Retrievers are natural-born swimmers. It is important that the Chessie maintain a healthy weight and avoid obesity.

The key to keeping your Chessie comfortable and happy in the final stages of the disease is patience on your part. Expect to clean up unpleasant messes and understand that your Chessie has lost control of his bodily functions and is distressed and frightened. Don't get frustrated by accidents. Your dog can sense your mood. Instead, be sure to give your Chessie plenty of love and support so he is as comfortable as possible and has the best quality of life he can have.

The Pros and Cons of Holistic Medicine for Your Chessie

Holistic medicine is gaining traction for humans, so it is only natural that we want to consider it for our dogs, too. This includes a number of alternative medical options, such as chiropractic care, massage therapy, acupuncture, sound and aromatherapy, acupressure, and more. The majority of times, holistic medicine is used in conjunction with traditional veterinary care, rather than in place of it. You may wonder if holistic medicine is a good choice for your Chesapeake Bay Retriever. Let's take a brief look at some of the individual components of holistic care to weigh the pros and cons.

Chiropractic Care

Veterinary chiropractors, like chiropractors for humans, specialize in relieving pain and discomfort of the joints, bones, and muscles by gently manipulating the spine and other parts of the body. Using slight pressure, the veterinary chiropractor will make adjustments that will put your Chessie's skeletal frame back into alignment, ease pain, and increase mobility. If you think that your Chessie may benefit from chiropractic care, discuss it with your veterinarian. Perhaps your animal care clinic has a veterinary chiropractor on staff or can recommend one to you that will work in partnership with your vet on your Chessie's care.

Massage Therapy

When humans get massages, it is a soothing, calming experience. It is the same for your Chesapeake Bay Retriever. A good canine massage can reduce your Chessie's stress levels, improve blood flow to the muscles, ease pain, and aid in digestion. Massage therapy can help your Chessie recover from a muscle strain or sprain quicker. Proponents of canine massage therapy even claim it can lower blood pressure, boost the immune system, and flush toxins from the body. The added bonus is that your dog will love it. It feels good and, if you learn some massage techniques so you can do it yourself, it is a good bonding experience for you both.

Hank had a massage one time. My daughter, a distance runner, signed herself and Hank up to compete in a doggie 5K race. We arrived early for the event and walked around to look at the vendor booths. One booth had a canine massage therapist who was giving out free massages to any of the dogs competing in the race. Hank was first in line! He seemed to love the massage; it put him in a state of Zen. Did it help him run the 5K faster? Nope. According to my daughter, when they had only about a half mile to go, Hank decided he was done with the race and lay down in a mud puddle. It took her about 15 minutes to get him going again. He probably could have used a deep-tissue massage after the 5K, but instead, we took him to the dog beach across the street for a quick swim. Hank waded out up to his neck and let the cool water ease his soreness.

Acupuncture

Acupuncture is a practice that dates back to ancient China about 5,000 years ago. It is used to restore the balance of energy within the body which will, according to acupuncture experts, aid the body in healing itself. Thin needles are inserted into the body at the points where nerves and blood vessels meet, called acupuncture points. Acupuncture has been shown to reduce inflammation, relieve pain, improve blood circulation, and lower stress levels. Although acupuncture for humans has been around for thousands of years, its use on dogs is a fairly new idea.

Never attempt to do acupuncture on your dog yourself. Only a trained and experienced acupuncturist that has an expertise in canine acupuncture should perform the procedure. Have a conversation with your veterinarian in regard to acupuncture to determine if this is a viable option for your Chesapeake Bay Retriever.

Sound Therapy

There is plenty of research to indicate that certain music can trigger impulses in the brains of dogs, resulting in a calming effect. Music can ease stress and anxiety, reduce barking and whining, and even lower blood pressure in your

Chessie. If your Chessie has separation anxiety or has to spend part of his day in a crate, try leaving music playing while you are gone. It has to be the right music though. Classical music and soothing instrumentals are best. Hard rock, heavy metal, and rap may be your favorite genres, but these styles of music will not have the same impact on your dog's brain as classical music. In fact, hard, fast, jarring tunes can actually increase anxiety and agitation.

Aromatherapy

Like sound therapy, aromatherapy is a form of holistic healing that uses pleasant, calming scents to relieve stress and anxiety. Smells impact brain function, according to recent studies. Specific scents have been proven to have relaxing qualities. There is, however, a big danger posed by aromatherapy. Some essential oils are toxic to dogs and can cause illness or death. Consult with your veterinarian before you introduce aromatherapy to your Chessie to make sure that you are using safe essential oils and in the proper amounts for your dog's sensitive nose.

Acupressure

Acupressure is, like acupuncture, an ancient healing art from China. Also, like acupuncture, acupressure relies on manipulating specific pressure points in the dog's body. By applying light pressure to these spots, proper blood flow is restored. Modern proponents of acupressure have found that it is an effective and noninvasive way to reduce anxiety and speed healing.

Potential Concerns with Holistic Methods

Much of the effectiveness of holistic treatment options center around the ability to reduce stress and anxiety in the dog. By doing so, the animal's body is better equipped to fight off illnesses and to heal itself, as nature intended. Holistic medicine is best used in conjunction with modern veterinary medicine and with the full awareness of your veterinarian. Never forego veterinary care in lieu of a holistic remedy. This is especially important if your Chessie is experiencing a medical emergency. Also, be open and honest with your veterinarian about your beliefs surrounding holistic medicine. You want the holistic treatments to complement the medical treatment that you vet has prescribed, not work against it. You will find that most vets are open to combining treatment options that include both traditional and holistic medical care.

What You Should Know About CBD Products and your Chessie

In recent years, the push for legalizing cannabis has spread across the country, with proponents touting the natural health benefits of CBD. That extended to dogs as well, as many dog owners are looking for an all-natural health supplement to combat the rising costs of standard veterinary care. But just because cannabis products are legal and deemed safe for humans doesn't necessarily mean they are safe for your pets. Before you give your Chesapeake Bay Retriever CBD, do your research, learn the facts, and seek the advice of your veterinarian.

IS CBD THE SAME AS MARIJUANA?

The short answer is no. CBD stands for cannabidiol. This is a chemical compound that is found in cannabis along with THC, tetrahydrocannabinol. While THC is the compound that possesses psychoactive properties—that is responsible for getting the user high—CBD contains no psychoactive properties.

WHY GIVE YOUR CHESSIE CBD?

There are a variety of reasons why dog owners choose to give their pets CBD. In studies, CBD has been proven effective at reducing pain and inflammation from arthritis, controlling seizures, and easing anxiety. Many people claim that CBD also improves a dog's joint mobility, prevents nausea, and even gives him a nice, shiny coat.

TALK TO YOUR VET ABOUT DOSAGE

To make sure that the CBD you are giving your Chessie is both safe and effective, talk to your veterinarian about the proper dosage. The dosage is based on your dog's weight and the strength of the CBD product. Giving your Chessie too much CBD can be harmful, but if the dose is too small, he will not obtain any health benefits. If your vet clinic does not sell CBD products for dogs, ask your veterinarian to recommend a specific product or two and to provide you with dosing information.

CHECK THE THC LEVEL IN THE PRODUCT

Thoroughly read the label on all CBD products. Look for the Certificate of Analysis, or COA, that is required by law to be printed on the label. This tells you that the product has been lab tested and will indicate the amounts of THC in the product. For dogs, look for a product with zero amounts of

THC. Even trace amounts of THC can be toxic to dogs. The COA will also detail the results of microbial testing, pesticides testing, and heavy metal testing. If the product you are reviewing does not have COA information on the label, put it back on the shelf and move on to another product from a more reputable seller.

BEWARE OF HEMP OIL

Many manufacturers offer a hemp oil product that they tout as a healthcare product. Hemp oil does not contain CBD, or only has trace amounts of it. While the hemp oil is not harmful for your dog, it lacks the health properties of CBD, therefore it will not benefit your Chessie. Get into the habit of reading labels. Find the COA information on the label to see how much CBD is actually in the product. If the product has "hemp oil" or "hemp seed oil" in the name, it may not contain CBD at all.

LOOK FOR BROAD SPECTRUM OR CBD-ISOLATE PRODUCTS

The best option for your Chessie is to use a broad-spectrum, CBD-isolate products. This means that the product contains only CBD, which has been isolated from the other chemicals found in cannabis. The label and the COA information will tell you if the product contains any other compounds other than CBD.

KEEP MARIJUANA AWAY FROM DOGS

Every veterinarian can tell you stories of dogs that have ingested marijuana, either because they found their owners' stash or because someone thought it would be funny to try to get the dogs high. While canine deaths from eating marijuana or cannabis edibles are rare, the high concentration of THC can make a dog extremely sick. The dog will experience neurological symptoms, such as becoming hyperactive, uncoordinated, anxious, confused, and vocal. Your dog may get a wild-eyed look on his face. He may drool, urinate on the floor, have tremors, or have a seizure. In severe cases, the dog may lapse into a coma. The symptoms typically go away in a short time, but your dog will be sick and quite uncomfortable until then. Always keep marijuana and cannabis products away from your pets.

The Pros and Cons of Pet Insurance

Just like we have health insurance to help us pay for medical expenses, there is pet insurance to help cover the unexpected costs of emergency medical treatment for your dog. A veterinary emergency can run thousands of dollars and many people simply don't have that money sitting around.

That puts them in a terrible position to make heart-wrenching decisions based on finances rather than on the best option for their dog. Pet insurance can help lessen finances as a factor when deciding on the treatment plan for your dog. Before you decide if you need pet insurance, however, you should weigh the pros and cons.

PET INSURANCE DOESN'T COVER EVERYTHING

If you are expecting pet insurance to cover all your Chesapeake Bay Retriever's medical expenses, you will be sorely disappointed. When shopping for pet insurance, be sure to read the fine print carefully so you understand what is covered and what isn't. For example, some policies don't cover routine veterinary visits and checkups; they are only meant to be used for emergency veterinary expenses. Others do not cover spaying, neutering, or other preventative care, including vaccinations. Some policies exclude the exam fee. Most pet insurance providers also exclude pre-existing conditions and have breed restrictions, meaning they won't cover certain breeds of dog.

WATCH FOR FEE SCHEDULES

Some pet insurance companies operate on a fee schedule basis. What that means is that they will give you a list of common diseases and treatments along with the projected cost that the insurance company claims the treatment will cost. They will only pay this amount. In reality, many of the procedures on the fee schedule cost much more at most veterinary clinics. You are responsible for the difference, which could be significant. There are pet insurance plans that cover a flat percentage of your vet's charges, typically 80 percent. These are better options because the coverage is not based on arbitrary numbers that the insurance provider sets.

YOU CAN CHOOSE YOUR LEVEL OF COVERAGE

Many pet insurance providers offer different plans with different levels of coverage. At the highest, and most costly levels, there are plans available that cover almost all emergency, accidents, and non-routine veterinary care, including medications and even cancer treatments. At the lowest and cheapest end, there are policies that only cover annual check-ups and vaccines. In the middle are policies that include a mix of both. To determine which option is best for you and your situation, you need to do your homework and find out exactly what each policy covers and balance that with the monthly premium you can afford to pay.

CHAPTER 18 Your Chessie's Health

THERE ARE DEDUCTIBLES

Just like our medical insurance, pet insurance policies often have deductibles that need to be met before the policy will pay out. Deductibles are often set based on the level of coverage for your plan option and the age of your dog, so be sure to compare policies from different companies to find what works best for you.

PREMIUMS ARE BASED ON BREED AND AGE

In addition to the level of coverage you chose, your monthly premium will also be determined by your dog's breed and age. Even where you live can impact how much you pay each month. The dog's age, however, is the biggest factor. The older your dog gets, the more you will pay in monthly premiums. If you are shopping for pet insurance for an older dog, your only options may be high premium, high deductible policies.

Photo Courtesy of Larry and Shannen Butcher

ALL VETS ARE IN NETWORK

You know how your health insurance only covers expenses if you go to doctors that are in their network? And, if your insurance coverage changes, you often have to switch doctors? You won't have to worry about that with pet insurance. It doesn't operate on an in-network/out-of-network basis. Your pet insurance should be accepted by all veterinarians. Just to be sure, however, ask your veterinary clinic if they accept the pet insurance you are considering. It pays to shop around and do your homework because not all pet insurance policies are created equal.

CHAPTER 19:
Traveling with your Chessie

When we go on vacations that involve hiking, car travel, and non-hotel accommodations, we often take Hank along. He does pretty well in new surroundings and seems to enjoy new experiences. Traveling with your Chessie can be a rewarding experience, but we found that things go much smoother if we do our research and know what to expect on the trip. Chesapeake Bay Retrievers are large dogs, so we have to consider how much room we have in the car and where we are staying so we don't have a repeat of the one time that Hank insisted on sleeping with me in a twin bed.

Photo Courtesy of Aastin Curtis-Atkins

CHAPTER 19   Traveling with your Chessie

Making Travel Preparations

When you are planning your trip, keep your Chessie's needs in mind during every step of the way. Doing so will make the experience much more enjoyable for him and less stressful for you. Thoroughly research your destination to find out if dogs are welcome on trails, at campgrounds, in parks, or at beaches. Look for dog-friendly restaurants and businesses, too.

I often use the BringFido app. It's free and it allows users to search by city. It lists dog-friendly hotels, Airbnbs, and other lodging options, as well as restaurants with dog patios, area activities that are open to dogs, and even pet-friendly events, like festivals and 5K races. I enjoy reading the reviews that app users leave; it gives me more insight into the places that are listed on the app.

> **CELEBRITY DOGS**
> **Tom and Timber Felton**
>
> Tom Felton, an English actor and musician best known for his role as Draco Malfoy in the film adaptations of the *Harry Potter* books, is the proud owner of a Chessie named Timber. In a 2011 interview, Felton said, "My biggest worry when I'm away working is what'll happen to Timber. I wanted a dog throughout childhood but wasn't allowed—responsibility and all that—so the first thing I did on moving out was get a puppy. She's a Chesapeake Bay Retriever. I love her."

The Importance of ID Tags and Microchips

Identification tags and microchips are important when you and your dog are at home, but they are doubly important when you are traveling. An excited Chessie may bolt out of the car when you stop for gas or yank the leash from your hand at a park. If he gets separated from you, the ID tag and microchip may be the only thing that will ensure a happy reunion.

Make sure that the information listed on your Chessie's ID tag is current. Use a pair of pliers to clamp the tag securely onto the collar and make sure the collar fits properly so your dog doesn't slip out of it. Personally, I prefer to use a harness because I know that Hank can't slip his head through it.

Visit your vet's office prior to your trip and ask them to check your Chesapeake Bay Retriever's microchip to make sure it is still in place and detectable. Update the contact information on it, if needed.

Find out if your destination has any specific vaccination requirements for dogs that differ from your region. If so, you will want to ask your vet about getting your Chessie that vaccine before you go so you don't run the risk of your dog bringing back a disease. Lastly, get a copy of your Chessie's vaccination records from your veterinarian. You probably won't need it—I've never been asked for it—but it is a good idea to be prepared in case you need to prove that your Chessie is current on his vaccines before he can enter an attraction.

Dog Carriers and Travel Crates

It may be a good idea to invest in a dog carrier or travel crate when vacationing with your Chesapeake Bay Retriever. This way, you can keep your Chessie confined during travel, which will be required for flights. You may also need to crate your dog when you are at your destination. For example, if you and your family decide to go out to eat, you won't want to let your Chessie have free run of the rental house. Left alone in an unfamiliar place, he may react by destroying things.

Be warned, however, that travel crates for dogs as large as Chesapeake Bay Retrievers are not cheap. They also aren't readily available at your local pet supply store. I had to order ours online. Pay attention to the dimensions. I ordered one crate that said "extra large" in the description, but it was too small for Hank. I had to return it and start over in my search. Since I'm a visual person, I held up a tape measure so I could get a better idea of the true size of the crate. This helped me eliminate several options before I found one that was big enough. The one I bought has nylon sides, so it is lightweight when it's folded up. So far, it has worked well. My daughter bought a similar nylon travel crate for her Husky, however, and he chewed through the fabric. You will have to factor in your Chessie's chew potential when making your final choice.

What You Should Know About Flying with Your Chessie

A generation ago, it was rare to see dogs on an airplane. Nowadays, it is common for dogs to accompany their owners on flights. Chesapeake Bay Retrievers, however, are much bigger than Chihuahuas and Pomeranians. They can't fit into a tiny purse that you carry onto the plane. Because of the

CHAPTER 19 Traveling with your Chessie

size of Chessies, you will need to work with the airline to arrange for your dog to fly with them. He will likely fly in the baggage hold or the cargo hold.

Each airline has its own policies regarding dogs on flights, but you can expect that you will be required to prove that your Chessie does not have fleas or ticks or any contagious diseases. You will also need to show proof that your Chessie is up to date on his vaccinations. All airlines will also require you to have your Chessie in a clean, approved crate. Check with each airline to get exact requirements. You certainly don't want to get to the airport only to find out that you don't have the right crate, or you forgot to bring your Chessie's vaccination records. Talk to the airline well in advance of your trip and follow all of their requirements.

The airline will charge you a fee for your Chesapeake Bay Retriever's passage on the flight. Since he will most likely have to fly in the cargo or baggage area, the cost will be higher than if you had a small dog that you could keep with you as a carry-on. Fees range greatly so be sure to talk to the airline in person. The fee will depend also on the size of your dog, the duration of your flight and if you have connecting flights.

Federal aviation regulations state that all pets must be eight weeks old or older to fly on commercial airlines. If you want to fly with a puppy that young, or if you will be traveling with your older Chessie or a Chessie with a chronic medical condition, you should schedule a veterinary visit to find out if your vet has any concerns about your Chesapeake Bay Retriever making the trip.

Plan to arrive at the airport with plenty of time to spare. That way, you can walk your dog outside for a while to let him burn off some energy and to relieve himself. If you're pressed for time, rushing, and stressed, your Chessie will become anxious. Keep food light the day of your flight and stop feeding your Chessie about four hours before your flight time. Don't give him treats or anything that may upset his stomach during the flight.

In the past, dog owners got a canine sedative from their vets to knock out their dog during air travel. The current advice from airlines and animal care advocates is to not sedate dogs prior to flight. When a dog is sedated, he can experience breathing trouble. He will also not be able to regulate his body temperature as well when he is unconscious.

The size of Chesapeake Bay Retrievers may make air travel challenging for many pet owners, but if you do your research, you should be able to find an airline that will work with you to get your Chessie safely to your destination.

Tips for Making Car Travel with your Chessie Easier and Safer

Although we have never taken Hank on an airplane, he has gone on plenty of road trips with us. His longest car ride was about eight hours. He did surprisingly well; however, it is important to note that he was not a young puppy when we took that trip. He was older so his energy level was not as high. A hyper, exuberant puppy and a long car ride sound like a less than ideal combination. We enjoy including Hank on family trips whenever we can, but we have learned over the years that it takes some patience and planning to make the experience easier on us and less stressful on him. Here are some tips that will make car travel with your Chesapeake Bay Retriever easier and safer.

GET YOUR CHESSIE USED TO CAR RIDES

From the day we brought Hank home from the breeder, we have taken him on car rides. He almost always accompanies me to pick the kids up from school or drop them off at various practices or events. Hank is fully acclimated to car travel, but if your Chessie is not used to riding in cars, you will want to do several practice runs with him. Vary the length of the trial runs. Also switch up where you drive with your Chessie, so he gets used to the noises of cities and the smells of the countryside. Make the practice car runs a rewarding experience for your Chesapeake Bay Retriever with plenty of praise and positive reinforcement.

GIVE YOUR CHESSIE A COMFY SPOT

Your Chessie will feel more secure during the road trip if he has his own place in the car. Make this spot as cozy as possible. We always bring along Hank's favorite blanket. The familiar smell and feel of it is comforting to him. Be sure your Chessie's place in the car is roomy enough for him to be comfortable yet confined enough that he can't jump around in the vehicle while it's moving. A travel crate is a great way to check both of these boxes.

FOOD AND WATER

On road trips, we try to limit how much food we give Hank. We typically leave on our trips first thing in the morning. We give him a small portion of his food in the morning, at least an hour before we hit the road. I know some dog owners prefer to withhold food prior to long car rides because a dog with an empty stomach is less likely to vomit in the car. We feel it is more important to keep Hank on his regular feeding schedule, albeit with smaller

CHAPTER 19 Traveling with your Chessie

Photo Courtesy of Sarah Hyde

amounts. We also provide him with a nice drink of water about an hour before we leave. We bring along a jug or two of water from our house—so it tastes familiar to him—and a collapsible water dish that we use to give Hank water when we stop.

MAKE PLENTY OF STOPS

We have learned to take our time traveling with Hank. Instead of pushing through to get to our destination as quickly as possible, we make it a more leisurely experience. Every two to three hours, we stop at a rest stop for a short break. Most rest stops have dog run areas, so Hank has an opportunity to stretch his legs and relieve himself. Of course, we always travel with a roll of doggie waste bags so we can be responsible pet owners and clean up after Hank. Prior to stopping the car, we will clip Hank's leash onto him. He is always eager to get out of the car when we stop and we want to make sure he can jump out quickly, but with one of us holding tightly to the leash.

BEWARE OF DANGERS

One of the biggest threats to dogs on road trips comes from overheating. Too often, people leave their dog locked in their vehicle while they run into a store or restaurant. The temperature inside the vehicle can rise drastically in just minutes, even with a window cracked open slightly. I know people who will leave their cars running and the air conditioning on for their dogs, but I am always leery of doing this. My car will shut itself off after a period of inactivity, cutting off the A/C as well. For these reasons, I simply won't leave Hank in the car unattended. On road trips, we go through drive-thru restaurants or order food to-go and find a dog-friendly park to have our lunch. When we stop at gas stations to fill up and take bathroom breaks, we take turns staying in the car with Hank.

Speaking of gas stations, take care that your dog isn't exposed to a chemical hazard in the parking lot. Gas, motor oil, antifreeze, and other vehicle fluids can spill out and sit in puddles on the pavement. If you let your Chesapeake Bay Retriever out of the car in a gas station parking lot, he may try to drink these fluids. Some of them, especially antifreeze, are quite tasty to dogs, but can be deadly. When we are on road trips, we usually pull over to a grassy median area in front of or adjacent to the gas station. One of us—it's usually me—will take Hank out of the car and walk him around the grass while the rest of the family fills the gas tank, buys snacks, and uses the restroom. When they are all done and back in the car, they will drive over to pick up me and Hank and then park in front of the gas station so I can run into the bathroom. It takes a little longer, but it is worth it.

CHAPTER 19   Traveling with your Chessie

What You Should Know About Staying in a Hotel with your Chessie

The good news is that more and more hotels are welcoming dogs as guests. In fact, about three-quarters of all hotels now allow dogs to check in with their owners. There are some caveats, however, that you need to plan for.

I would suggest that you take your Chessie on a trial run to a dog-friendly hotel in your community. That way, if your dog freaks out, you can just head home.

SIZE MATTERS

A hotel may advertise that it is dog friendly but read the fine print before you book your accommodations. Many hotels place size restrictions on their doggie guests. They may not allow a dog as large as a Chesapeake Bay Retriever to stay. If you have two Chessies, your odds decrease as some hotels have a maximum total weight requirement for dogs. Since regulations vary from place to place, it is best to call the hotel directly to speak to a manager, instead of booking online or through a hotel reservation website. You will be able to explain the breed and size of your dog to the manager who will let you know if they can accommodate your Chessie. Just to cover your bases, when the hotel emails you your reservation confirmation, ask that it also confirm that your Chessie will be able to stay with you. Also ask the manager to put a note on your reservation so that the front desk attendant that checks you in is aware of the situation. This will save you some hassle and save the front desk clerk from having to call the manager.

EXPECT A PET FEE

A few hotels allow dogs to stay for free but most of them charge a per-night pet fee that will probably fall in the $50 range. Sometimes this fee is negotiable. For example, if you are staying in the same hotel for several nights, ask if your dog can stay free the final night. If you are traveling during the off season, you could ask for a 10 percent discount on the pet fee. The worst that can happen is the manager says no.

RULES AND REGULATIONS

When you are booking your dog-friendly hotel, ask about the hotel's dog rules. A standard rule at many hotels is that dogs cannot be left unaccompanied in the rooms. That means, your dog has to go with you everywhere you go. Find out where the dog run is outside. Ask if they close the run for the night or if you and your Chessie will have access to it at all hours. Are there any places in the hotel where dogs are off limits? It is better to find that out as soon as you can, so you don't violate a hotel rule.

DOG AMENITIES

Find out if the hotel offers any special dog-related amenities that can make your stay even better. Some hotels have a doggie happy hour time every afternoon on their patio as an opportunity for all the dogs and dog owners staying in the hotel to meet for cocktails and play time. Some hotels have an on-staff dog walker and dog sitter if you need to leave your Chessie for a few hours. There are even boutique hotels that have doggie spas on site where your Chessie can go to get pampered.

PLAN AROUND YOUR CHESSIE'S BEHAVIOR

You know your Chesapeake Bay Retriever better than anyone. Use that information to make the best choices when booking a hotel. If your Chessie is older, has arthritis, or suffers from hip dysplasia, you should ask for a room on the ground floor to avoid the stairs. If your Chessie barks when cars pull up or when people walk by his window, you may be better off with a room on the second or third floor.

PACK YOUR CHESSIE'S SUITCASE

When you pack your suitcase for your trip, be sure to pack your Chessie's bag. Hank has his own duffel bag with his name on it that we use for traveling with him. In it, we pack all the items that Hank will need. We have two collapsible bowls: one for food and one for water. I always measure out Hank's food into individual baggies, so I don't have to bring a measuring cup. I bring extra servings of food, just in case. I also pack a small baggie of Hank's favorite treats.

In his suitcase, I also pack Hank's favorite blanket since it is his comfort item. He has a few balls that he really likes, so I pack those as well. I pack an extra collar and extra leash in case one gets broken or lost. You may want to bring along your Chessie's dog bed, too, though it is possible that the hotel will have dog beds for you to use. I include a small towel and a larger one in Hank's duffel bag. The small one is to wipe off his paws before we get back in the car or go into the hotel room. The large one is to dry him off if he goes swimming at a dog beach. Hank has an impressive collection of bandanas. We pick out enough fresh bandanas for him to wear a different one each day. A dapper dog is a happy dog.

I also always pack some health-care products for Hank, such as a small bottle of dog shampoo, a brush, and a doggie toothbrush. On one trip, Hank

CHAPTER 19 Traveling with your Chessie

ate a yellow jacket—he does this periodically. When he gets stung, his face swells and we have to give him Benadryl. I didn't have Benadryl with us and had to make an emergency trip to the closest pharmacy. Since then, I bring along Benadryl whenever we travel.

Photo Courtesy of Abigail Hughes

Leaving your Chessie at Home

We do plenty of travel without Hank, too, which he hates, but there are simply times when he can't go with us. If you prefer not to travel with your Chesapeake Bay Retriever, you will need to make arrangements for your dog's care in your absence. Fortunately, you have numerous options.

Pros and Cons of Boarding Kennels

Your veterinary clinic may offer a boarding kennel as part of its services. Or you can contact an independent dog kennel to arrange for your Chessie to stay there while you are gone. Not every dog handles being boarded well, although many dogs seem to have a great time at the kennel.

When you board your Chessie at a kennel, you have peace of mind knowing that he will have professionals taking good care of him. He will have the chance to play, get exercise, and socialize with other dogs. He will be fed on time and will be given fresh water several times a day. If there are any issues or concerns, the trained staff at the kennel can address them immediately. It's even better if the kennel is affiliated with your vet clinic because your Chessie's regular veterinarian will be right there to attend to him, if needed.

Boarding your Chessie might be the best choice for you if you don't want to have people at your house when you are not there; however, keeping your dog at a kennel can be quite costly. For your Chesapeake Bay Retriever, it can be a stressful experience. Not only will he be away from his people, but he will be away from everything that is familiar to him. Some dogs are quite adaptable and quickly accept kennel life as their new normal. For dogs with separation anxiety or ones that don't adapt well to change, staying for a week or two at a boarding kennel can be an upsetting experience.

While most boarding kennels offer a safe, secure environment and are staffed with trained professionals, there are some risks to your Chessie. Perhaps the biggest risk comes from infectious diseases. One sick dog can infect the entire kennel before the staff even realizes it's ill. During play time, there is the risk of one dog injuring another, though the kennel staff is trained to watch for signs of impending aggression in dogs and to take immediate action.

CHAPTER 19   Traveling with your Chessie

The Pros and Cons of a Dog Sitter

If you decide that boarding your Chesapeake Bay Retriever while you are away is not the best option for you or your dog, you can hire someone to dog sit for you. You can do this a few different ways. You can find someone who can stay at your house—more of a house sitter/dog sitter combo—or you can hire someone to stop by a few times a day to feed your Chessie and take him for walks. You can also hire someone you already know or use one of the gig services, like Rover.com, to find someone near you. Naturally, there are pros and cons to each one of these options.

Having someone come and stay at your home to care for your Chessie is less stressful on your dog. As an added bonus, this person can feed your cat, take the trash can down to the curb, bring in your mail, and water your plants while they are dog sitting your Chessie. It is typically cheaper to hire a dog sitter/house sitter than it is to board your dog at a kennel. But you have to be careful about allowing someone to stay at your house. You want someone who will be responsible and respectful of your home. That's why hiring someone you know can be a good idea but know that dog sitters on Rover and other similar websites have been fully vetted by the company, have been interviewed, and have undergone a background check.

If you don't like the idea of someone staying at your house, you could hire someone to come by several times a day to check on your Chessie, give him potty breaks, take him for walks, and make sure his water bowl is full. This form of dog sitter is typically the least expensive, but there are some drawbacks. First, your Chesapeake Bay Retriever will be left home alone for long stretches of time. Your dog's routine will probably be upended, which can make him anxious and confused. You also run the risk of your dog sitter forgetting to stop by or having some other sort of issue (car trouble, called into work, lost the house key) that prevents them from caring for your dog.

What do we do when we have to leave Hank? My niece, Maggie, has been our go-to person for dog sitting for several years now. She started staying at our house when we were away when she was a junior in high school and she is now finished college. Since she's family and we know she's a good kid, we have no qualms about letting her stay at our house. She loves Hank and he loves her, so even though he may miss us, we know he is getting plenty of attention and love in the comfort of his own home.

CHAPTER 20:
Your Chessie in his Golden Years

The worst part of sharing your life with a Chesapeake Bay Retriever is that his lifespan is tragically shorter than our own. You will watch as your Chessie goes from a curious, roly-poly puppy to an elderly, gray-around-the-muzzle senior dog in less than 10 years. The average lifespan of a Chessie is between 10 and 12 years. Maizie was 13 when she died, and Hank is currently eight years old. That means he is transitioning to his golden years, which is a heartbreaking thought. During that time, he will experience some changes to his physical health and personality. Our task is to help him transition into this next stage of life.

Photo Courtesy of Celia Wright

CHAPTER 20   Your Chessie in his Golden Years

The Changing Care of a Senior Chessie

When your Chessie gets to be Hank's age, he will begin experiencing age-related changes. Most of these changes come on so gradually that you may not even notice them. Some of the first signs of aging you may see involve joint stiffness and pain, along with some mobility issues. Chessies are prone to joint disorders, such as arthritis and hip dysplasia, that often manifest as the dog ages. You may also start to notice that your Chessie's hearing and vision are not as sharp as they once were. Your Chessie may also seem to slow down. I know Hank appreciates lying on the front porch much more now than ever before. He is still an active dog, but he does like his downtime.

As your Chesapeake Bay Retriever ages, you might also observe changes to his appetite, bowel and bladder habits, and dental problems. All of these are part of the natural aging process; however, they can have an impact on your Chessie's quality of life. Work with your veterinarian to address these changes and take any necessary steps to make things easier on your dog.

Changes to your Senior Chessie's Vision and Hearing

Typically, a dog's vision and hearing will decline so gradually that it is not noticeable right away. Vision and hearing loss can masquerade as other things, like stubbornness or laziness. When Maizie was in her golden years, I remember calling her to come to me and she just sat there, looking the other way. At first, I thought she was ignoring me, which made me angry. But then, it occurred to me that perhaps she couldn't hear me calling her name.

As your Chessie ages, it is important to be patient with him. It is easy to get frustrated and think your dog isn't listening to you, but he is not being obstinate or defiant. It could be that he can no longer hear your commands or see your hand gestures. If he barks when a family member walks into the house, it could be that he can no longer see well enough to recognize them. He is reacting as if a stranger has come in because, to him, that is what has happened.

Be sensitive to your Chessie's declining vision and hearing. Don't move his food dish or toys to a new location. Don't rearrange the furniture. Help him navigate the stairs or jump out of the car. Be careful that you don't startle him by sneaking up on him. Above all, show him patience and understanding. His declining vision and hearing are not his fault. He is probably just as concerned and frightened as you are.

Changes in your Senior Chessie's Temperament and Behavior

There will be some changes to your Chesapeake Bay Retriever's temperament as he ages. We jokingly call Hank a "grumpy old man." While he is still great with the kids, he is less tolerant of the cat (of course, it could be that the cat is being more of a jerk than normal). When his favorite people come over, Hank is just as exuberant as he always was, but he no longer runs to greet everyone who stops by. Some dogs become more timid as they get older. It could be that they are making up for some hearing and vision loss

Photo Courtesy of Amy Houston

CHAPTER 20   Your Chessie in his Golden Years

Photo Courtesy of Diane Prat

by cautiously approaching unfamiliar situations. Their apprehension could also be because they are more easily confused.

Just as humans suffer from memory loss as we get older, your Chessie may forget things from time to time. Occasionally, dogs will become aggressive in their senior years. This, too, is a sign that the dog is confused and doesn't understand how to react to an unfamiliar situation. Just remember that your Chessie is not turning into a "bad dog"; he is acting in the way he thinks is best in response to the situation. Instead of punishing him, return to the old, familiar positive reinforcement tactics that he knows so well. It will be comforting to him to follow a familiar routine.

Mental stimulation is just as important for an older Chessie as it is for a younger dog. Replace rigorous exercise with other forms of stimulation. A puzzle feeder or a puzzle treat toy will keep your Chessie busy trying to figure out how to get the treat. Of course, human interaction is also key to keeping an older Chessie mentally stimulated. Even if his exercise is reduced, your Chessie will still reap the benefits of going places, like the dog park, a dog beach, or a restaurant with a dog-friendly patio. New places and new experiences will keep his mind sharp. Cuddles and companionship will stave off boredom and keep your Chesapeake Bay Retriever happy.

Nutritional Changes for your Older Chessie

In each stage of life, you Chesapeake Bay Retriever will have different nutritional needs and his golden years are no exception. As he ages, his metabolism will slow. He will no longer need to consume as many calories as he did when he was a puppy or an active adult. It is important to adjust his food to accommodate his new metabolism so he doesn't gain weight. Talk to your veterinarian about your Chessie's diet and gradually make a change to his food intake. Your veterinarian will most likely suggest switching your Chessie's dog food to one that is formulated for senior dogs. Most pet food manufacturers offer the same variety of dog food in several different formulas, designed for each stage of life—puppy food, adult dog food, healthy weight food, and senior food.

It is not uncommon for older Chessies to experience some dental pain that makes eating more difficult. Tooth and gum problems can cause so much discomfort that your Chessie simply won't eat. Schedule a visit with your veterinarian if you see why your Chessie is not eating his food or if he is losing weight. It could be that a simple antibiotic will take care of his dental issues and allow him to eat without pain again. If the condition is more chronic, you should talk to your vet about switching your Chessie from dry kibbles to wet, canned dog food that is easier to consume.

There are a few other benefits to feeding an elderly dog canned dog food. Some older dogs have diminished senses of smell and taste. The stronger odor and taste of canned dog food is more appealing to them. Wet dog food is also higher in water content so it can help keep your Chessie hydrated.

> **FUN FACT**
> **Arthritis and Senior Chessies**
>
> Chesapeake Bay Retrievers have an average lifespan of 10 to 13 years. Senior Chessies may experience arthritis in their later life. There are several types of arthritis that require a diagnosis from a veterinarian. Identifying arthritis early on can decrease discomfort for your dog. Signs that your Chessie may be experiencing arthritis include:
> - Limping, lameness, or abnormal gait
> - Reluctance to move or climb stairs
> - Swollen joints that are tender to the touch
> - Lack of interest in play and an increase in sleep
> - Irritability, especially when joints are touched
>
> There are many treatment options for senior dogs with arthritis, so don't hesitate to reach out to your veterinarian if you notice any abnormal behavior in your senior dog that could indicate this condition.

CHAPTER 20   Your Chessie in his Golden Years

Photo Courtesy of Melissa King

Exercise Changes for your Older Chessie

"Our matriarch Rosa (10 years old) does not know she is getting older. She still wants to be included in all the activities that she has been for a decade, but her needs are changing. When we take her for a swim, we make sure to not let her get overly tired. After 5-7 retrieves, she is tired. She will attempt to retrieve as many times as we throw the dummy, as will most any Chessie, so we need to know when she is at her limit. If we are not observant, she will likely be sore for several days. Not helping an older Chessie to know their limits also can result in injuries for them."

LEAH SPRADLIN
Hickory Creek Chesapeakes

As your Chesapeake Bay Retriever ages, his exercise needs decrease. You can cut down on the frequency and lengths of his walks, especially if he seems to tire earlier than normal or if he shows signs of joint pain or stiffness. If your Chessie is experiencing joint pain and discomfort, he won't let you know. It is in their nature to hide their pain; it's an instinctual habit from long before dogs became domesticated. Keep a close eye on your Chessie when you go for walks and take your cues from him. If he slows down or turns to go back home, he may be signaling to you that he has had enough. You will also know if he has been overexerted if your Chessie immediately lies down when you get home from a walk and if he struggles to get back up. His muscles and joints might be stiff and sore.

Talk to your veterinarian about your Chessie's stiffness. There are a number of things you can do to relieve some of his discomfort, including health supplements and medications. Chondroitin and glucosamine are two of the more common ones.

If you live near a dog beach, you can try replacing some of your Chessie's walks with swims. Chessies love the water and enjoy swimming. This is a great way for your dog to get some exercise without putting added strain on his joints.

You know how an old mattress can make your back hurt in the morning? The same thing can happen for your Chessie. The padding and cushioning in older dog beds gets worn down over time and they lose their support. Try spoiling your Chessie with a new orthopedic dog bed that distributes his weight more evenly. It should ease some of his discomfort and make him less stiff when he gets up in the morning.

CHAPTER 20 Your Chessie in his Golden Years

Photo Courtesy of
Sherry & Roy Ebel

Common Age-Related Ailments in Chessies

Aside from an increase in muscle and joint pain, arthritis pain, and stiffness, your Chesapeake Bay Retriever may see the onset of diseases, such as congestive heart failure and progressive retinal atrophy that were covered in Chapter 18. In addition to these, your Chessie may experience changes to his bowels and bladder as he ages that result in messy accidents in the house.

It is important for you to remember that bowel and bladder accidents are a natural, though unpleasant, part of getting older. When accidents happen, remember that your Chessie is probably just as alarmed as you are. He knows that he is supposed to relieve himself outside, but he lacked the body control to make that happen. And he knows he displeased you. Show patience, even if you are angry and frustrated. He is not peeing in the house because he is being naughty or trying to get back at you for something. That's not how dogs operate. It is simply an accident because of his changing bowels and bladder. Don't yell or punish him for something that is beyond his control. Instead of getting upset, try giving your Chessie more bathroom breaks, reduce his water intake when he will be home alone, and use puppy pads to contain the mess. Also, take him to the vet just to rule out a kidney or bladder infection that could also cause frequent accidents.

What You Should Know About Dog Euthanasia

Euthanasia is the most heartbreaking decision that a dog owner has to make, yet it is the most humane. The decision is made out of love for the dog. When your Chesapeake Bay Retriever has become so ill or so old that he is suffering or has a poor quality of life, the right thing to do is to end his suffering.

Discuss your Chessie's condition and his quality of life with your family and your veterinarian to help you make your final decision. It will help your family to understand why it is best for your Chessie to be put to sleep. It also allows family members to say their final goodbyes and to show your Chessie how much they love him. It will be a painful time for everyone, but they will be able to make peace with what is about to happen.

Some veterinarians make home visits to perform euthanasia. Or, if you go to the clinic, when you take your Chessie to the veterinarian one last time, take steps to make him as comfortable as possible. Bring his favorite toy and blanket. It will provide him comfort and help him relax.

Your veterinarian will escort you and your Chessie to a quiet room away from the hustle and bustle of the front lobby. Some vet offices will light a special candle on their front counter to alert others that a family is there saying goodbye to their beloved dog.

You will be able to stay with your dog to comfort him and speak in a soothing way during the process. In many cases, the veterinarian will administer a sedative to help your Chessie relax. The medication that will euthanize your dog is called pentobarbital and is administered intravenously. It will very quickly and painlessly render your dog unconscious. His heart and brain function will stop soon after. The entire process takes only a minute or two, and your Chessie will not feel any pain.

Afterwards, your veterinarian will step out and let you remain in the room with your Chessie for as long as you want. As per the arrangements you have made with the vet, you can either take your Chessie home for burial or allow your vet clinic to handle the remains.

When Your Chessie Crosses the Rainbow Bridge

"With an aging Chessie, always cherish the time you have. The hardest thing you'll experience is losing your Chessie. They hold such a special place in your heart, and you will never forget or get over the loss. But while you can never replace your Chessie, it helps if you get another one sooner, rather than later, to start a new chapter in your life."

ANDREA HURT
Chessies R Us

Your goal in raising your Chesapeake Bay Retriever from puppyhood through old age is to give him the best life possible. Unfortunately, as he ages, you and your family may have to make some difficult decisions. I was in that situation with Maizie and I know how heartbreaking it can be. You must balance your emotions against the quality of life your dog is living. This is where I struggled. I could not imagine life without Maizie, and I felt like I was betraying her by considering euthanizing her. But her congestive heart failure had progressed so far that she could no longer stand, was soiling herself, and was struggling to breathe. It was time to say goodbye.

The death of a dog is devastating. Psychologists and mental health experts now recognize that the loss of a beloved dog has the same impact on a person as the loss of a family member. The grief is just as intense and raw. That only makes sense. After all, your Chesapeake Bay Retriever has been an important member of your family. You will all need time to process the loss and go through the stages of grief. Give yourselves time to do this.

Photo Courtesy of Dave Lowther

CHAPTER 20   Your Chessie in his Golden Years

There will be some final decisions that you need to make regarding your Chessie's remains. Check the local laws in your area before you make plans to bury your dog in your backyard. Some municipalities have regulations surrounding this. You will also be prohibited from burying your dog on public land, like his favorite park or hiking trail. Find out if your town has a pet cemetery where you can have your dog interred. Lastly, you could ask your veterinarian if they offer cremation services. Many of them do. You then have the option of keeping your Chessie's ashes as a reminder of him or scattering them in his favorite place to honor his memory.

We made a Maize memory book. Her collar is on the outside cover and the pages are filled with photos and short stories about her antics. We even put her Christmas stocking in it. The kids and I put the memory book together and, although there were plenty of tears, we found it to be therapeutic to relive her life and remind ourselves how lucky we were to have her in our lives, even though the time passed too quickly.

www.ingramcontent.com/pod-product-compliance
Lightning Source LLC
Chambersburg PA
CBHW071429070526
44578CB00001B/44